THE OLD LAND
AND THE NEW

The Journals of Two
Swiss Families in America in the 1820's

EDITED AND TRANSLATED BY

ROBERT H. BILLIGMEIER &
FRED ALTSCHULER PICARD

sketches by Hans Erni

UNIVERSITY OF MINNESOTA PRESS, *Minneapolis*

Library of Congress Catalog Card Number: 65-15544

PUBLISHED IN GREAT BRITAIN, INDIA, AND PAKISTAN BY THE OXFORD
UNIVERSITY PRESS, LONDON, BOMBAY, AND KARACHI, AND IN CANADA BY
THE COPP CLARK PUBLISHING CO. LIMITED, TORONTO

Acknowledgments

IT PROVIDES us pleasure to acknowledge our appreciation for innumerable courtesies and help given by Mr. Armin Müller, curator of the Heimatmuseum of Toggenburg, and Dr. Dominik Jost, professor at the Cantonal College of St. Gallen. Mention must also be made of the encouragement of Professor W. A. Liebeskind of the University of Geneva and Pastor Schlump of Hemberg. We are deeply grateful for the excellent suggestions given by Mr. Joseph Shechtman of the University of Minnesota Press. Above all our appreciation goes to Hanny Salvisberg Billigmeier, whose knowledge of German and English as well as her native Schwyzerdütsch was invaluable.

Note on Translation

⟨⟩ ───

JOHANNES SCHWEIZER and J. Jakob Rütlinger, whose ac-
counts of their journeys from Switzerland to America are here translated,
thought of their writing partly as diaries for their own use and partly as
detailed letters to their friends and relatives at home. Writing in a conver-
sational style, they readily lapsed into the Swiss dialect that they would
use in speaking. Many divergences from standard German grammar appear in both texts, some of which arose from the differences in usage between written German and the Swiss dialect.

The Reverend Christian Kranich, a friend of Schweizer's, edited his
book but made only a few corrections. Errors in spelling and in sentence
structure remained. The authors were addressing themselves, after all, to
an audience not likely to be critical.

Besides contributing a foreword to Schweizer's book, Pastor Kranich
included a number of his own comments as footnotes. We have set these
off in a different series from our own notes and appended his ini-
tials (C. K.) to each one, because though we cherish every one of them
we have no wish to claim credit for them ourselves. Our own footnotes
are numbered and unsigned.

In translating the two books, we have changed as little as possible.
Every effort was directed toward rendering the account with as much of
the original flavor as possible. Only where referents were obscure, as they
often are in conversation, were sentences substantially clarified.

A conscious effort was made in translating to refrain from making the text flow more smoothly, or removing repetitious words, or in general polishing the language.

The authors' thoughts are recorded in the accounts as they occurred to them; not much effort was made to be systematic. A roughly chronological framework is used by both, but even in this they are not consistent. Rütlinger makes substantial use of topical organization in the latter part of his book. Although parts of the accounts are supposed to have been written as daily journals, it is clear that many entries were written retrospectively, as is indicated by the frequent shifting from past to present tense and retrospective asides. These features, too, have been left unaltered in the translation.

Schweizer and Rütlinger used a number of English words and phrases — not always accurately. Soon after his arrival Schweizer began to add English words to the text: Heamboats (steamboats), Stor (store), Cort (court), Steage (stage), Schmokous (smokehouse), Diacon (deacon), Lac Counti (Lake County), Flaur (flour), Troubels (troubles), Yänkies (Yankees). Mrs. Schweizer in her letter to her parents writes of the Shoolmester (schoolmaster), Feshon (fashion), and so on. Schweizer spelled personal names as he heard them; Peggy was written Peke, and Jack, Tschek. Only in part does this reflect imperfect mastery of the new language; after all, *Stor, Cort, Flaur, Yänkies*, though not spelled the English way, give a German reader a more accurate idea of how to pronounce the word than the conventional spelling would.

In both books several common English verbs were soon assimilated into German: setteln (to settle), renten (to rent), and klaren (to clear land).

Table of Contents

THE OLD LAND
AND THE NEW

Introduction

by ROBERT H. BILLIGMEIER

←—————————————————————————————

OUT of the torrential influx of nineteenth-century Europeans into America, the greatest population movement in all history, came an extensive literature of immigrant accounts portraying the new Americans' first contact with American society and their early efforts at integration. In the 1820's, when the flow of immigration was still small, two Swiss immigrant families wrote accounts of what seemed to them to be the most decisive experiences of their lives. These particular accounts relate to a period in the history of American immigration that is less well known than the more spectacular colonial and post-Civil War movements. They are particularly vivid and insightful personal documents affording valuable perspectives upon the integration of the "Old Immigration" of ante-bellum days.

In 1820 Johannes Schweizer, his wife, Anna, and their nine-year-old daughter, Salomea, left Switzerland to establish a home in America where, as the Göttingen historian Arnold Heeren wrote, "a younger Europe is blossoming." Only the broad outlines of Schweizer's personal history before his emigration are known. He was born in Hemberg in the Toggenburg area of Canton St. Gallen in 1785. He died in America in 1831.[1] Shortly before departing for the United States Schweizer and his family lived for a time near Basel where he served as manager of an estate. Even a most careful search in Hemberg and the Toggenburger Heimatmuseum in Lichtensteig yielded not much more than these fragmentary references

[1] "Bürger Register der Gemeind Hemberg. Evangelisch Religion," Item No. 370.

3

to his early life. He reveals many dimensions of his character, however, in the account which he wrote of his emigration and his early adjustment in America. His *Reisebeschreibung nach Nordamerika und durch die bedeutendsten Teile desselben* was published in Ebnat in the Toggenburg in 1823. It was widely circulated; nearly four hundred people are included in the list of subscribers, most of whom lived in the Toggenburg itself or in nearby areas of eastern Switzerland.[2]

One of the subscribers to Schweizer's book was an old friend, Johann Jakob Rütlinger, the teacher of the Bächli school in Hemberg. In 1823 Rütlinger followed his friend to the United States and joined him first in Lancaster, Pennsylvania, and later in Middletown, Maryland. As Schweizer had done, Rütlinger published an account of his journey down the Rhine and across the Atlantic, and, what is more significant, of his experiences as an immigrant in the America of the 1820's. His *Tagebuch auf einer Reise nach Nordamerika im Jahr 1823* was published in Ebnat, St. Gallen, in 1826, by Abraham Keller, who had published Schweizer's earlier book.

Rütlinger was born in Wildhaus in the Toggenburg in 1790. "In a high mountain valley in eastern Switzerland . . ." he wrote in the introduction to a book of his poetry, "specifically on the meadow where the birthplace of the reformer Ulrich Zwingli is still to be seen, I received a simple rearing, along with five other children, in the bosom of poor but respectable parents. My father was a teacher who for more than thirty years taught his 50 to 60 pupils. For the miserable salary of 18 to 20 florins he gave his undeniably simple and meager instruction every winter for 20 to 22 weeks. In this school I was not able to learn anything but the mechanics of writing and a smattering of reading. That was all. My father wanted me to be a schoolteacher too. The new system of public instruction had just started in our canton. The estimable minister and educator Steinmüller had opened a course of instruction for new schoolteachers in Rheineck. By almost completely exhausting the economic resources of my father, I was able to become one of the first to attend this institute. The course lasted nine weeks. Now I was already a schoolteacher. This was all of my formal education. I received the position in the winter school in my home town. I had to promise to keep the position for several

[2] This book followed by several years a work of J. U. Büchler, which was perhaps the earliest account of an immigrant from eastern Switzerland: *Land- und Seereisen eines st. gallischen Kantonsbürgers nach Nordamerika und Westindien, über Amsterdam nach Baltimore, . . . in den Jahren 1816, 1817 und 1818* (St. Gallen: Zollikofer und Zühlin, 1819).

years. The following year blind luck provided another job for me in the summer school in Hemberg, which is five hours away from Wildhaus. In the spring of 1809 I started teaching there.

"I was seventeen years old when I began to teach school. If I wanted to maintain the position of schoolteacher, I could clearly see that I would have to pursue my education further through my own efforts. I began to read everything I could get my hands on. I had no books of my own and neither did my father."[3]

Rütlinger admired poetry and the profession of poet. His attempts at writing poetry revealed to him what he called the problems of "meter, expression, and smoothness." His desire to improve his work led him to read and then to write, and again to read and to write further without discouragement. "No matter how far I was from becoming a poet, these hours in which I studied poetry were the most pleasant hours; it pleased me endlessly when I had again put something down on paper."[4] After reading Johann Peter Hebel's *Allemannische Gedichte*, he tried to write poetry in popular speech, in the Swiss-German dialect (Schwyzerdütsch). "But dear God! I fooled myself in this as much as I had in trying earlier to write the other kind of poetry."[5] He was aware of the slender talent he possessed, but his poems were nevertheless read and appreciated for their homey, endearing quality. On departing for America in 1823 he presented his friends with a volume of poems, *Ländliche Gedichte*, published as a souvenir. He would not have published them, he said, under other circumstances. His second volume followed in 1824 and a third in 1826, and his collected poetic works were published in 1835. A later, unpublished manuscript sent to Switzerland in 1841 contains some fifty poems from the period 1824 to 1840 and a short account of Rütlinger's life in Ohio. Summary notes on this material, and excerpts from several family letters published in 1913, are presented as a supplement to the present translation of the *Tagebuch*. Rütlinger died in Ohio in 1856.

Schweizer and Rütlinger were but two representatives of a large contingent; as they both make clear, emigration to America was a significant option to the Swiss of their day, as it had been in the previous century and was to continue to be all through the nineteenth century. The Swiss

[3] Johann Jakob Rütlinger, *Ländliche Gedichte* (Ebnat: Abraham Keller, 1823), pp. iv–vii. (Our translation.)
[4] *Ibid.*, pp. vii–viii.
[5] *Ibid.* See the discussion of Rütlinger in Samuel Voellmy, *Das Toggenburg in der schönen Literatur des 19. und 20. Jahrhunderts* (Wattwil: Der Toggenburger Vereinigung für Heimatkunde, 1961).

came in significant numbers to colonial America, settling largely in Pennsylvania. Along with settlers from Württemberg, Baden, and the Palatinate, they formed the "Pennsylvania Dutch" population. Early settlements were also formed in the Carolinas. In the 1820's and 1830's rural Pennsylvania and urban New York were the principal areas of Swiss settlement. In succeeding decades increasing proportions of Swiss immigration established farms in Ohio, Illinois, Missouri, and Wisconsin. The Swiss tended to form areas of particular concentration, usually in good dairy lands. Despite efforts of the Swiss government to discourage emigration it grew rapidly in the 1850's and in the post-Civil War period. Relative to the total immigration from all countries, however, Swiss immigration diminished. By the end of the century New York and California emerged as the states with the largest Swiss-born populations.[6]

The reasons for this steady flow of population are of course bound up with the conditions of life in the Switzerland of the time, and, in the two instances we are considering here, with the conditions of life in the canton of St. Gallen in the early nineteenth century. (Though the far lower rate of emigration from the French-speaking portions of Switzerland suggests that subtler forces than the purely economic ones were at work.)

The two emigrant families' assessment of the political, social, and economic problems of the time provided in part the motivation for leaving St. Gallen. These assessments also explain the solicitous feeling Schweizer and Rütlinger both had for their country. Upon departure for America and indeed after establishing themselves there the Swiss families continued to express love and deep concern for the native land then so torn by bitter partisan discord and dissension in every canton and in every city. They hoped for the return to Switzerland of prosperity and stability. Its welfare remained a matter of vital importance to them despite the fact that they had committed themselves and their family fortunes to America.

One clear indication of this persisting identification with their native land is found in Schweizer's continual concern with anything that might have economic utility or practical advantage at home. He recorded in fine detail various processes, tools, implements, trees, approaches to work, crops, or recipes that might be adapted in Switzerland to the advantage of the people. Rütlinger's concern for Switzerland is still reflected in his last letters to his sisters written in 1855, shortly before his death.

The invasion of Switzerland by France in 1798 brought an end to the

[6] See John Paul von Grueningen, ed., *The Swiss in the United States* (Madison, Wis.: Swiss-American Historical Society, 1940).

6

ancient Confederation. A unitary Helvetic Republic was first created, but in 1803 a more federative political system was instituted under the Act of Mediation. Though some of the political and social changes that were introduced in the period of French ascendancy in Switzerland were popular — many anachronistic impediments to effective economic and political life were abolished — the relationships between Switzerland and France, which the French established largely in their own interests, brought serious difficulties to Switzerland. The frontiers were violated by French troops; thousands of Swiss were conscripted into the armies of Napoleon. Switzerland was forced by France to participate in the continental system which, in general, did great damage to Swiss commerce and industry.

The wars that marked the end of the Napoleonic era left Switzerland suffering keenly the consequences of alien political and military intrusion. Disease and poverty had followed in the wake of the successive waves of armies which crossed the country.

Between 1815 and 1830 Switzerland experienced grave internal confusion and disunity. To an extent the old cantonal particularism was restored. Each canton collected its own customs and minted its own money. In some of the cantons old patrician families sought to regain the positions of power they had held in the old regime. Tariff restrictions imposed by the French and Austrians affected Switzerland's economy. British textile manufacturers established their advantage in the world textile market, and this affected critically those areas of Switzerland in which textile manufacturing was basic to the economy.

The crop failure of 1816 led to widespread hunger in parts of Switzerland to a degree rarely known in that country. In certain areas of Graubünden and other cantons of eastern Switzerland many children were conducted in groups to Germany for summer employment that would at least give them sufficient food. Wages were low in Switzerland and opportunities for employment severely restricted. Agricultural efficiency was at a low ebb.

The Toggenburg district of St. Gallen, from which Schweizer and Rütlinger came, was severely stricken by the economic distress that prevailed generally throughout the country. Inflation was especially critical in 1816 and 1817. The price of food rose to an astonishing height in the face of severe shortages that could not be readily remedied by importation of foodstuffs. The village of Hemberg, from which the emigrants departed, suddenly had a staggering relief burden. In a population of approximately 1700 the public welfare rolls in mid-1816 included 53 persons. By November the number had risen to 137. In August 1817, the number receiving public relief had reached 272, to which 204 were added by December of that year. Soup kitchens were established to supplement the financial assistance which the community was able to provide. At Christmastime in 1816, and again a few months later, collections were made at the church door to buy bread for the poor. Private donations added to this fund. The Poor Commission tried to find work for the unemployed in home industries.[7] Rütlinger made petition to the government of St. Gallen to help people help themselves by providing the raw materials and equipment for cotton and wool manufacturing.[8]

The health of the population suffered, as is clearly indicated by a sharp increase in mortality, especially among children. Sixty-three women were left in widowhood at the end of the two-year period. The costs of social welfare and medical aid reached an alltime high.[9]

The inflation diminished after the excellent harvest of 1817, and in two years prices were near normal. The acute distress disappeared, but the economy of the Toggenburg area, like that of Switzerland generally, did not fully recover for years. Rev. Christian Kranich of Hemberg, who edited Schweizer's book and wrote the introduction to it, could say to his congregation in 1824, "The horror of the past inflation — we have all experienced what that means — has now disappeared. What the goodness of God has made to grow already promises an ample harvest. The golden sun shines down on our alpine pastures covered with abundant grass."[10]

In the Toggenburg area, as in many other areas of eastern Switzerland, the manufacturing of textiles had long been important in supplementing the basically agrarian economy. Home industries were faced with competition from large-scale enterprises, but the local spinners, weavers, and dyers were flexible enough to adjust to such competition to a considerable extent. There were times of difficulty, of course. Later in the century a shift to mechanical embroidery occurred and Bühler reports seventy embroidery machines in the commune.[11] Except for occasional periods of distress, as during the Napoleonic period and immediately afterward, the

[7] J. Bühler, *Geschichte der Gemeinde Hemberg* (Lichtensteig, St. Gallen: J. U. Furrer, 1879), pp. 21–22.

[8] Oskar Frei, *Johann Jakob Rütlinger von Wildhaus (1790–1856), Sein Leben, Seine Dichtungen und Schriften* (St. Gallen: Historischer Verein des Kantons St. Gallen, 1915), p. 5.

[9] Bühler, *op. cit.*, pp. 21–22.

[10] Christian Friedrich Kranich, *Schöne und Gute unseres Vaterlandes* (Ebnat, St. Gallen: Abraham Keller, 1824), p. 1.

[11] Bühler, *op. cit.*, p. 30.

Toggenburg area enjoyed fair prosperity, and financial need did not create heavy pressure for emigration.

The period of internal reconstruction began with a struggle between liberal and conservative forces within the country. Schweizer and Rütlinger were distressed by the bitterness of controversy. They feared, moreover, the loss of civil liberties traditionally enjoyed. Conservatives sought to re-establish as far as possible the social and political institutions that had existed before Napoleon invaded Switzerland. Liberals in each canton energetically promoted reforms in agriculture, land distribution, the monetary system, education, the system of tariffs and taxation. They sought to strengthen the national political authority as opposed to the extreme states-rights philosophy which underlay the old, loosely bound confederate system. In the current political issues, religious issues were often intricately intertwined, a fact which generally impeded mediation of the problems.[12]

The liberal forces after 1830 became increasingly ascendant. Roads were constructed at a faster rate. Commercial activity quickened, and the particular kind of decentralized industrialization characterizing modern Switzerland began slowly to emerge. Progress was greatly accelerated after 1848 when constitutional reforms strengthened the powers of the national government.

By mid-century the hopes the emigrants Schweizer and Rütlinger had earlier expressed for their country were clearly being fulfilled.

Patterns of emigration from Switzerland, Alsace, and Rhenish southern Germany had become well established in the eighteenth century. A stream of settlers came to America from these areas. In the late eighteenth and the nineteenth centuries another pattern of emigration, to southern Russia, became important. Colonists were first introduced into Russia in 1763 by Catherine II, who wished to have the underpopulated and undeveloped southern regions made more productive. It was hoped that the introduction of western European settlers would not only bring modern agricultural methods to the steppes but also stimulate trade and industry. The German settlements were to grow until their inhabitants eventually numbered two million. With the exception of the Mennonites from the Danzig area, the Germans leaving for colonies along the Black Sea, the Volga, and the Caucasus were almost entirely from Württem-

[12] Valentin Giterman, *Geschichte der Schweiz* (Thayngen, Schaffhausen: Augustin Verlag, 1941), pp. 418–445.

berg, Baden, the Palatinate, and Hesse; a lesser number of Swiss from Zurich and other areas also emigrated.[13] These were the general areas from which the German-speaking population in America was to come. There were Mennonites, Lutherans, Separatists, and Catholics among them.

At the time Schweizer and Rütlinger left for America some of their fellow countrymen were leaving for Zürichtal in the Crimea. Many others were leaving their homes in the Rhenish territories through which the authors traveled, some for North America, some for Russia. Some of the religious sects mentioned by the authors, the Separatists among them, were establishing colonies both in America and Russia in the same period.

The movement of German-speaking people to Russia bears some similarities to the contemporary movement to the United States. Certainly the push exerted by local conditions was identical. There were also some very significant differences. The emigration to Russia was sponsored by the Russian government. Catherine II was of German origin and had family connections with the ruling house of Württemberg. Agents of the Russian government were active in recruiting colonists in the Rhenish territories, especially in Württemberg. They entered into contractual relationships with groups of people interested in emigrating. Certain guarantees provided inducement: an initial grant of land, almost unlimited possibilities of expanding holdings by purchase, freedom from taxation, freedom from military service, local self-government, and complete religious freedom.[14]

Many potential emigrants weighed the United States and Russia in a balance. In this sense America and Russia competed for millions of German-speaking emigrants. The inducement provided by Russia seemed highly encouraging. The difficulties in travel to Russia, however, were far greater than those of the Atlantic crossing, though the ocean voyage seemed much more formidable to many.

The settlers established themselves in colonies from Bessarabia to the South Caucasus and from the Volga to the Crimea. The conditions of life were extremely strenuous and only by the most unified effort

[13] Cf. David G. Rempel, "The Mennonite Colonies in New Russia: A Study of Their Settlement and Economic Development from 1789 to 1914" (unpublished Ph.D. dissertation, Department of History, Stanford University, 1933), and Georg Leibbrandt, *Die deutschen Kolonien in Cherson und Bessarabien* (Stuttgart: Ausland und Heimat Verlag, 1926).

[14] Karl Stumpp, *Die deutsche Auswanderung nach Russland, 1763–1862* (Stuttgart: Landsmannschaft der Deutschen aus Russland, 1961), p. x.

within colonies and among them could the settler survive. Schweizer and Rütlinger stressed the great advantages of planned emigration projects of organized colonies or at least of groups of families over the moving of isolated families or individuals. They advocated government responsibility in such emigration. In Russia, if not in America, such corporate enterprises were the only means by which the colonists could hope to make a place for themselves in the economy of the region. After the initial period of severe struggle a stable position was achieved. The major flux was over by 1824, but parent colonies expanded. Daughter colonies were established in peripheral areas as the prolific settlements increased their populations.

In the 1870's the colonists became increasingly conscious of a shift in governmental attitudes toward them. Indications of tendencies toward Russification became more and more clear. The rights and privileges originally granted in perpetuity were modified as pressures for assimilation increased.

Many of the German colonists descended from emigrants of the authors' generation fled Russification and emigrated to the United States and Canada. In the decades following 1870 they settled on homesteads on the Great Plains, particularly in the Dakotas, Nebraska, and the prairie provinces of Canada. Thus many of the descendants of emigrants who left the Rhenish areas on long journeys in opposite directions were reunited within one country after several generations of separation.[15]

The adjustment of the two Swiss families to the American environment was made easier, linguistically and in other ways, by the fact that Pennsylvania and northern Maryland were heavily infused with cultural elements introduced by the many immigrants of the colonial period from Rhenish areas of Germany and Switzerland. In certain areas a stable Pennsylvania-Dutch subculture had emerged, with its own speech, an Allemannic-Swabian dialect that reflected the speech of the Rhenish Germans and Swiss and was also influenced, of course, by English. By making certain kinds of choices with regard to place of residence, friends, and associates, individuals could live in a cultural environment to a degree transitional between Europe and America. These choices were determined by individual self-identification and by external pressure.

Neither Schweizer nor Rütlinger appears to have contemplated emi-

[15] See John J. Gering, *After Fifty Years* (Pine Hill Printery [?], 1924), for an interesting account of the difficulties encountered in the settlement of South Dakota in the 1870's.

11

gration to Russia, but Schweizer knew at least one person who went there, as Pastor Kranich points out in his Introduction.

Schweizer and Rütlinger had something to say about the particular reasons they had for writing their books. For each of the authors his book was a personal account of a decisive experience in life and was valued as a private monument to it. That alone would explain the act of writing the book, if not of publishing it. It is clear from the intentions they profess in introducing and concluding their works — and indeed from what appears in every page as well — that the books are essentially extended letters to friends and relatives in Switzerland. The books represent personal communications in which old ties are reaffirmed and the momentous experience of immigration is related in personal terms. Writing in this manner is a way of going home again.

Schweizer explained that as he wrote he imagined he was conversing with a friend in his native Toggenburg, now one friend, now another. The authors' intimate knowledge of the attitudes and interests of their primary audience led them to anticipate replies and questions; they did this consciously. The monologue almost became dialogue. The people, the familiar setting, the context of communication were firmly set. The reaffirmation of connection may well have served to diminish their own sense of isolation from their past, enabling them to return to their new surroundings with greater fortitude and better heart.

Both Schweizer and Rütlinger addressed the far-off Swiss mountains and fields as warmly and personally as they did their friends, treasuring the memories of people and places both. In their last farewells to the Rhine in Holland, they attributed human qualities of friendliness and benevolent concern to the river which also flows through their native canton of St. Gallen. Their lives had been spent thus far in intimate alliance with an environment of great natural beauty. The love of nature they felt was not generalized and impersonal, but rather a most intimate, pantheistic love. In leaving their native land they both seemed to tear themselves consciously away mountain by mountain, stream by stream, river by river, tree by tree, and friend by friend.

But more than the wish to commemorate their own odysseys and record their feelings impelled these travelers to write. Their concern with passing along any American materials or processes that could be used in Switzerland was matched by their desire to increase the chances for success of those who might emigrate after them.

It is a fair proposition that some of the hazards of a journey can be eliminated by foresight, knowledge of the most common vicissitudes, and intelligent planning. Each trip, however, besides the general characteristics it shares with other contemporary trips along a similar route, has its own unique qualities. Certainly in the early nineteenth century no amount of planning or organization, advice, information, aid, or even money could altogether eliminate the considerable difficulties of a long journey. The Atlantic crossing and long land journeys were still, in actuality and even more in popular imagination, formidable enterprises. At that period and even more so in later decades one traveled at risk of life and health and with little comfort, however inexpensively.[16]

Many immigrants, spurred by their own difficulties in making the journey to America, wished to help others contemplating the same enterprise. Attempts were made to provide essential factual information. Greatly needed by prospective emigrants was some general measuring stick by which to evaluate the rumors, advertisements, blandishments, and anecdotal accumulations of the time. Schweizer and Rütlinger attempted to point out a number of specific ways in which strangers en route were victimized in land transportation, freight arrangements, food purchases, ship contracts, and various other transactions. For many immigrants the practice of indenture which Mittelberger [17] had condemned in the 1750's still meant a condition of virtual enslavement and personal debasement.

Schweizer and Rütlinger both felt keenly the waste and human suffering that attended immigration of individuals and single families having only meager resources. They were exposed to vicissitudes and exploitation far more than larger groups. The authors saw great merit in a movement of people carefully planned to include immigrants with needed and complementary skills, going to a previously chosen destination that had an economic development suitable for the requirements and abilities of its new inhabitants. In the 1840's as immigrant streams increased, a large number of books began to appear offering guidance to emigrants; their titles indicated their primary purpose: "guide book for emigrants," "practical handbook for emigration," "the emigrants' adviser," and "practical instruction for travel and settlement."

[16] Alan Conway, ed., *The Welsh in America: Letters from the Immigrants* (Minneapolis: University of Minnesota Press, 1961), p. 3. Earlier, people were taken on as passengers largely as ballast; as increasing numbers sought passage such transport of persons became a lucrative trade in itself.

[17] Gottlieb Mittelberger, *Journey to Pennsylvania*, edited and translated by Oscar Handlin and John Clive (Cambridge, Mass.: The Belknap Press of Harvard University Press, 1960), pp. 9–10.

13

Much thought was given by immigrants to the questions frequently asked by their friends and relatives at home: Who should come to America? Who has the best chance of competing successfully? What groups have most success, what occupations, age groups, classes? What personal qualities seem relevant to success? To what factors, other than simple luck, may success be attributed? There were also the more mechanical aspects of immigration which had to be considered. Like Mittelberger in the 1750's, Schweizer and Rütlinger addressed themselves as well to instrumental queries: how far is it; how long does it take; how much does it cost to get there; how dangerous is it; and what will we find?

The answers individuals gave, in letters or books, were not easily formulated. If they were serious answers, they involved an evaluation of the immigrant's own total experience, an evaluation including personal factors that are not readily measured by the historian.

Despite the fact that many millions have in recent centuries moved from one country to another, relatively little is known concerning the personal impact upon immigrants of the voluntary act of uprooting themselves from their native environment and replanting themselves in an alien environment. To understand the highly significant phenomenon of the emigrant-become-immigrant more fully, a systematic study of a large number of personal accounts is needed to provide greater insight into the personal aspects of this immigration.[18]

It is true, as Theodore C. Blegen writes: "There has been all too often an air of impersonality in accounts of American immigration. The coming of thirty millions of people was a movement of such magnitude that to many it has seemed futile to try to disengage personalities from the mass. Many writers have forgotten the individual man in the surging complex of international circumstances. . . . But the pivot of human motion is individual life." [19]

Popular interest in North America grew rapidly among western and northern Europeans in the nineteenth century. The avid interest with which the British and later the Germans read letters and books on America in the seventeenth and eighteenth centuries now came to be shared more generally in western Europe and, after the first quarter of the nineteenth century, in Norway, Denmark, and Sweden. The reading public was being

[18] The most extensive use of such personal documents is found in the monumental work of W. I. Thomas and Florian Znaniecki, *The Polish Peasant in Europe and America*, 2 volumes (New York: Alfred A. Knopf, 1927).

[19] Theodore C. Blegen, *Land of Their Choice: The Immigrants Write Home* (Minneapolis: University of Minnesota Press, 1955), p. 7.

rapidly expanded with current improvements in popular education. General interest in the United States and the literature on the subject were mutually stimulating.

Because immigrant letters and accounts were so often published and so widely read back home by ordinary people throughout the nineteenth century, it is important to recognize in them a significant factor in forming the popular image of America. Deriving from that fact is their influence upon potential emigrants earnestly weighing the advantages and disadvantages of leaving home.[20]

In this considerable immigrant literature the careful scholar may find thousands of mirrors held up to America, each with the unique perspective of a time and place and person. In no mirror is the image complete or unblurred. Taken collectively they may provide many helpful constituents of the image of national life; certainly much may be learned about the assimilation of the ethnic components of the "Old Immigration."

Later generations are likely to find in these accounts much that is faulty, partial, biased, and superficial — at least according to their retrospective notions of reality. But the immigrants' conceptions of America and Americans — accurate or inaccurate — were the working conceptions with which these men and women attempted to adjust to a new environment and deal constructively with it. The conceptions which were used by immigrants to guide their behavior cannot simply be discounted upon the discovery of inadequacies in them. It is important for the student of social relationships rather to study the conditions under which conceptions of the new society emerged and how they were reflected in the relationships of immigrant and native-born.

While describing even commonplace and routine matters, the immigrants in their accounts were cataloguing and evaluating significant aspects of their new environment. However prosaically they seemed to speak, they could not consider what they described in terms unrelated to their vital concerns; they were approving or disapproving, liking or disliking, accepting or rejecting, finding hope or despair. Careful reading of such accounts reveals the immigrant in his intimate efforts to come to grips with the complex new environment in the most basic areas of daily life.

Interpretations of life in the United States presented by letters and books were taken seriously, both among the new settlers themselves and

[20] Carlton C. Qualey, *Norwegian Settlement in the United States* (Northfield, Minn.: Norwegian-American Historical Association, 1938), p. 60.

in Europe among local, regional, and even national publics interested in America and emigration. They became subjects of much discussion and debate. The interpretations defined aspects of American life, generalizing, summarizing, and ordering the confused events and impressions. It was the interpretation, not the event, that provided the cue to behavior.

As John Steinbeck observed in his recent travels in search of America, external reality is not very external after all.[21]

In part, observations were an individual matter and depended upon individual sensitivity, intelligence, breadth of interest, and other personal qualities which vary within each ethnic group. But to a significant extent membership in a cultural community was associated with certain regularities in the kinds of observations and comparisons made.

What the immigrant observed and experienced was also closely related to the niche he was able to find in the new society. The niche he won gave him one particular perspective upon the new world – a vantage point. It determined in large part the particular segment of American life which was exposed to his vision.

People compete for a place in the economy both as individuals and as members of groups. This is true as well of immigrant groups establishing themselves in a new society. The manner in which the popularly defined ethnic groups are evaluated is determined largely in the context of economic relationships. The relevance of group identification to individual welfare did not escape these immigrants. The Germans, Swiss, English, and Scandinavians in the early nineteenth century were conscious of the significance of this categorization to individual members. They did not feel they had to be gravely concerned about it; they did, however, contrast their positions favorably with the newly arrived Catholic Irish.

Nevertheless, both Schweizer and Rütlinger, soon after their arrival, became concerned over reports that the reputations of German and Swiss immigrants had suffered of late. "I cannot describe what a bitter, poignant experience it is to hear these facts about the people to whom one belongs," Schweizer wrote in his journal. He repeated the allegations made to him: "Earlier they could be trusted with anything, the Swiss contending with the Germans for highest honors. A German or Swiss hired man or maid generally received double the pay of an immigrant from any other country. Since that time, however, they have excelled other national groups in thievery, cheating, laziness, and drunkenness. What a sad obser-

[21] John Steinbeck, *Travels with Charley in Search of America* (New York: Viking Press, 1962), p. 206.

vation! Has the entire German population deteriorated? Or does a different class emigrate now? Whoever wanted to take the trouble could without much difficulty gather material for a universal chronicle of crooked tricks which are attributed to German immigrants." (Page 105.) The fears aroused by these allegations made to Schweizer and Rütlinger early in their life in America did not seem to find confirmation in the authors' own experience, and they apparently disappeared.

Much of what happens in a competitive economy depends upon the distinctive values of the groups competing. The immigrant groups of the colonial and early national period competed for a place in a largely agrarian economy. Certain values were particularly advantageous in such economic activities as that economy required. There was a very extensive agreement in values among Americans and the English, Germans, Swiss, Dutch, Scandinavians, and Scotch-Irish of the "Old Immigration."

These groups did not differ greatly in economically relevant knowledge and skills, although some contrasts could be drawn, as Schweizer and Rütlinger have done. Similarities were extensive in levels of specific knowledge as to the most useful crops and their proper cultivation, knowledge of husbandry of animals, familiarity with a money economy. Attitudes toward individual effort and personal responsibility were also similar. No great competitive advantage, then, fell to any particular group. There were compensating advantages and disadvantages which inhibited the emergence of any long-enduring system of ethnic stratification. This situation contrasts sharply with the predicament of the later "New Immigrant" groups from southern and eastern European areas; these immigrants had to compete under very serious disadvantages in American industrial centers.

The immigrant, especially in his first years, seems to have engaged in an almost continual process of consciously or unconsciously evaluating his position. He tested the utility of tools, implements, clothing, and other items of material culture brought along from his homeland. He tested as well the adequacy of nonmaterial aspects of culture. Immigrant letters and books reveal something of the dimensions of this process in innumerable contexts.

Evaluation also involved measuring goals and expectations originally providing motivation for migration against the day-to-day realities of the present, as well as the future possibilities. In this personal bookkeeping, dreams and expectations were set against reality as it was perceived; fears in anticipation against difficulties actually encountered; dread at

17

leaving home against the challenge of the new now being fulfilled; what might have been at home against what is now and is likely to be. This elaborate weighing and measuring of human experience was not susceptible to objective methods of cost accounting.

There were moments of hope and despair, sometimes in quick succession. It is easy to understand why the people at home sometimes received contradictory evaluations not only from different friends and relatives but from the same person as well. Some individuals could sustain over a long time the conviction that America was the best hope for the masses of their fellow-countrymen. For most immigrants the reality of America was too confusing and complex to be readily set into clear focus in a short time.

While to Schweizer and Rütlinger the truth about the United States seemed to lie near midpoint between strenuous condemnation and unqualified praise, others made judgments ranging along the whole continuum. In the 1750's Mittelberger had written from Germany, to which he had returned after several years in America: "For before I left Pennsylvania, when it became known that I wanted to return to Württemberg, numerous Württemberger, Durlacher, and Palatines (a great many of whom live there and spend their days moaning and groaning about ever having left their native country) begged me with tears and uplifted hands, and even in the name of God, to publicize their misery and sorrow in Germany. So that not only the common people but even princes and lords might be able to hear about what happened to them; and so that innocent souls would no longer leave their native country, persuaded to do so by Newlanders, and dragged by them into a similar kind of slavery." [22]

Some immigrants found land more fertile and life more satisfying in America than even their dreams had allowed them to hope for. Those at home needed only the courage to emigrate and the willingness to work in order to reap an abundant harvest.

"Oh! you unhappy Welshmen, why do you not emigrate to the New Purchase in Iowa instead of quarreling over the lack of land and poverty in the mountains of Wales?" [23]

"You, my true friend, together with many others of my acquaintances probably censure me for my emigration considerably, and perhaps even yet believe that I regret having left Ødefjeld. No! not so. In no circum-

[22] Mittelberger, *op. cit.*, pp. 9–10.
[23] Cited by Conway, *op. cit.*, p. 110.

stances would I return to live in Ødefjeld, not even if I could be the owner of half of the Annex. . . . Here in America a much better mode of living is open to every honorable citizen . . .

"Every poor person who will work diligently and faithfully, can become a well-to-do man here in a short time, and the rich man, on the other hand, has even better prospects, for he can work out his career with less drudgery and fewer burdens and thus have a much more peaceful life here than in Norway. . . . I have never lived better than at present."[24]

The economic situation of the United States was a major topic of popular conversation when the authors arrived. In their journeys through German territories they had heard constant complaints about the deterioration of economic conditions in Germany. They were convinced by many visible evidences of the substance of the widespread lamentations. In the United States the complaints concerning the economy were not so abundantly verifiable. The authors were left somewhat puzzled by the ubiquity of complaints and reflected upon the relativity of definitions of "poverty" and "economic distress." What they heard was naturally disconcerting and yet in a sense encouraging in that despite lamenting almost everyone they actually observed lived in what appeared to be rather decent circumstances.

When President Monroe delivered his first message to the Congress on December 2, 1817, agriculture, manufacturing, and trade were flourishing. Peace had been restored, and the young republic, freed from the concerns of war for the first time in years, was able to concentrate its attention upon domestic affairs. A period of rapid development was inaugurated, but not before the new nation passed through the severest economic crisis in its early history.

Immediately after the war, attention turned to the construction of roads, particularly in the western wilderness where there had been only trails before. Cities were founded as the population shift westward accelerated. Land speculation became feverish as investors bought vast holdings for rapid resale at extravagant profits. The speculators often established small equities, hoping to make their large profits before their own loans fell due. The inflation of land values became serious and the boom in sales collapsed.[25]

Major factors contributing to the economic difficulties of the time

[24] Cited by Blegen, *op. cit.*, pp. 180–182.

[25] W. P. Cresson, *James Monroe* (Chapel Hill: University of North Carolina Press, 1946), p. 329.

19

included the disordered currency and the unsound condition of credit generally. Paper currency was issued by more than four hundred sources, including chartered and unchartered banks, factories, private institutions, municipalities and towns, as well as individuals. Such issuance was poorly regulated and paper currency became seriously debased. During the war the country had suffered a sharp decline in specie circulation. The loss of specie was further aggravated by a heavy demand in Europe for precious metals.

The Bank of the United States, which had been re-established in 1816, attempted to solve the monetary crisis. Under its less than mediocre president, William Jones, it first encouraged speculation by permitting overexpansion of credit and then abruptly altered its position and drastically curtailed credit. Many state banks were ruined by this abrupt attempt at deflation. There was considerable popular reaction against the Bank, which both Schweizer and Rütlinger record in detail, but though the Bank of the United States was legitimately open to criticism, it was not because it adopted a deflationary policy but because of its timing. If restrictions on credit had been applied earlier, it is likely that the severe depression would not have occurred.

Immediately after the war, New England mill towns were still prospering from the increased demands for textiles which characterized the war period. Thousands of European immigrants were attracted by prospects of working in these industries. By 1818 American manufacturers were beginning to feel the competition of British manufacturers, and soon their problems became acute. British industry, responding rapidly to the removal of wartime commercial restrictions, found a ready market in the United States. The British were intent not only upon exploiting the market, but upon inhibiting the development of American manufacturing enterprises. With goods dumped on the American market, many new and fragile manufacturing enterprises were unable to survive British competition and collapsed. Thousands of persons were left unemployed in the North and East, as American mills retreated to half-time operation or closed down entirely.[26]

American shipping interests also suffered. Great Britain closed her West Indian ports to American shipping. Prices of American agricultural products fell with the loss of this important market and much perishable food and grain spoiled.

American manufacturers began efforts at organization to advance their

[26] *Ibid.*

20

interests in this critical situation. Tariff protection of American industries was increasingly regarded as a vitally important measure for economic development. But the tariff question did not immediately become a major national issue. Only after 1824 did the movement for protection gain strong support; even then sectional economic interests were clearly evident in the struggle for tariff legislation.

During the last months of 1818 commodity prices declined rapidly. After several years of agricultural shortages Europe had bumper crops. These considerably reduced American food exports. The prices of cotton and tobacco fell by almost half between the summers of 1818 and 1819. Rütlinger and Schweizer refer to various points of view about land speculation, currency difficulties, commodity prices, the dumping of British goods; they mention the inclination of Americans to hope for another war in Europe for the advantages that war might bring.

The American people strongly felt its youthfulness and this made difficulties seem less serious, for all the complaints of the moment. Associated with feelings of youthfulness is the conviction that however serious the crises may be, time and unfettered maneuverability, unnarrowed by old commitments, will present opportunities for solution. Immigrants soon sensed this fundamental optimism even when they remained unconvinced of its validity.

There is, of course, no way of knowing how many people considering emigration were deterred by news coming back to Europe describing the American depression. It is obvious from the accounts of Schweizer and Rütlinger that some people who knew about the state of the American economy came anyway. They were convinced of the rapid recovery of the economy or believed that in any case conditions in a depressed America would offer them an advantage over the circumstances of life in Europe.

The two Swiss were struck by the unique elements in the American character as much as by the physical and economic differences. Both of them were strongly drawn to the American atmosphere of personal freedom. They gloried in it. They made much of the fact that in this nation no free man had to bow his head or tip his hat to another as a symbol of his subservience or inferiority. In his last pages, Rütlinger spoke of his hope that America would remain "a free, happy refuge for all those who are forced from the old world by oppression and misery." Yet freedom was not for all men. It was hard for the authors to reconcile the principle of freedom universally professed and widely practiced in Amer-

21

ica with the enslavement of Negroes, their humiliation and debasement. This was, Rütlinger said, America's "stain of shame."

There has been a notable persistence in the American character and values since the beginning of the nineteenth century despite intervening changes in technology, urbanization, industrialization, and rapid population growth.[27] This persistence is clearly apparent from the observations of the Swiss immigrant families.

The Swiss families, as immigrants often did, noted how different personal relationships were in Europe and in America. Hospitality seemed boundless, incredible. The kind of hospitality that here was given to complete strangers was extended in Europe only to one's dearest friends. They admired American openness. It meant companionability, amiable familiarity, neighborly concern over another's well-being, generosity with advice, and practical aid in building a new neighbor's house or husking his corn. The new immigrants, on the other hand, did not observe the kind of intimate human relationships which they had left behind and now so sorely missed. Perhaps they witnessed them among the members of the religious sects, but not in the general community. The transitory nature of the attachments they observed in America left them concerned that relationships of a less superficial intimacy did not exist at all in this mobile, traditionless world.[28] Judging from what they could observe of intimate family life, the relationships of husband and wife and of parents and children seemed to the Swiss strangely casual, although mutual affection was obviously not absent.

If America promised opportunities for persons of certain backgrounds and skills, there was a price that its citizens paid for their good fortune. There was truly great opportunity for social mobility unhampered by old attitudes, ways of working, and institutions. Yet the Swiss families found

[27] See Henry Steele Commager, *America in Perspective* (New York: Random House, 1947), pp. xvi–xvii; W. W. Rostow, "The National Style," in Elting E. Morison, *The American Style: Essays in Values and Performance* (New York: Harper and Brothers, 1958); and Lee Coleman, "What Is America? A Study of Alleged American Traits," *Social Forces*, 19:492–499 (1941). Seymour M. Lipset, using foreign travelers' accounts of American life, manners, and traits of character in the nineteenth century, challenges Riesman's theory of a transformation in American character as a result of technological development, urbanization, and industrialization. Specifically he uses such materials to argue against the contention in *The Lonely Crowd* that these factors led to a shift from inner-direction to other-direction. See *A Changing American Character?* Institute of Industrial Relations, Reprint No. 180 (Berkeley: University of California, 1962), pp. 136–171.

[28] See Clyde Kluckhohn, *Mirror for Man: A Survey of Human Behavior and Social Attitudes* (New York: McGraw-Hill Book Co., 1949; Greenwich, Conn.: Premier Books, 1957), p. 181 of the Premier edition.

a disconcerting formlessness, a lack of structure, attitudes of impatience with all traditions — those which seemed good as well as those which seemed obviously restrictive. Freedom was immensely appealing when wisely manifested in social relationships. There was a haunting uncertainty about the lack of discipline, the disregard for order, and the little respect paid to law — even to a law that could not be counted unjust or oppressive. They observed that children were taught little discipline at home or in school. People professed to believe in education but were unwilling to make much financial sacrifice to pay for teachers' salaries. "Practical" knowledge was esteemed above "learning."

In the final pages of his *Reisebuch* Rütlinger affirmed both his uncertainty as to how the great experiment would turn out in the end and his determination to remain where he was to find out what the consequences were to be. The decision, he thought, would not be long delayed. "I do believe this, however; America is still capable of anything. I mean to say that it lies in the balance between benediction and curse. . . . Which way the balance will shift is not yet determined." And finally, "Let things be as they may, I would like to see the wonderful working of destiny in America as long as the good Lord . . . grants me life."

Many other important aspects of American life come within the compass of attention of the two Swiss immigrants: the American character; social and physical mobility; agriculture, trade, manufacture, and transportation; tools and equipment; the church, religious life, communitarian socialist utopias, the camp meeting; political institutions and the fluctuation of popular political interest; the litigious inclinations of a society in which contractual relationships are more important than relationships defined by traditional association; popular attitudes toward money; fashion and other symbols of pecuniary success; family relationships and rearing of children; the Indian and Negro slavery; common diet and recipes for apple butter; attitudes toward law and punishment; the court system and the jury; indenture; flora and fauna; and so on.

Both authors are keen, talented observers, with an exceedingly great range of interests. Each from his own perspective makes a broad survey of American life. They are amazingly intent upon informing themselves, learning as much of their new milieu as their capacities permit. In the commonsense approach of these accounts there is much wit, humor, and human understanding.

Schweizer is more the self-educated man in the quality of his interests and in concern for detailed observation. A long letter written by his wife to her parents (and reproduced after his journal) reflects the different interests and sensitivities of a woman. Rütlinger writes less critically of the United States and its inhabitants than do the Schweizers. He is more imaginative. In the preface to a book of selections from Rütlinger's *Tagebuch*, published in 1962, Dominik Jost writes, "Rütlinger is worthy of not being forgotten. He has the gift of wonderment and knows how to communicate it. . . . He forever experiences the wonderful or at least the astonishing because he is perceptive." [29]

Another native trait that impressed both men was the American's careless — sometimes shoddy — performance of work in the interest of getting things done and over quickly. Schweizer and Rütlinger mentioned this, as other immigrant books and letters of the period do, as an apparent national characteristic which manifested itself in various contexts. The American's wastefulness of food and resources caused distress to people trained by less abundance to abhor wastefulness as sinful. The carelessness in regard to quality of work and the wastefulness might have afforded the immigrant a competitive advantage over the native American but for the compensating quality both the Swiss immigrants quickly recognized, namely, a creative and inventive ingredient in the utilitarianism of Americans which led them to devise new tools, implements, and ways of performing specific tasks with minimum effort. The new arrivals often openly admired the dexterity, facility, and inventiveness which were a response to the challenge of obstacles in a society where self-reliance was already traditional. Immigrants were not generally reluctant to adopt American techniques when their utility was obvious. G. Lowes Dickinson's characterization of the American as "contemptuous of ideas but amorous of devices" finds confirmation in this period.

Schweizer and Rütlinger noted that Americans were given to asking new arrivals how much they liked America, as if they themselves were extravagantly proud but yet so uncertain of the object of pride that they continually needed confirmation from immigrants. Americans are still inclined to ask the same question upon meeting those who are newly arrived. They are plainly disappointed if newcomers voice anything but enthusiastic sentiments and extravagant praise. Sensing this, and wishing to please their new countrymen, immigrants have often deliberately fed the hunger.

[29] Dominik Jost in the Preface to an excerpt from Johann Jakob Rütlinger, *Tagebuch von einer Reise nach Nordamerika im Jahre 1823* ([St. Gallen:] Zollikofer & Co., 1962), p. 8. This edition of the book was published by apprentice typesetters and printers as part of their examination for journeymanships.

Deeply ingrained in national consciousness is the grossly oversimplified proposition which was so succinctly stated by Crèvecoeur in the eighteenth century. "What attachment can a poor European emigrant have for a country where he had nothing? The knowledge of the language, the love of a few kindred as poor as himself, were the only cords that tied him; his country is now that which gives him his land, bread, protection, and consequence; *Ubi panis ibi patria* is the motto of all emigrants."[30]

Most Americans would be reluctant to apply this to the origin of their loyalties, but they have generally assumed it valid with respect to immigrants. This disposition and national pride have led Americans generally to underestimate the love and ties of sentiment that continued to bind the new arrival to the land of his origin. It has not always been understood as well as it needs to be how difficult it has been for many immigrants to shed their old loyalties and to change their old identity of a native in a beloved land to that of an alien in a strange, even though challenging, land. It has been easier to appreciate the excitement of emigration than the self-torture that also was often part of it.

The influence of migration on the individuals that experienced it was profound; equally profound, in its very different context, was the influence on the land they came to. From the time of the founding of the first settlement to this generation, immigration has had such significant effects on America that to consider the history of the country without close attention to it would be to pull apart the tapestry of national development.

American settlement and the expansion westward were intricately bound up not only with the fertility of the native-born but with the continual movement of people into America from abroad. The settling of new regions, the growth of villages into towns, towns into cities, and cities into large metropolitan complexes are a part of national history which intrudes upon almost every other part. The most rapid period of urbanization and industrialization, which came in the late nineteenth and early twentieth centuries, coincided with a greatly accelerated immigration. No historian can afford to minimize the effect upon political, economic, and social institutions of an immigration that in some years brought a million people to America's shores from many different nations.

The perspective of the United States on migratory movements has been largely determined by its experience as the greatest receiver of immigrants in the long history of human movements. Understandably, Ameri-

[30] Michel-Guillaume Jean de Crèvecoeur, *Letters from an American Farmer,* Letter III: "What Is an American?"

25

can scholars have paid far less attention to the effects of emigration upon the yielding nations, although these have been of considerable significance. Also, the personal dimensions of emigrating-immigrating as well as of assimilation have been more competently dealt with by novelists and autobiographers than by scholars. Questions about the number, quality, and condition of immigrants have always been matters of informal public attention and concern from colonial times to the present.

In the early nineteenth century the number of immigrants was not large, but the stream flowed continually. Before the end of the first decade, it had become illegal to bring slaves from Africa into the country. The immigrants, arriving almost exclusively from Europe, came largely from those areas of the continent from which the white colonial population had been drawn. Transportation available for individual and family travel by land and sea was limited. The more effective communication facilities which stimulated later population movements remained to be invented. The capacity of the American agrarian economy in the Napoleonic period and in the period after the Peace of Vienna to attract and absorb immigrants remained relatively restricted.

In the early decades of the national period, there were no formal impediments to immigration, but there also was no special inducement beyond that provided by the opportunities it promised.[31] In addition, generally favorable official attitudes prevailed and there was an equally favorable public opinion toward the kind of ingress which by then had become traditional in America. The Congress, however, voted down proposals which would have stimulated a more rapid immigration.

In 1819 the young republic decided that it might be well to learn more about immigration than could be determined from decennial censuses, and a system was established by the government for recording immigration. The Congress enacted a law which required the captain or master of a vessel arriving at an American port from foreign ports to deliver a list or manifest to the collector of customs of that district. The officer of the vessel was required to designate the age, sex, and occupation of the various passengers, their country of origin, and their probable destination.[32] Although the system did not produce complete and accurate statis-

[31] Marcus Lee Hansen, *The Atlantic Migration, 1607–1860* (Cambridge, Mass.: Harvard University Press, 1940), p. 56.

[32] United States Immigration Commission, *Statistical Review of Immigration, 1820–1910* (Washington, D.C.: Government Printing Office, 1907–1910), Vol. III, p. 3. See also Conrad Taeuber and Irene Taeuber, *The Changing Population of the United States* (New York: John Wiley & Sons, 1958), pp. 52–53.

tics, it represented a notable improvement over the dearth of information that had prevailed until then.

The ship captains reported 8385 alien passengers in 1820, the first year the statistics were gathered by the customs collectors in American port cities. By 1825 the annual immigration had reached more than 10,000. By 1828 it had passed 20,000. In the decade of the 1830's the ingress rapidly accelerated and almost 600,000 entered. They were drawn by the developing might of the new nation — which they in turn increased — as well as spurred by dissatisfaction with their home conditions. By the 1840's the industrial expansion of the United States was making notable progress. In the West, settlements were rapidly spreading as transportation facilitated expansion in all directions. The famine in Ireland and the political unrest in Germany and elsewhere in western Europe gave impetus to the movement. In this decade 1,713,000 immigrants arrived in the United States. In the 1850's more than two and a half million came, and in the two decades of the Civil War and early postwar period the stream of immigration remained at an even level. After 1880, however, the flow of immigration increased spectacularly as large contingents arrived, for the first time, from eastern and southern Europe. From 1901 to 1910 the United States received 8,795,000 immigrants, the largest number recorded in any decade in the nation's history.

In the introduction to his book *The Uprooted*, Oscar Handlin commented, "Once I thought to write a history of the immigrants in America. Then I discovered that the immigrants *were* American history." A bit of that history is contained in these accounts by Johannes Schweizer and J. Jakob Rütlinger, Swiss immigrants and American pioneers.

PART ONE

JOHANNES SCHWEIZER was born in Hemberg, St. Gallen, May 6, 1785, and died September 21, 1831. He was the only son of Anna Elizabeth Schweizer (née Hänin) who died in 1810 and Conrad Schweizer (1735–1806). In 1808 Johannes married Anna Grob (born in 1788), daughter of town-councilor Abraham Grob (1763–1837) and his wife Salomea (née Hemisegger, 1766–1847). The daughter of Johannes and Anna Schweizer born in 1811 was named Salomea. The "Bürger Register der Gemeind Hemberg, Evangelisch Religion," Item No. 370, contains the single note that Anna Schweizer remarried in 1834 in America, three years after Johannes' death in 1831, and that their daughter married in America (no date given).

The author of the Foreword and the original editor of Schweizer's journal, CHRISTIAN FRIEDRICH KRANICH (1781–1849), was the Protestant minister in Hemberg for thirty years. He delivered his first sermon in Hemberg in 1818 and the last shortly before his death. He was a strong and beloved community leader, known for his freshness and vitality as well as for the sense of inner peace he seemed to reflect. Some of his sermons were collected and published as *Andeutungen der Sichtbaren vom Unsichtbaren in mehrern Predigten* (Glarus: Freuler Buchhandlung, 1822), and as *Schöne und Gute unseres Vaterlandes* (Ebnat, St. Gallen: Abraham Keller, 1824).

Account of a journey to North America and through the most significant parts thereof

by JOHANNES SCHWEIZER

←⊣ ————————————————————————————————

Foreword BY THE REVEREND CHRISTIAN KRANICH

SINCE the world-famous sailor Columbus,* after countless difficulties, dangers, suffering, and sickness of all kinds, happily sighted and discovered the other hemisphere of our earth, the younger sister, America, has become more and more familiar to the elder one and a more intimate friend. Many were spurred on by the desire to see the fresh, enchanting, blooming daughter across the sea, and did see her. Difficult travels by land and sea did not hold back the foot eager to wander. What cannot man dare and endure?! Not infrequently, the amount of money available for travel greatly affected the outcome. Many found good fortune; many did not. For in America, too, Dame Fortune steers with a double rudder — good and evil fortune. Where on earth would it be otherwise??

However, be that as it may, America, most particularly the northern part of it, the United States, interests and tantalizes exceedingly the mind

*Columbus is the Latin, Colombo the Italian, and Colon the Spanish form of the name. He was born in 1447 in Cagureto in Genovese territory. He died on May 20, 1506, in Valladolid, in the 59th year of his life. He possessed a noble heart and an unshakable courage which has rarely been equaled. He deserves that magnificent memorial which has been erected in Seville with the inscription: "For Castile and Leon / A new world was discovered by Colon." [C. K.]

31

of our time. Why? We have neither the space nor the authority to answer this. Enough that a general interest reigns, and that each account of travel from the old world to the new is read with great attention. This is proved by the rapid sale of these accounts among us, even when they do not deserve it.

The Account of a Journey to North America and through the Most Significant Parts Thereof, which is presented here, is the work of a level-headed, well-informed Swiss, born in Hemberg in the canton of St. Gallen. We believe we can recommend this book with good reason to the honored public, and not for the motives for which a merchant sometimes recommends his wares. In the announcement of this work, the worthy Pastor Frey of Schönengrund expressed an opinion of this work that is certainly not exaggerated or veiled by artificial praise. He wrote, among other things: "The talent of this capable man was so valued in his community that he was frequently consulted about his observations and newest judgments concerning those things attracting the attention of Europeans. In these pages one will find as much character as in the highly prized writings of the poor man from Toggenburg.[1] The versatile knowledge of the author is reflected everywhere, and the appealing language will win the reader. What the author tells of his trip by water and by land is always highly entertaining. The new information concerning the character and customs of Americans, their country, and their way of life is extensive. The account of the pros and cons of emigration is excellent, and rarely has the subject been illuminated more clearly from all sides. Seldom have recommendations been so clearly given concerning the classes of people who would or would not benefit by emigration." (The complete announcement can be found in the supplement to the *Schweizerboten,* No. 33, 1822.) Although we could add much more to the recommendation of this work, we consider it superfluous. We are convinced that it will by means of its content recommend itself sufficiently to readers of all classes. The saying is appropriate, *Factis virtus colitur, non sermonibus.*

Yet in another respect we must take a moment to talk with the various readers of this book so that each will, as far as possible, read this book

[1] The poor or, better, the ordinary man in the Toggenburg was Ulrich Bräker, a weaver of Näbis (1735–1798). His three autobiographical volumes, making pointedly humorous observations upon society and his own character, were popular and influential in the German-speaking parts of Switzerland. Many editions have appeared, including recent ones in Switzerland and East Berlin. See "Ulrich Bräker," *Toggenburgerblätter für Heimatkunde,* 25:5–9 (1962).

with an unbiased mind and will not put it down without a sense of satisfaction.

To you numerous friends and relatives of our distant Swiss-American friend we now turn. Naturally, you have wished for the publication of this travel journal for a long time. Do not be displeased with us because it was delayed longer than we would have liked. We realized that you, at least some of you, were looking forward to the journal of your friend with as much eagerness as once a heroic, far-wandering son of Ithaca longed for his distant home. We can think of no more appropriate comparison. We tried to follow the author's wishes as much as possible, but since he was not close at hand much remained to be done which could not be immediately resolved. Therefore we had to content ourselves with the adage: Slow and steady wins the race. I trust you will forgive us.

In addition, we would like to give you the latest news of your friend as of May 14. The recent communication was brief and concerned mostly with family matters of his immediate relatives in Switzerland and cannot be related publicly. He discovered late that a ship was about to sail for Europe and had to be contented with a brief note to his dear ones.

This much we can tell you: He is still in Lancaster, and he and his family are in good health; he thinks of you often in fond remembrance; he is still completely Swiss and because of this cannot easily favor the American character; he does not regret being in America, but many years must pass before he will be able to say that he likes it. In short, his letters reveal that he is still, in all ways, the same and that Americanism has not been able to take anything from him yet. To the author, the friends who urged him in sincerity to pick up his walking stick and go to America remain unforgettable. How warmly and sincerely they live on in his memory one example of many will serve to illustrate. In his last letter to the undersigned he wrote, among other things, "Give a thousand greetings to the dear, distant M.O. [He met her in Cologne.] What a wonderfully united and yet widely spaced clover-leaf — Odessa [where this friend now is], Hemberg, and America! What a curious association of ideas surges through my mind at this thought!" And in the end: "Farewell. The Lord be with you until He brings us all together again in the next world, when the long sustained chord of Odessa, Hemberg, and America is dominated by a mighty Hallelujah." (The author is a friend and student of harmony.) All his friends will understand him completely on every page of his diary, in which form his travel account appears. Nothing there will strike them as strange.

33

There are other things which should not be withheld from those who do not know the author. To them a few words in advance. The smooth language of one acquainted with polished manners and modish customs has always been alien to the author. He had to speak as he felt, not any other way. He hated flattery and was repulsed by a lie. His moral sense was always strongly expressed and readily identified him. He never wished to offend, but he had to speak the unvarnished truth. His opinion was written on his broad, curved brow even when he remained silent. His eyes sparkled when subjects of learning, which he loved, were discussed, they became fiery and burned in anger when he saw deceit, malice, injustice, and stark self-seeking. To trim his sails to the wind, as the proverb puts it, he could not and would not do. As a citizen of his native country, he was a fiery republican; he held in high esteem freedom established by law. He praised harmony and true patriotic unity often with fiery eloquence. Why then did he leave his beloved fatherland? About this matter he himself gives an honest account. The first cause lay in his own individual circumstances and in other conditions of which it would not be appropriate for us to speak. All this the gentle reader must take into consideration in order to understand thoroughly and to estimate the author justly, especially when he expresses himself strongly or appears to be arrogant.

For less educated readers, we have added a comment here and there. They are not more numerous because space did not permit. Outside of these comments the author speaks throughout for himself. We have left his writing almost completely unchanged. We believe that this will not displease his readers.

Now go forth, dear diary of a faraway friend, and begin your travels. Greet affectionately all true friends of the author. Tell them on every page how faithfully he thinks of them and continues to love them, how sacred these things are to him: the places on mountains and valleys in the shade of heavily leafèd trees, by the rushing river or by an awesomely majestic waterfall where he walked for pleasure with them, and how friendship endures even though they breathe different air. Stop in at the little house in the country and entertain the members of the family by the faithful light of the lamp. If entry is granted you to the mansions of the great, say to them that you cannot be genteel and adroit, but that you mean things honestly and perhaps they may prefer this to many a strutting gallant with his fashionable obeisances. Then return again to him who sent you over the sea. Greet him a thousand times and tell him that we will never cease to remember him with sincere Swiss love and that our homeland still enjoys freedom, peace, and prosperity. May you cross the great ocean without shipwreck and arrive safe and sound in the land which bears the name of Vespucci Amerigo!

KRANICH

Hemberg, Nov. 6, 1822

The Schweizer journal

TO MY FRIENDS

Broad lands and the wild, deep ocean separate me from all of you, and hearing news from you seems almost like a message from gray antiquity. But in my heart you are all still so close, in my memory still so fresh. I feel as though I were sitting with you in the cozy room and were singing songs in German with you about God and youth, the blessedness of friendship, our homeland, and friendly Mother Nature, and that I were chatting and dreaming with you about the welfare of our country and our families, about new discoveries and improvements. I hear you — interrupt you — argue with you. But I quickly make up with you again. I wander at your side into the quiet, remote alpine valley and climb with you the dizzying heights. I feast with you on the boundless view before us and race down the glaciers, shouting jubilantly. Eagerly we search for rare plants and for the petrified fossils of adamic times. Richly laden with treasures, we rest in the shepherd's hut, and we are restored by the song of the shepherd which comes to us from far off in the valley. We feast our eyes upon the golden sunset. That I am by your side I often imagine on my solitary walks through the American oak forests which extend for hours. I share with you my amazement when suddenly a mighty river lies at my feet, bringing light and air and life into the wilderness. I exchange opinions with you about American life and ways. I stop in with you at the home of a hospitable planter, and marvel with you at the shrewdness with which he gets what he wants. When at last reality awakens me from this sweet, blessed illusion, I call out with streaming eyes, "Oh, if only you were here!"

So these pages originated. You will find here no journal in which every event is described with anxious care, no physical or geographical account

35

of travels, nothing farfetched or classified in terms of material or execution. No, I have only sought to share with you my endeavors in a foreign land. Sometimes it was one of you, sometimes another, who was in my mind and with whom I actually conversed as I wrote. Hence this mishmash. Accept with love what your friend gave with love. If I have been able to entertain you for an hour, if you think of me with love as you read, if by means of this book I have tightened again the invisible bond that surrounds us in spite of great distance, then this will have given me a rich reward outweighing all other gains.

Should these pages be read by someone besides my friends, I ask for friendly judgment. It must be remembered that I enjoyed no scholarly education and I would never aspire to being an author. I only wrote now and then, and exactly as I would have told you orally. I never wanted, even if I had had the time and the talent, to write a logical treatise concerning the life and ways of the inhabitants or of the States of North America, because for the sake of form one often steps on the toes of truth. Rather I wanted to describe what I discovered principally by presenting facts. Do not be concerned about the contradictions in these facts. America is the land of contradictions. Want and superabundance, freedom and slavery, unrestrained liberty and coercion, dove-like simplicity and the cunning of the snake, the highest culture and the lowest barbarism — nowhere in the world do they stand so close together.

Say what you will, America is still a child, an ill-bred child, but blessed with many fine, enviable gifts. That is why sometimes the good and sometimes the bad appears in it. One should remember this in order to understand more readily not only the many contradictions in these pages but the contradictions of genuine writers who in their praise and blame of America do not agree with one another.

I took care to judge the truth of things according to my best knowledge and conscience. What I did not myself hear or observe, I got mostly from honest men whose evidence and judgment I held to be above suspicion, or I gave the source from which I drew. I sought to be impartial and consulted as many people as possible. I made my judgments without regard for my own lot or for my prospects which up to now are not bright.

You pages, dedicated to friendship, go forth! May favorable winds bring you soon to the hills and valleys where my dear ones live. May you spread many tender thoughts for the faraway friend and convince them anew that our friendship will endure through time and space!

For those who do not know me and who perhaps may read these pages, it might not be superfluous to provide some insight into what it was that awakened thoughts of emigration and brought me to the point of journeying forth.

With few worldly goods, I found myself ignorant of all the little arts of earning and saving. While not a spendthrift I was also not a penny pincher, especially when there was a possibility of acquiring something which seemed to me good and useful or something related to my favorite fields of knowledge. I could see that in spite of anything I might save in the costs of food and clothing we were always going backwards. The high cost of living, the unemployment of the time, and the increasingly somber outlook for the future multiplied my worries. I made many plans and experienced many a depressing hour.

I knew many who despite the difficult times were getting ahead and whose prospects were promising. Sometimes this was the result of an extraordinary frugality combined with the ability to endure almost anything. Sometimes it was the skill of squeezing and sucking out whatever remained to be squeezed or sucked and of cooking the gelatin out of bones on which there was no longer any meat. The first I could not do, and the second I would not do. I saw many others who, in spite of their industriousness, came daily closer to bankruptcy. Sometimes they were not even aware of what was happening to them and so almost unaware tumbled into poverty. I saw how such a state of affairs worked to the detriment of morality. I observed and heard a philosophy * become commonly held which in other times one would have been ashamed to espouse. Not only did I fear the serious consequences that could arise directly out of my own situation, but I feared more the general effect of such evil influences. The thought that perhaps I would never be able to pay my debts made me recoil as I would from torture. And with my limited means, and considering the difficulty of the times, such an eventuality was not altogether unlikely. My health, I felt, could not stand even greater efforts and deprivation than I was already making and so arose the first thoughts of emigration.

But now on the other side the crushing thought: my friends, my country, my treasured fatherland which had become so dear to me with all

* More accurately, a pseudophilosophy or cynical sophistry whose basic tenet is self-gratification or whatever flatters the senses. A good example of this is given by Plato in the dialogue between Euthydemus and Dionysodorus. [C. K.]

its hills and valleys and where I often felt so happy. Here in house and hut so many hearts beat truly with mine — to leave all this cost me many a difficult battle.

During this time I received unexpectedly an offer of a position as overseer of an estate near Basel. After an interview with Mr. F. I accepted the position gladly, because I felt that with an assured income there was still hope of staying in contact with my friends.

I began my new job and found my superior a personable man who treated me more like a friend than like a subordinate. I wish to thank him here from my heart for this treatment and for the many other kind things he did for us. But in other respects I found much that was unpleasant in my job. Part of this was due to my unfamiliarity with the local conditions and part was due to other things which I cannot now further explain. Mr. F. could not at the time put a stop to these drawbacks, so thoughts of emigration arose stronger than ever. At any rate I was already estranged from my beloved homeland: America and Basel now seemed to me equally distant from my Toggenburg. Although I had dear friends in Basel and enjoyed their unearned trust and many other blessings, I missed my own quiet hearth, which I hoped to find again in America, combined with an honorable livelihood. To this I offered now my final sacrifice, my position in the quiet, familiar Basel which had become for many reasons very agreeable to me.

It is often difficult to decide whether good sense or sentiment most affects the making and execution of important decisions. My feelings inclined me toward a quiet hearth of my own where I would not have to tremble at the heavy footsteps of creditors, and good sense led me to believe that emigration was the best way of achieving this end. Both sentiment and reason had a share in this decision. I believe I had complete freedom in choosing to remain or to leave for America. The good Lord in Heaven, I believe, allows His children to try things out in this way, but when we undertake something that threatens to turn out disastrously and we call Him in all earnestness to take the reins into His own hands, He often guides us safely over the way we chose ourselves, over field and stone. He allows us at times to see the places where we, depending on our own devices alone, would have broken our necks.

The long-anticipated and long-dreaded day was approaching. We were just waiting now for relatives to arrive who to our great joy had agreed to make the trip with us. For three days we waited impatiently for the

38

relatives whom we had not seen for a year and a half and who were now about to share so much danger and joy with us. But instead of the arrival of our traveling companions came the news that they had decided not to go along. We were stunned. The decision to give up the position in Basel had been made in anticipation of their traveling with us. Now the plans for departure were too far advanced for us to be able honorably to give them up. But to make the trip alone with my wife and child seemed daring and ill-advised at best. I relate this because it was the first but not the smallest test we faced on the road we trod. Because of the change we had to alter our earlier plans to travel down the Rhine in favor of a journey overland as far as Mannheim or Mainz.

On May 15, 1820, we left the city of Basel and with it our native land. You don't know what that means until you see village and steeple, valley and hill of the native land pass from view as you gaze in vain into the gray distance in hope of having one more glimpse of the beloved country. Now in the moment of parting, Basel, too, had become my native land, although I had never felt that way about it before. I had always wanted a Toggenburg where a Basel was. The inhabitants of Basel I had often compared unfavorably, though sometimes favorably, with the inhabitants of my Toggenburg. I was not objective enough to see good readily but I was quick to perceive the bad. Here I would like to set forth the nature of my error and injustice: The bitter would have been far outweighed in the balance had I put the helpfulness, compassion, and friendship that a single man in Basel had shown us from the moment of our arrival against the unpleasantness I found in my business affairs. It would please me greatly to name this man here, but I would not want to offend his modesty. But my friends know him, as does God in Heaven, whom he serves, and many another blesses him as I do. Oh, may the Almighty bless you, your wife and child, worthy sir! May He preserve you for a long time for the sake of souls in need of advice and help! In the strange land we shed many a tear of thanks and loneliness for you. God willing, we will see you again in the hereafter.

Only too quickly the small boat moved down the Rhine. Soon the city was disappearing and of the high cathedral tower only the spire remained visible. The hills of home were no longer before us — the Rhine curved a few more times — we could still see Basel behind its woods and in the blue background the hills of Solothurn still beckoned. So it is that a son, going out into the unknown, looks back many times upon his father's house. Ah, there on the hill from which she can see far into the distance, he sees his beloved mother waving goodbye. The pain overwhelms him. He hides his face, looks back once more, and turns the bend weeping. Thus his homeland is lost from view forever.

So, farewell, beloved Fatherland. I shall never see you again. Farewell to your majestic mountains on which I so often felt I could rise above all earthly problems! Farewell to your soft hills and beloved valleys where I often felt such childlike contentment and joy. I thank you a thousand-fold for everything that you were to me and that you gave me. From you I learned appreciation of the beauties of nature, appreciation of many nobler and more elevated pleasures which in another land would probably have remained unknown to me. Through you I learned to value freedom and virtue, learned to suffer at a brother's sorrow. In another country I would perhaps have learned contempt for them. Through you I learned the value of friendship. In what other country would so many staunch hearts have beat at one with mine?

O Fatherland, may you some day be again completely free, happy, and contented. May all your children know happiness and contentment. May the hydra of discord, of narrow regional feeling and mean party spirit, find no more foothold in your hills and valleys! I would be content to die in a foreign land if I could hear this news. Like the old Simeon this would give me courage.

And so farewell, my precious, unforgettable friends! I thank you from the heart — fervent thanks for all your marks of tender friendship, your warm compassion for our lot. Few, perhaps none, of you will I ever see in this life again, but not a one of you, not one, will I ever forget!

So sail on, in God's name, tossing boat! Lead us ever farther from fatherland and friends. They are both with us in our hearts. Indeed, we are all going to the same last homeland, whether our way leads us along the Mississippi or the Rhine.

From Neuburg on the Rhine we went on foot and now and then by good chance on some wagon through the fruitful, pleasant land along the Rhine. Everywhere we stopped we were met with the question, "Are you really going to America?" Sometimes we were pitied; often we were wished good luck. Our decision was sometimes regarded as that of a madman; at other times it was seen as an example of enterprise and mature judgment. Thus it is, I often thought, even in situations in which we expect a child would be quickly able to see the truth. Daily we see the most perceptive people with the same fund of knowledge making completely different judgments about the same thing. Somebody must be

40

wrong, although we find it very difficult to entertain any mistrust of our own understanding. We want to grasp, with our limited intelligence, things that the space between the planets is not large enough to encompass.

It is truly a pleasure to travel through the river towns of Baden from Basel to Freiburg. One can only note the cleanliness, the order, the health in body and soul of these towns and their inhabitants. Such a people was worthy of a ruler like Karl Friedrich[2] and such priests as Dalberg and Wessenberg. What a shame it is that there are so few of them!*

For unforeseen reasons we had to stay in Freiburg a few days. I say this reluctantly, but it is nonetheless true, in few cities of Switzerland have I found such a friendly, kind, and congenial atmosphere as here. Also the discipline of the troops deserves praise. There were about 1600 infantry troops in the city, and yet I heard not the least noise. Even less did I find among them that kind of ridiculously stupid pride and crudeness often found among young people who believe a uniform to be a privilegium † for an undisciplined life.

Here, where more industries ‡ have engendered a larger population, we also heard more complaints about poor earnings. I was astounded at the unbelievably low prices of articles manufactured here. In the country, too, there did not seem to be the prosperity existing farther up. In the earliest hours of the morning, farmers' wives with cans of milk were already at the door, having carried the milk for two or three hours. And young girls, poorly but cleanly dressed, tried to sell lilies of the valley (*Convallaria majalis*) and other flowers; they offered forty to fifty flowers for two pfennig,[3] and the milk was also sold at the lowest price possible.

[2] Karl Friedrich (1728–1811) was a Grand Duke of the German Duchy of Baden. During his long reign (1749–1811) he established many reforms and won a reputation abroad as a ruler of unusual wisdom and humanity. He was strongly influenced by the Enlightenment in France and corresponded with a number of eminent French intellectuals. See Hellmuth Rössler and Günther Franz, *Biographisches Wörterbuch zur Deutschen Geschichte* (Munich: R. Oldenbourg, 1953), pp. 435–436. There were in this era several important personages bearing the names Dalberg and Wessenberg. The particular persons to whom Schweizer was referring in this context remain obscure.

* Would not anyone who knows these names well echo a fervent amen to the words of this honest traveler?! [C. K.]

† An exception from ordinary law. [C. K.]

‡ Including crafts, factories, manufacturing, trade, and handiwork. [C. K.]

[3] The accounts of both Schweizer and Rütlinger make mention of many of the common coins used in the early nineteenth century along the Rhine. Each German state and Swiss canton minted its own coins. Coins bearing the same name often varied considerably in value from state to state and within each state from time to time. Because of this confusion, English bank notes were often preferred in business transactions. The confused state of coinage makes it very difficult to render precise equivalents. The table below was devised largely from data in Valentin Giterman,

41

It would have been difficult to find anyone in Basel who would have even delivered milk for that price.

I do not really understand economics, but I wonder if the money being spent for maintaining the soldiers here could not have been put into circulation in a more beneficial way; and whether people are really so utterly depraved that the golden dreams dreamed in the land of the chimera can never be realized in the land of actuality; and why it is that, of all the wishes for the good fortune of the sons of earth and for the lessening of their griefs, nine tenths would be reckoned by sensible people as fit only for the dust-heap of foolish fancies; and why the realization of the remaining tenth is so laborious and demanding that one would often rather keep the disease than expose oneself to the rigors of the cure. Is it that way everywhere? Must it be so, or could it be otherwise? It is true that the wisest of kings said: "All is vanity under the sun," but perhaps a Joshua would never have said that had he been king. In a word, I agree with the poet who said: "Let us become better and soon it will be better." But if only ninety-nine become better, and the hundredth one remains bad, and unfortunately has more power than the others, then indeed things will get very little better.

If the good in this world is ever completely to conquer the evil, the world will have to endure for many more thousands of years.* An uncharted field is yet to be crossed. If in one century a few inches are gained, then in a following century half of that gain is lost.

The poor, clean, hardworking Freiburg tradesmen wakened in me many a melancholy thought and called forth many a pious wish. Poverty accompanied by spiritual depravity shakes one, indeed. We despair of the possibility of improvement and try to push the memory from our minds. On the other hand, poverty linked with order and virtue touches us only in a pleasant way. How happy one could make these people, if, instead

Geschichte der Schweiz (Thayngen, Schaffhausen: Augustin Verlag, 1941), p. 479, and the Muret-Sanders *German-English Dictionary*.

4 pfennig = 1 kreuzer		1 florin = 1 gulden	
4 kreuzer = 1 batzen		11 florins = 1 louis d'or	
15 batzen = 1 florin		90 kreuzer = 1 reichsthaler	
25 stüber = 1 florin		25 batzen = 1 reichsthaler	

Rütlinger helpfully points out that 3 kreuzer was the equivalent of 2 American cents in the 1820's.

*This cannot be reckoned mathematically. Let us persevere with courage for the common good. Let us not allow hope to diminish. Let us show, as Epictetus did, moral greatness through patience and endurance. Since Christ, after all, there has been improvement, if not in general, then in specific ways. And it will get better!! [C. K.]

of spending many a hard thaler for a game at which one yawns, or sacrificing louis d'ors for finery and fashion which after a few weeks will be thrown in the corner because one had the vexation of seeing similar items at a neighbor's, if, I say, one were now and then to find amusement — this could also become quite a new fashion — in buying from these poor people and paying four times what they ask. Or, to be a bit more romantic and adventurous, such a poor family should be ambushed by night and fog; for their rags, new clothes should be given, and for their wretched potatoes, sausage and ham should be tossed to them. Such a Mardi Gras prank might be as entertaining as any robber drama. At a concert we often come upon disharmony, at a ball unhealthy blood. We see on the stage what we could see at home in the flesh, or see what we are ourselves, or what we do not want to become. Not much would be sacrificed if the suggested new entertainment were introduced.*

On the twentieth of May we left Freiburg after paying our accommodating innkeeper a very small sum, and rode with a farmer as far as Ringsheim. In body and soul our driver was a crippled piece of humanity. A massive head, a horrible mouth, a pair of spindle legs, a shrieking, raucous voice, all in all the physiognomy of a malevolent ape made his appearance both ridiculous and repulsive. In my conjecture he was like an old lawyer or pettifogger who, from sheer corruption and crooked dealing, was on the verge of losing his senses. To his twelve-year-old son he related tales of his underhanded dealings with great self-satisfaction. If the boy burst forth with an occasional comment that here or there he had gone about things wrong, the man would clap his dry claws together and with hissing laughter cry, "Do you hear? That boy will someday be the devil's apprentice." No doubt of that, I assured him.

We were not much luckier in our choice of an inn in Ringsheim. An appalling filth prevailed. Clothes, rags, bread, excrement, children, dogs, chickens, and so on lay and crept over one another on the floor. Behind the table sat a female upon whom was to be seen practically everything that was on the floor. I inquired after the mistress of the inn, and this picture of horror informed me that it was she. What could one do? It was already night and outside the rain poured down. We just had to be patient. Although we were hungry, patience could not restore our appetite. In the night the innkeeper came home drunk, and even by morning he could scarcely stand up. He cursed and orated endlessly. Sometimes he consigned his wife to the devil, sometimes his children, his house and

* How well said! [C. K.]

43

yard, and, indeed, the whole kit and caboodle. On top of that, for all he cared, the d——d weather could knock everything to bits, so that Lucifer* would get everything in pieces. Not until noon did we finally have the opportunity of moving our belongings out of this dog kennel.

In Friesenheim we encountered a somewhat better inn, although here too there was a veritable Bacchanalia.† Until late into the night the racket went on; two common rooms of the inn were filled. Never have I seen a Whitsuntide so spent and never myself spent one so unrestfully and unpleasantly. How superior are the people in and around Freiburg to these people. As one approached the south district of Alsace from the Rhine, the better qualities of popular character were lost.

On the Monday after Whitsuntide, we went by way of Offenburg to Appenweiher, a friendly place. Here we turned in at The Sun and found the innkeepers both friendly and fair. All was quiet and peaceful. But in an inn across the way there was noise until morning made by people dancing and bowling. Finally, several men beat each other up thoroughly as a farewell gesture. From Freiburg to where we are now, one can find many examples of that well-known observation based on wide experience, namely, that where there are many well-built inns, most of the homes will have broken windows and many dirty, ragged children.

From Appenweiher to about an hour above the town of Rastatt, the countryside is uniformly pleasant and picturesque. Beautiful, fruitful valleys are surrounded by wooded heights on which here and there the ruins of old castles are visible between clumps of spruce.

The vegetation is luxurious. An innkeeper in Aalsbach showed us hemp sixteen feet long, and that was male hemp. The rye stood like a wall before us. On these fruitful fields corn, potatoes, cabbage, beets, and low beans were planted together. As disorganized as such mixed cultivation looks, this method must not be too bad for small farm holdings. Early-ripening plants make room for later-ripening ones. The beans entwine themselves willingly around the strong cornstalks. In the shade of the potato plant the white beet flourishes.

Rastatt is an attractive city. The castle in which the famous, tedious,

---

* Literally, "light-bringer," the morning star. It is also, however, the evening star. Thus it has come to mean "the prince of darkness." [c. к.]

† Feast of Bacchus, god of wine, honored by the pagans. The most important celebration consisted of a procession which depicted the triumph of Bacchus. The celebrants, both men and women, enraptured by wine, swarmed about in a frenzy and abandoned themselves without restraint to their senses. [c. к.]

useless Congress [4] held its meetings is truly a regal edifice. But the humane concern characteristic of the innkeepers of Freiburg we did not find here. We were turned down in seven inns. For a while we thought we might have to spend the night on the street, until one innkeeper finally let himself be talked into taking us. Our innkeeper informed us that while the Congress was in session he got one louis d'or a day for the little room in which he settled us. It seems that the innkeepers of Rastatt are still nostalgic for that golden time. Or they have grown so fat on louis d'ors that the measly kreuzer and batzen of the honest wayfarer are no longer palatable to them.

The region from Rastatt to Karlsruhe is a boring, unfruitful wasteland. The eye is no longer delighted by the fresh green of the fields. Pale, sparsely growing rye and here and there a stunted cherry tree characterize the scene along the road. Off in the distance to the right the fir forest extends for miles beyond the wasteland, offering a welcome diversion from the monotony of the scenery.

We stopped to refresh ourselves in an inn we found in Grünenwinkel, a little village near Karlsruhe. We found a room full of ragged children, an equally ragged and drunken innkeeper, and his wife, her face showing the marks of deepest misery. All of this permitted us no pleasant moment of refreshment. We made haste to leave the place. Grünenwinkel looked very poor in general. Large but more or less neglected and damaged houses appeared to have known far better days. Outside of this village we crossed a new and costly bridge over a murky and meandering stream. Soon thereafter on either side of the street began a row of giant poplars. We rubbed our eyes to awaken from the bad dream of Grünenwinkel's poverty. Soon to the right and left parks and woods alternated. When one had passed through the row of some eight hundred poplar trees, suddenly as at the magic touch of a fairy the royal city appeared out of the desert.

Morning, noon, and night, large numbers of magnificently equipped troops with ringing military music moved through the streets. Busily the officers in charge and the public officials hurried to the castle and left again, proceeding from there in every direction to carry out their orders. Everywhere the eye was met with luxury and art. This is no mere Euro-

[4] The Congress of Rastatt opened in December 1797. Representatives of the various states of the Holy Roman Empire and of France were present. The negotiations were brought to an end with the outbreak of the Second Coalition War (1798–1801).

pean city, this is a Palmyra,* a Heliopolis.† Who could dream of Grünenwinkel after this?

But in the closed room, with soft voice, his eye straying toward the door, the heir of all this fine art complained that there was no taste for it, that art now catered to the popular taste, and the lowest popular taste, too, and he mourned over past golden days. The official complained about great expenditures and money due to the soldiers. Many businesses were daily becoming more and more pressed financially. The sons of Mars complained about the rations that were too meager, and their poor pay for hard, oppressive service. The townsman and the artisan moaned about the great number of duties and taxes which they would soon be unable to scrape together. They complained about the recession of trade and commerce, and chattered about happy bygone days. Actors, musicians, officials, and soldiers were blamed for destroying the vital heart of the land. Everyone thought it could not go on as it was and each person thought he alone carried the burden; it was time to lead the Trojan horse into the city. Who was right? I think that there is basic validity in each complaint, but to perceive the fundamental nature of the evil not many are bright enough to do.

We paid the innkeeper's bill, and a fair one it was. For us it was really something out of a golden age. The night of May 25 we made a pilgrimage as far as Schreckheim. Thus we pursued our fortune by land and sea — the good fortune, which we were told, had also emigrated from this land.

In Schreckheim we were fortunate to find a boat bound for Speyer. We embarked immediately. The boat had a galley and two elegantly papered rooms. About a hundred feet from our boat a crowd of people were milling about, busily trying to salvage something from the wreckage of a ship which had sunk two days earlier. The ship had been carrying eighty barrels of sugar and several tons of iron. So quickly had the accident occurred that the entire crew was lost. This was a rather unpropitious introduction to a sea journey.

The crew of our ship was a rough, unholy lot. The Skipper was hardly in his cabin when they began to brawl and fight like wildcats. Nevertheless I must say to their credit that to us they were very friendly and ready to help. By noon we reached the Bavarian customs port of Germersheim.

* A famous ancient city in Syria. It was especially rich and powerful in the time of the Roman emperor Trajan. It lay in a palm forest in a valley lying in the midst of a desert. Later it was ravaged. Now Palmyra, under the old name Tadmor, is a poor village. So things change on earth! [C. K.]

† A city in lower Egypt which was famous for its temple to the sun. [C. K.]

Here there is a pontoon bridge. We had an unfavorable wind, and because of that there was much noisy argument and complaining between the ship's crew and the bridge guards, until finally we were able to slip through the opening made for us. Then the customs officials boarded the boat to ascertain whether the cargo was in accordance with the declaration. After that the whole crew went into town to have a good time. It was three o'clock before we left Germersheim, and we did not reach Speyer until ten o'clock. We had already been turned down at three inns and were about to try a fourth one when a half-naked fellow emerged from behind a caved-in wall.

"D——n it all," he cried, "I believe they don't want to put you up for the night! You are Swiss, aren't you? The D——l take me if I don't break all the innkeeper's doors and windows if he doesn't let you in this minute!" With these words, he ran hard against the door and threatened the innkeeper's body and soul if he did not open the inn quickly. These courteous attentions were not at all appealing to us, and we would have liked to sneak away. But the innkeeper actually appeared and was quite polite and moreover apologized for not having opened the inn to us sooner.

This rough, tattered quarters-finder of ours was a character. By trade he was a ship's servant, he told us, and he had sailed twice to Amsterdam in this capacity in ships carrying emigrating Swiss. He recognized us by our Swiss dialect. The man painted a terrifying picture of the fate of the Swiss who emigrated in 1817. Many of them perished in Holland from hunger and lice. From his own experience he could tell us that most of those who had perished had not even survived the boat trip to Amsterdam. He tried, sometimes by cursing and sometimes by imploring, to persuade us to turn back.

Only in the morning did our quarters begin to appear interesting to me. The inn was part of an extensive and partly ruined building in which the royal court of justice had once held its sessions. Our housing agent and his family lived in one room very close to the former courtroom which was now completely in ruins. My imagination took wings. I envisioned this ship's servant as the ghost of an ancient German knight who was now and then awakened from his slumber by the inhospitable spirit of the present-day Germans.

With great pomp the birthday of the King of Bavaria was celebrated today. What events must have been feted here several hundred years ago? What events would be celebrated here several hundred years from

47

now? In these ruined walls where sovereigns often stopped, terrible judgments had been pronounced which often made princes tremble. Now only a few day-laborers sought shelter here. In the courtroom crows and owls now made their homes. In the distant future certainly herds would graze here, and a father would tell his son the almost forgotten tale of the city of Speyer which was supposed to have stood here long ago.

Until May 29 we waited here for the chance of getting passage on a boat, but in vain. For a boat trip as far as Mannheim we were asked to pay two thaler. We had the luggage that we had with us shipped to Mainz, and we started off on foot. Because our child was not well, we failed to get any farther than Mannheim this day. There again we met a hospitable and fair innkeeper in the red house near the Neckar gate. Madame von Grymberg and Mr. Akermann, to whom we had letters of introduction, took us in with such cordiality and good will that I never think of them except with deep gratitude and love. May God in heaven reward them for it.

Everywhere in Mannheim they were talking about the execution of Sand.[5] What the people had to say about it and how they expressed themselves gave little indication that they were satisfied with the situation. Sand's execution was, indeed, not the way to greater harmony. Without the care and protection which Sand was accorded during the trial, and which the people must really have appreciated, the death of this visionary patriot could easily have been the signal for revolutionary action.

Mannheim is a large market center for agricultural commodities. I found several articles for sale which were completely new to me, for example, dried and hulled peas and beans. Moreover, it has its own mill

[5] In Mannheim on March 23, 1819, a student of theology, Karl Ludwig Sand, stabbed to death August von Kotzebue, a prolific but minor dramatist and a propagandist in the service of the Russian Empire. Kotzebue was particularly hated by young liberals because he opposed their demands for more democratic political institutions. Sand was a member of one of the most radical of the secret societies among the newly formed *Burschenschaften*, the German university student associations. Sand was executed for the crime. He was widely regarded as a martyr to the movement for national unity but a somewhat misguided one. The murder of Kotzebue gave Metternich, Austria's powerful foreign minister, the opportunity to suppress liberal and nationalist sentiments in the interest of preventing chaos. Metternich called a conference of representatives of German rulers to meet in Carlsbad. Out of the conference came a series of decrees designed to suppress expressions of liberal and national ideas. A commission was established to combat what were defined as revolutionary doctrines. The decrees were passed by the federal diet in September 1819, but their execution varied greatly within the many German jurisdictions. See G. Mann, *Deutsche Geschichte des neunzehnten und zwanzigsten Jahrhunderts* (Frankfurt-am-Main: S. Fischer Verlag, 1958), pp. 122–123, 127.

for grinding rye. The half-ripe rye heads are cut off, placed in baking ovens, roasted, and then dried. Then at the mill they are just cracked a bit. This is delicious as soup or mush. Also the local pearl barley is superior, to my thinking, to the famous *Ulmergrütze*; the *Speltzgrütze* or the so-called grits are also far more carefully prepared here than in Switzerland or Swabia.

Here too I saw the preparation of Mannheim sausage. The desired quantity of meat and bacon was cooked a bit, then the meat was finely chopped. The bacon was cut coarsely and then mixed with pigs' blood and kneaded into a dough. After the desired amounts of salt and spices were added, the mass was stuffed into large intestines and quickly cooked once more. Then it was hung up in the smoke room.

Anyone who is about to travel down the Rhine to America and wants to bring his own provisions, in part or completely, can buy the best here the most advantageously.

Once again neither a large skiff nor any other suitable boat was to be found to take us down the Rhine, so we left Mannheim on foot at noon on the thirtieth. We went by way of Frankental and Worms and finally reached Osthofen this day. Here again the most ungodly, inhospitable spirit haunted the innkeepers of this town. Unfortunately, no housing provider came to our rescue here. Instead, we had to travel three quarters of an hour more at night till finally in a little tavern we found a hospitable reception. The innkeeper had served with English troops and had participated in the last campaign against the United States directed from Canada. His wife had accompanied him as a canteen woman. They had not been back very long. They provided for their livelihood through this little tavern and a garden which was beautifully and diligently tended. These people left a country whose language and customs they knew and turned away from everything in order to cross the wild ocean to return to their native land. This they did even though many tales of need and poverty had reached them while they were abroad in the foreign land. And we were leaving this land for one in which we might become poverty-stricken – a land which they so happily left. So we all search, often by completely divergent paths, for fickle fortune, which, like a ventriloquist, seems to call us first from this corner and then from that one until our feet are sore. Finally we get clever enough, as Rückert[6] says,

[6] Frederick Rückert (1788–1866) was a professor of Oriental languages at the University of Erlangen and later at Berlin. He wrote *Sonnets in Harness* and other works of poetry. He was particularly known as a translator and interpreter of Persian and other Oriental poetry in Germany.

> "... *länger mit Schnaufen*
> *dem Narrn nicht nachlaufen.*"

> "... no longer, panting,
> To run after fools."

From Osthofen to Mainz the countryside is lovely. Here and there a valley garlanded with vine-covered hillsides and occasionally a ruined castle make the whole scene so charmingly romantic. In Nierenstein (literally, Kidney Stone) we stopped to sample the famous grape juice which has given the area its name. This famous juice has, it is claimed, melted away the kidney stones of many a jaded gentleman. But our host overdid it and poured us such a tart, sour wine that I am sure it could have dissolved flint, not just kidney stones.

From Nierenstein we took a boat to Mainz because we were fatigued. As soon as we arrived, we immediately sought Mr. Kayser to whom we had sent our baggage. I found him to be an honest and friendly man. I was not a little astonished at the high freight charge made by Mr. Fischer, the freight dispatcher in Basel. Therefore, I would advise anyone making this journey to be more cautious with Mr. Fischer than I was or, better yet, not to use him at all. Mr. Kayser sent a commercial agent with me to find a booking on a boat going to Cologne. There was a boat there which we engaged to take us and our luggage for an acceptable price. They would have a few more days' layover awaiting cargo, but we were granted permission to board the boat the next day.

On June 1 we boarded the boat, which bore the name *Herck Hin*. I had purchased a bucket, a small coal brazier, a sack of coal, bread, bacon, and barley meal, and so we took our effects into the rear of the hold. There, on top of several hundred bushels of wheat, we set up our housekeeping quarters and congratulated ourselves on having escaped from the whole breed of innkeepers. Most of them are a depraved and uncouth lot. From this day forth, I will give selections from my diary.

June 2. The boat *Herck Hin* can hold a cargo of approximately two thousand hundredweight, is uncomfortable and not a little leaky. Almost every half hour the water has to be pumped out. But the boat is going to Cologne first, and the Skipper seems to be a fairly honest man. These are grounds enough for preferring this boat.

Mainz seems almost to be a seaport city. At a rough count about two hundred boats are tied here. In the harbor there are boats with hot and cold baths. The bathrooms are equipped with all possible conveniences.

Out of the cabins emerge groups of well-groomed ladies and gentlemen. The pontoon bridge is never empty. The sixteen mills along the Rhine intensify the picture of industrious activity.

It is a very stormy, blustering day. Rain, drizzle, storm, and sunshine alternate and mix together. The wind rages mightily in the masts and rigging. Often it is so powerful that you have to cling to the deck to keep from being swept over.

Just now my trunks arrived on the ship. Impatiently I ripped open the one with letters from my faithful A. and G. and R. I had not been able to read them in Basel. Oh, it was a painfully sweet pleasure! The enclosed pictures! What a precious, tender, thoughtful gift! So many other priceless souvenirs of our loved ones. Oh, how close I feel to you and yet how very far I am from you. Oh, may merciful God reunite us again in the land of eternal peace.

June 3. Today I bought a jug of double-strength brandy for 27 kreuzer. Brandy is considerably cheaper here than in Switzerland; other food supplies are a bit more expensive than in the cities on the upper Rhine, cheese and butter by almost half. Iron tools are very reasonable. There does not seem to be much money in circulation in Mainz, despite the fact that it is a transportation and commercial center and that the upper class enjoys considerable luxury. Complaints about unemployment, taxes, and duties are loud and widespread.

I will grant you that in monarchical states many improvements are introduced more quickly and more successfully than in republics. But in not a single monarchy is there a just division of burdens. It is true that even in republics the rich, relatively speaking, bear the smallest burden, but the contrast is not as screamingly apparent as in monarchies. Many a Swiss, in spite of poverty and need, would bless his government and constitution were he able to look around outside of his native country, although I readily admit there are many reasons for complaint.

June 4. Last evening our Skipper, Härling, left Mainz. Because three of our crates had not yet arrived, I had to stay behind. I was able to leave Mainz in a small boat just this afternoon. It was raining as hard as it could, and a strong back wind spun us over the Rhine like a piece of down. Only late at night did we arrive in Bingen, where Skipper Härling had dropped anchor. Again our campsite on the wheat, under cover, seemed very attractive to me.

This morning I stopped at Weissenau, about an hour from Mainz, to conduct business. A large procession was taking place. A celebration like

that is interesting because it often reveals quite precisely at what level the people are in their religious, spiritual, ethical, and aesthetic interests. Every house that the procession passed was decorated with pictures, flowers, ribbons, and so on. Candles burned everywhere. The roads were all strewn with grass and flowers and in certain parts covered with bowers of green branches. Musicians and the military were mixed up in the parade; but the thing that really makes a procession solemn, the religious element, was completely missing. Boys and girls tussled with one another; laughter and chatter were general. Yet I found in several places in Mainz the posted announcement of "plenary indulgence" for every person who on a designated day, at a specified church, would take part in the procession and mass. What Luther said on one occasion came to mind: "Reason is often like a drunken peasant on horseback; if you help him up on one side he falls down on the other." Indulgence-peddling is indeed a strange phenomenon in an epoch of disbelief.*

June 5. Spent the whole day in Bingen. The little city has an unusually picturesque setting, a narrow valley enclosed by high, steep mountains. Through the middle of the valley flows the Rhine which below Bingen swells to fill the whole breadth of the valley. The mountains are terraced †and planted in vineyards, and in this fashion every bit of land is used. Here and there on the uppermost heights are little fields of rye, like green ribbons hanging down from a hat. Occasionally a castle stands out boldly and even in its ruinous state looks large.

The price of a morgen⁷ of vineyard property ranges from 1000 to 2800 gulden. Still one cannot expect a big return because the grape plants are cultivated only to knee height. I asked the Skipper for the reason behind this strange way of raising grapes. Instead of giving me further explanation, he simply answered, "This method would be used everywhere, if vineyard cultivation were also understood in other areas." How often one is talked down to in this tone, in almost every field of human knowledge!

June 6. Today at ten o'clock our boat left Bingen. About half an hour's time below the little city is the infamous Bingenloch.⁸ When we were still

* Very true! Who in our time cannot make the sad observation that superstition and atheism are the two poles which influence one another greatly and merge with one another?! [c. k.]

† A terrace in agriculture is a gradually rising elevation of earth, each layer often artificially secured by rocks, lawn, flowers, etc. [c. k.]

⁷ A morgen was about nine-tenths of an acre in area.

⁸ The Bingenloch is a famous whirlpool which has long inspired awe and has added to the attraction tourists have found in this portion of the Rhine valley.

some distance from it, the sailors began to cross themselves and to pray. I did not anticipate anything ordinary, because this religious attitude on the part of our crew seemed foreboding. But I found the danger not at all as great as I feared. A reef, fifty to sixty feet wide, seems to stretch across the Rhine, but it can be navigated even at low tide. Toward the western shore crags project here and there. When the water level is of average height, probably half of the Rhine's width can be navigated.

There is nothing prettier imaginable than the boat trip down the Rhine from Mainz to Koblenz. Below Bingen the Rhine is always surrounded by mountains, and often sheer cliffs rise precipitously above the water. The rocks seem to be slate containing ferrous material. Wherever the slate had crumbled, or a little soil existed, or even wherever a few shovels of soil could be carried in, grapes were to be found, planted like dwarfed bean plants. It seems incredible that the yield could cover the expense of constructing and maintaining the many walls and the culverts through which the little streams can rush down to the Rhine.

Often stone walls of two or three hundred cubic feet are needed to permit the planting of thirty or forty vines. If as a result of frost or rain a boulder is loosened, this may result in destroying in a quarter of an hour what twenty or thirty men could not possibly rebuild in a month. Almost every half hour we came upon old fortresses built on projecting ledges, so that from a distance they often give the appearance of floating on air. Only with difficulty could the tooth of time gnaw away at them. Rastatt, Karlsruhe, and Mannheim will scarcely last as long as these. In the old days strength was more important than elegance; now it is just the opposite.

The towns and cities along the Rhine often appear to be completely pinched in between the cliffs. All bear evidences of former prosperity, and, to a degree, of present prosperity. Diligence and industriousness are manifested everywhere. Is it possible for a country which so carefully utilizes every speck of valuable land to become as poor as the trade centers of Switzerland are now? And what kind of fate is in store for these areas when wine brings barely half of its present price? I think that a manufacturing society and one that strives exclusively to develop commerce are in about the same situation, their welfare dependent upon many circumstances beyond their control.

This evening we made a stop in Koblenz. A ship with emigrants lay next to us. Their ship was examined to the last detail, as was every passenger down to his skin. The previous week several thefts by such emi-

54

grants are supposed to have occurred. This made the drastic measures necessary. They were not applied in our case; not even our passport was asked for. On our crates we had to pay only a paltry sum.

Such acts of thievery on the part of emigrants naturally cast a bad light on emigrants in general. Sometimes it is difficult to prove oneself a convincing exception. The famous Franklin * once sent the English government a barrel of rattlesnakes as a return gift for a boatload of outcasts. Even today this must often seem an appropriate repayment for many of those who enter the country. After I had seen a boatload of them close at hand, I must say that the thought of making a sea voyage with a large group of emigrants is horrifying. This boat was going to Antwerp, but even if it had been going to Amsterdam it would have been difficult for me to decide to travel with them.

This evening I still had time to visit Mrs. von S., who had prepared a very friendly reception for me. I spent a most enjoyable evening with her. My conviction was strengthened anew that neither religious nor political boundaries delimit the kingdom of the good and noble.

June 7. Today we had already departed by 3:30. In an hour we were already in Neuwied. Earlier I had decided to stay here a day and let my wife and child travel ahead to Cologne. However, we had become convinced that from more than one point of view it was not advisable to leave the ship. The Skipper did not want to make a stop here, so I was not able to make any use of the letters of introduction to people here. I was sorry about this.

From Koblenz to Neuwied the country is flatter; farther on the mountains become steeper again. Here and there vineyards reappear, and occasionally a patch of rye was seen — hung on the slope, I should say. We Swiss certainly do not use our soil nearly as well as they do here. They use fertilizer in an annoyingly neglectful manner, however. If the soil were not incomparably more fertile than ours, the crops would long ago have stopped growing.

I have noticed many times how the wash, laundered only in the cold waters of the Rhine, gets white so easily and so quickly. An ordinary soaking in lye would not have done more for us in Switzerland. I have never seen such results in Switzerland from the waters of a stream. Is there

* Benjamin Franklin was born in Boston, January 17, 1706. He is the inventor of the lightning rod. He was also the first to explain the nature of the northern lights, and the electric kite is his discovery. He also invented a unique, fuel-saving cooking stove. Although he perfected the harmonica, he was not, as was formerly believed, its inventor. [C. K.]

much alkaline material present in the water here, and has it combined with certain oils and animal fats to form soap? Granting the availability of these things, why are they not stabilized by acids, which must be equally as available as alkalines? Is the composition of the atmosphere noticeably changed because of the lower elevation? And does this difference in some way or other have an effect upon washing and drying?

A barge carrying lumber bound for Holland passed us today. A tremendous thing! It could have been perhaps 1100 to 1200 feet long. Six fairly sizable cottages, equipped with doors and windows, stood upon it. In an enclosure stood two head of cattle apparently destined for slaughter. There were perhaps fifty to sixty people on it. In case of an adverse wind, these barges go faster than a boat because the wind finds little resistance. With a favorable wind, of course, a boat sails much more rapidly because of the sails. The rudders at the front and back of the barge serve only to steer. Unmarried men who want to work as bargemen often find an opportunity to get to Holland free or perhaps even earn a little by it. This is not suitable for families and they are rarely taken on.

Near Linz the countryside becomes flatter again. Here and there one still sees considerable areas of vineyards, but far too little grain is cultivated. Food staples are markedly higher here.

Often when I saw the quantity of lampblack being loaded and unloaded I wondered if lampblack production could possibly become a branch of industry suitable for various areas of my native land. This enterprise is carried out with very little expense and could certainly be combined with the production of charcoal and potash. Also the preparation of lampblack would give some of our people in the Upper Toggenburg employment. There are areas in St. Gallen and Appenzell where wood cannot be used for other purposes. I am certain that there could hardly be a lack of a market for lampblack.

I have also often thought that the manufacturing of noodles would be a worthy enterprise. From Basel to where we are now, I found their use quite general and also their price high. Rarely is flour as white as in Canton Appenzell and in the Upper Toggenburg seen elsewhere in Switzerland and along the Rhine. If the noodle industry were developed there and if a mechanic were to devise some original ideas for making a noodle machine, perhaps in a short time they could compete with Italian macaroni and possibly even surpass it.

We had an unfavorable wind all day. We dropped anchor in some out-of-the-way place. Cologne must still be five hours away.

The customs officer, who came on board our boat in Koblenz to make certain that nothing was unloaded in the Prussian states, is a very friendly and fairly well-educated man. I spent the time very pleasantly with him. He told me many amusing stories of the tricks people use to smuggle things. Clear proof, this is, of how tariff and customs barriers undermine the morality of a people. The Prohibition System is a veritable *Aqua Tofana** for the already weakened moral life and a certain way of converting Europe into a huge Botany Bay.[9]

June 8. Today we left very early with an adverse wind. The land is becoming increasingly more level. There are no longer any vineyards to be seen. A cold north wind is blowing, and here and there windmills swing their gigantic wings. Little by little Cologne, with its many towers and its forest of mastheads, appears on the horizon. As we get nearer, we hear the raucous noise of the seamen and the sound of the bells on the floating bridge which reaches from shore to shore. Our ship is anchored approximately in the middle of the harbor. We were thus completely hemmed in by a forest of masts and ropes.

Immediately I went to Mr. Böker to see about my crates, which I had expected in Mainz. I found the people in the office to be very friendly, especially Mr. Böker, who is a very congenial man. He was truly interested in helping me. He informed me that it would be very difficult to get to Amsterdam on a merchant ship, because the Dutch skippers did not want to be bothered with such traffic. Smaller boats rarely if ever sailed down. Still he promised to do whatever he could. Then I went to Mr. Huyssen and Maria O. and discovered here, too, a cordial reception. Mr. Huyssen even sent a travel agent with me to aid in arranging passage. More than twenty places turned us down flat. Most of them said that Mr. Böker had already made inquiry on my behalf.

Finally a boatman from Utrecht agreed to take us and our belongings. He escorted me to his boat, showed me the little room we could occupy, and then pointed out his fine quarters which consisted of four papered rooms in which were tables, armchairs, couches of mahogany, costly

* *Aqua Tofana,* a poisonous drink. A Sicilian woman named Tofana was the discoverer of this drink. She is said to have put several hundred people to death with it. The drink itself is supposed to be a tasteless, clear liquid, five or six drops of which are sufficient to be fatal. This poison acts very slowly without pain, inflammation, spasms, or fever. Just a weariness of living, gradual loss of strength, loss of appetite, and constant thirst are the symptoms. Finally a complete wasting away results. [C. K.]

[9] A penal settlement was founded on Botany Bay in New South Wales, Australia, in 1788, near the present city of Sydney.

mirrors, silver and porcelain service, golden pendulum clocks, paintings, and other evidences of Dutch luxury. He told his wife that he was going to take us along, that we had recommendations from Mr. Mandach and Mr. Quien and were also highly recommended by Mr. Böker and Mr. Huyssen. His wife, however, wrinkled her forehead disapprovingly and gave him a strong sermon. Occasionally I could puzzle out a fragment, and its implications for me as an emigrant did not appear courteous. The Skipper finally said that his wife would absolutely not approve of our transaction, but that he would think the whole thing over again tonight. I should, therefore, come again in the morning.

I went away with the intention of searching every possible place before I would again disturb marital peace. For the next two days, I searched every corner where anything even resembling a boat could be found. A couple of places asked for ten louis d'ors in good clear Dutch. By chance I met the man from Utrecht again. He told me that his wife had agreed. I was not a little astonished, however, when I inquired about the price of passage and found that he wanted fifty florins for the three of us. I bargained quite a little with him, and he lowered the price. The following day we boarded the ship.

June 9 to 19. The 365 churches that Cologne once had[10] have been reduced to 36 through the events of the last two decades. The city has many dirty, dark streets. All the sweepings, ashes, garbage from factories, workshops, and kitchens are dumped into the streets. If you wander into a side street, you would think that you had stumbled into a latrine. Moral and spiritual trash was not missing here either. According to the assurances of several reliable citizens, there are quite a few houses of prostitution here whose inhabitants are protected from all possible censure by law. In contrast, almost every week in one church or the other, at this service or that, an indulgence — sometimes long, sometimes short, but always a full indulgence — is available at reasonable prices. The posters explained in painstaking detail how, when, and where these means of purification were available. Provision is thus made for washing away the ugliness of sin, but for all that the filth in the streets is almost suffocating.

There is a church festival in honor of every patron saint. Everywhere

[10] Early in the Middle Ages the wealthy archbishops of Cologne built a fortified residence which formed the nucleus around which the medieval city grew. Cologne became the principal ecclesiastical center of Germany and its many old churches were among the most notable features of the city. The great Gothic cathedral, started in 1248 and completed in 1880, remains the main architectural monument of Cologne.

you see printed posters stating: "Such and such a Sunday is the feast-day of St. N———. The innkeeper of the N——— has provided for good dance music and will serve the respected guests who honor him with a visit all possible refreshments and will strive to grant all their wishes."

Everything here in Cologne is quite expensive. A pound of butter costs 24 stüber (120 Prussian stüber are the equivalent of 1 neuthaler). A pound loaf of white bread costs 7 stüber; black bread, the so-called Pumpernickel,* is to a Swiss almost inedible. It is made of cracked rye. If it gets a little dry, you can almost choke on the kernels; and still this horse fodder costs 4 stüber a pound. A measure of wine costs almost three times as much here as in Mainz because of the high import duties imposed.

For emigrants, traveling on a merchant ship is indeed most agreeable. There is no worry about theft, dirt, wanton depravity, and so forth, but it is a costly way of travel. It is often necessary to remain six or eight days in one place. Besides this, emigrants are not held in high repute, and it is often difficult to get on a boat. The Dutch boat owners are for the most part wealthy gentlemen and think it degrading to take common people on their boats if the people lack louis d'ors to throw away. It is always best for emigrants to arrange transportation in Basel through to Amsterdam; this makes for quick progress. It is well also to insist on being allowed to stay on board the boat in Amsterdam or Rotterdam or wherever one is going, until the large ship can be boarded. Unless you are taking many things with you, which would possibly involve you in difficulties in transit through France, you are better off going by way of Havre de Grâce. Mr. Jersing in Aesch, a suburb of Basel, can supply information about transit through France, and he can expedite merchandise through France. He is known in Basel as an honest man.

In the Prussian Rhine provinces and in Cologne the brandy distilleries are generally good. If ever a tax had a beneficial effect on a business, it is true of the distilling tax in Prussia. Taxes are assessed according to the time and the size of the still. As long as a still has not been sealed shut by the officials, the owner must be prepared to distill as much as possible in the shortest period of time. The stiff competition makes it necessary at the same time to pay attention to improving his product. Certainly through the changes in equipment both purposes have been fairly well achieved. Here and there I have discovered a fairly unadulterated brandy.

* A single loaf of bread often weighs up to 60 pounds. Its name supposedly is derived from a witty remark of a Frenchman, who declared that the bread was *Bon pour Nickel*, by which name, however, he referred to his horse or his servant. [c. k.]

I would like to try to describe what seems to me to be the most practical method.

The stills are mostly quite low. The diameter depends on the height, in the ratio of four to one or often five to one. The burning pots are generally hung in the fire vault by several pot hooks so that the bright flame touches at least two thirds of the surface and there is no draft. I was assured that the danger of burning up the spirits is seldom to be feared with this fire installation. The towers are mostly twice as high as the burners and are often surrounded by a collar or stillhead in which cold water can be quickly poured to prevent overflow of the spirits. From the towers of this singlings still the steam pipes lead into the condenser which stands about two feet higher than the mouth of the still. In the condenser is a Gedda refrigerator which is filled with mash on the inside and surrounded with water on the outside. The refrigerator at the same time forms the pre-warmer. From this condenser the vapor goes into a metal or tin vat B, which holds about a third of the amount a singlings vat holds. This vat B often stands in a water pot or more frequently in vat C, which is filled with water to be added to the mixture. It is heated here and the steam generated could boil potatoes. In vat B most of the vapor is condensed. In its towers two metal plates with tiny holes were soldered on opposite sides and each stretched across a little more than half. In going through these, more vapor is condensed. This vat B has a pipe underneath with a petcock by means of which it can always be discovered if there is still alcohol in the flow. If there is, then the water in C is heated more. Then the alcohol often passes through oval vessels and then to the condenser by means of coils. If all the solids have been used up, the swill is discharged, the vat rinsed out with water and filled again with the mash from the refrigerator.

By this arrangement the brandy is passed through twice without being touched by air and without much time being lost in the transfer. This is also economical of fuel. The fire that warms the water to be added also warms the singlings. For an added flavor, if that is wanted, spices are placed on the perforated metal plates in the towers of vat B.

In this area you rarely see other cheese than Dutch cheese. The cheeses are almost spherical in shape, high in fat content, but a bit sour to the taste. The very lean cheeses have caraway seeds or other spices mixed into them. Cheese is inexpensive here; you can buy lean cheese for four stüber a pound. It is best to buy it outside of the city or on board ship, however, because the import tax has not yet been added. The gates to the harbor, with the exception of one, are opened very late, from twelve noon until two o'clock, and are closed very early at night, too, in order to lighten the work of the customs officials. The poor devil who needs the services of these kind gentlemen must see to it that he is on time and is granted the favor of being allowed to wait until it is convenient for the officials.

Today another emigrant ship went by on its way to Antwerp. They had to stay here until their papers were all in order. The people were packed in so close that they could hardly move. They were accusing each other of thefts. I felt sorry for the decent people among them who had to suffer at the hands of the riffraff.

You cannot imagine a prettier kind of boat than these Dutch Rhine boats. As you step into the cabins you would guess you were in a palace. The floors are generally covered with Turkish rugs; the furniture is truly the epitome of luxury and magnificence. Not infrequently a fine piano is to be found. In front of the windows are flowerpots. In short, you can hardly believe you are on a boat. Sometimes, of course, such a ship is the lifelong home of a family; at most they occupy a house in winter for the short period when the rivers are completely frozen over.

As to my possessions and the Bibles I have for sale, Mr. Böker and Mr. Huyssen both advised me not to declare them at too low a value, as the Dutch customs officials have the right to take whatever pleases them, paying a 12 per cent markup. They also warned me to conceal nothing, for the officials could take any undeclared things that they found without paying the least compensation, and in addition healthy penalties could be assessed.

June 19. Today the sails were finally raised. I was not unmoved at leaving Cologne. Here, too, I spent many hours in the enjoyment of friendships, and I was richly compensated for the unpleasant things.

It rained all day, but we had a good wind so that we arrived in Ruhrort at six o'clock in the evening. The countryside along the shores of the Rhine is no longer as picturesque as above Cologne. A monotonous, melancholy atmosphere prevails. Everything proclaims the nearness of the North. Herds of small, ill-favored cattle search for the low sparse grass. Treeless plains only occasionally relieved by clumps of bushes weary the eye.

Ruhrort seems a prosperous little city, very attractively built. The Ruhr and the Rhine join here and the coal boats that come down the Ruhr are often reloaded here. These things enliven the place. This coal, locally referred to as Ruhr-coal, is shipped from here to Mainz and as far as Amsterdam.

June 20. Today we departed by three o'clock. It is cold, rainy weather with an adverse wind. Our crew, however, know how to make use of it very well. Partly because of the many bends in the Rhine and the occasional shallows, the sails have to be changed at every moment. This is accomplished with so little noise and shouting of commands that I can hardly believe I am living on a boat. As far as Cologne you hear a raging noise on board ship, but down farther all goes along so quietly and peacefully that involuntarily the idea springs up that either the lowland Germans and the Dutch understand their business better than the upper ones or the character of the people is very different from those above Cologne.

From Cologne downstream the boat did not take a "foreign" pilot along (which above Cologne every boat must do from place to place). Now and then, however, pilots came in small boats from the shore and boarded the ship in order to guide it through dangerous spots. Since the water is very murky, the shoals are not easy to recognize. The pilots ask for fifty to sixty stüber for a short distance and in addition are liberally refreshed.

From Cologne on, as was also true of our trip from Koblenz, we were accompanied by a man whose job it was to see that nothing was unloaded in secret. A despicable arrangement, an infringement of honor! It implied that the Skipper was not an honest man, and that he had to be watched and guarded day and night. Certainly between the skippers and these customs officials there prevails a unique, bitter-sweet relationship. This relationship is manifested in a marvelous intermixture of base pride, fragments of self-respect, and nefarious tricks. The proverb "A fool often makes a hundred fools" has been made an incontrovertible truth by the introduction of the Prohibition System. One can add, "One thief makes a hundred thieves." (Are these infamies the fruit of the Holy Alliance? of the *Bundesverein?*)

We made a stop at Nieder-Wesel. There is a pontoon bridge here and a toll station. I went with Skipper Wilsing into the city to make some purchases. Everything here is expensive with the exception of malt vinegar and lettuce. I bought seven large heads of the latter for two stüber.

Wesel is quite well fortified, with extended outworks. The moats can be filled to a considerable depth with water. The streets are narrow, dark, and exceedingly dirty. I did not feel I could breathe freely until the city was well behind me. At the waterfront I spoke for quite some time with a couple of old, disabled Prussian soldiers who were employed here in the warehouse as watchmen or something of the sort. One of them had worked in Switzerland in his youth as an artisan and cherished the happy days he had spent there. If only he were still there, he felt, things would be going very well for him. His friends would receive him with joy. He spoke of his employer and friends as though he had just left them a few months ago. All of a sudden, he realized that sixty years had passed by since those happy days. "Oh, my God!" he cried out, and a large tear rolled down into his gray beard. "What a fool I am! My good friends there must long be in their graves, and within the year it will be thus with me too." I think I shed a tear. Memory and hope smiled cordially for a moment on the old man, but hardly had he begun to warm himself in their rays than the gloomy, cold fog of reality made him shiver again. Will these guardian angels desert me often on my pilgrimage? Never for long, I pray, dear Father in Heaven! "One may fail, but never both."

In the afternoon we arrived in Emmerich, on the border between Prussia and Holland. We had to stop again and another inspection was made. Two officials came from the city to make certain that nothing upon which duty remained unpaid would be taken out, and that the contents did not contradict the reports of inspections made in toll ports upstream. Crates and barrels were ripped open, everything turned upside down and searched through. My crates remained unexamined. The officials were satisfied simply by looking through the declaration.

In the evening we put down anchor at the first Dutch customs house. Only a few houses were scattered along the shore. The ship's manifest had to be presented at the customs office. I received notice to write another declaration itemizing my things in columns, for example: No. 1, feathers, No. 2, cotton goods, No. 3, linen goods, No. 4, ironware, and so on. It seems that things are going to be pretty detailed and boring, because the Skipper says we will not get away for three days.

June 21. This is a hateful formality and truly a torment, to be so detained by these proud bloodsuckers to our detriment, only for their own amusement. Almost a dozen of these customs harpies * came on board today. If some left, others came. All of them had to be lavishly entertained by the Skipper. I don't doubt that I will have to feed these turkey

* Harpies, the robbing, rending ones, therefore the storm goddesses. In Homer they lived in the abyss of Hades. If someone had been away from home for a long time, so that no one knew what had become of him, and no one could believe he was among the living, one would say: "The harpies have taken him away." [C. K.]

cocks from my meager coffer yet. Today I had to go to the office three times. The first time, after waiting for hours, I had to leave without being heard. The second time, it seemed my passport had not been made out according to proper legal form. They expected me to deposit 600 Dutch gulden in cash, and then travel to Arnhem to arrange for a permit to continue my journey. With this permit, I was to return to Lobith again. The 600 florins would be returned as soon as I had made travel arrangements with a ship's captain. The third time, they said I was not to be allowed to transport my guns through Holland, and all that sort of nonsense. It is a maddening, shameful extortion! Here it is not law that counts, no, indeed, but rather the caprice of these bloodsuckers.

After much arguing back and forth on the boat and in the office with reference to our piddling stuff and our paltry selves, and after I declared that I would seek counsel in Amsterdam before I would agree to their demands, which to me seemed illegal, there no longer appeared to be any further obstacles in our way. The Skipper puffed himself up considerably and declared that it was his intercession and offer of bond that we had to thank for this. I do not know how much there is to this contention, but I do believe that not without reason did he insist upon such a conscientious declaration and appraisal of my belongings. Apparently my honesty screened his laxity. Perhaps it was not without design that my crates were right on top and plainly visible.

June 22. We are still here. Today they started customs examinations and the affixing of lead seals. In the meantime two other ships have arrived. These must wait until the business with our ship is completed.

The countryside around here has something pleasing about it. Here and there a village built on a little knoll is to be seen, while above it windmills swing their powerful wings. Everywhere one sees well-fed herds. Boats fill the canals that cut through the land and disappear behind the soft hills.

Right along the Rhine lies infertile sand. In many places it can be observed how the vegetation has adapted itself. First there are a few *Jancus* kinds and *Trilicum repens*. These are followed by *Alchemille millefolium, Convolvulus soldanella,* and a *Trifolium* species. Then *Potentilla anserina, Verbascum thapsus, Spergula arvensis,* and *Euphorbia pithyusa* begin. Beyond this, ordinary vegetation begins. Often in this sandy flatness, you imagine you see a little hill in the distance, but it turns out to be a bush of the *Crataegus* species which frequently grows to be from twenty to forty feet in diameter and four to six feet high.

64

You do not see any more cultivated fields here. Now and then an enclosed cabbage patch or a potato field appears. I would like it here despite the lack of cultivation. The wide, unfenced fields, the frisking of the cattle, have brought to mind pictures of my homeland. The clear sky, the song of larks, the droning of flies and insects, heightened this even more. Everything seemed so wonderful again. When we look at the world in the mirror of comforting memories, the sandy waste becomes paradise.

June 23. This evening the customs inspection finally came to an end. Immediately the sails were raised, or as the ship's crew would say in their low German: *that Schipp is klor gewurdten.* We sailed far enough so that Arnhem was in sight. Not far from Lobith the Rhine divides. One branch flows through Nimwegen and the other through Arnhem. Our Skipper chose the latter way because the water was deep enough to accommodate his boat and he could bring his cargo to Amsterdam more quickly and less expensively.

It is a pleasant evening in every way, and a romantic area. The setting sun is mirrored in the water with indescribable splendor. In the distance the bells of a village ring, their tones blending beautifully. Along the shores milk herds graze and gather about the milkmaid. Farther in the distance can be heard the sound of oars from the little boats and in between the chirping of crickets. Today for the first time I understand Matthisson's "A Golden Glow Covers the Grove." [11]

June 24. This morning we left very early. About five o'clock we got to Arnhem. Here there is another customs office. We will certainly have to remain here today.

Arnhem is the first Dutch city we have seen. It is not laid out systematically, but there are clean, attractive homes and many beautiful buildings. The streets are paved with bricks and are washed and scrubbed as clean as a table every morning. Everything gives evidence of Dutch wealth and luxury. Around the wharf swarmed attractive little boats that might be thought of more as costly chests or couches than as boats.

Today at noon the B. Brothers of Arnhem sent word to me that letters to them and to me from Mr. von Mandach had arrived yesterday. On the supposition that Captain Wilsing's ship was still in Lobith, they had sent the letter for me there. At the same time, Mr. von Mandach had written to them that I should be in Amsterdam by the 26th at the latest so as not to miss the chance of a good passage to New York. Taking that good

[11] Friedrich von Matthisson (1761–1831) was a German poet particularly known for his description of pastoral scenes.

advice would have been expensive. Our boat was not leaving here till morning and had to be unloaded in Saart, which is ten hours above Amsterdam. To take a wagon there seemed too expensive to me. Furthermore, the Skipper and the customs officials did not seem willing to unload my belongings. I finally decided to trust in Providence and let things go the regular way, which is to go from Saart to Amsterdam and to consult in person with Mr. von Mandach.

I cannot possibly transcribe this part of my diary without giving my heart the satisfaction of naming this noble Swiss publicly, even if by doing so I infringe upon his modesty. The friendship of this worthy man and true Christian accompanied us from our entry into Holland all the way to America, to our unceasing benefit. To him, to his wife, and to the cordial, loyal Mr. Isler, I owe so much, so infinitely much. May God in Heaven bless you in body and soul, in this world and the next, and all the noble souls as well who, because of your intercession, came forward so kindly to help us.

June 25. Last evening all the customs and travel arrangements were cleared up, and early today we left. The area we have traveled through today is very attractive; meadows, woods, hills, dwellings, whole towns, are mixed together in a pleasing disorder. Everything bears the stamp of industry and prosperity.

As one continues down river, the hills disappear. Already in some areas the land is hard won from the sea. Only the masterfully constructed dams prevent the sea from rushing down upon the land below. Should Holland's wealth ever be laid waste, one would perhaps have to ask in a few decades, "Where was Holland?" This thought spoiled many a pleasure for me today.

Not far from Wageningen there was a tremendous uproar. The Skipper was called to stop the ship, but he would not. In a minute a whole crowd of ruffians gathered along the shore and threatened to stop the ship by force. Some had already jumped into boats. The Skipper threatened that the first man to approach his boat would be thrown into the water and ordered his sailors to carry out his command. Finally they abandoned efforts. The Skipper told us that they had accused him of getting too close to a dam.

We got to Saart at nine o'clock. A large number of boats lie here and in Syanen, across the river. All of them are lit up with numerous torches. It is a pretty and stirring sight.

June 26. Early this morning I went to Utrecht, two hours' distance from here, in order to take the first packetboat to Amsterdam. The road is completely paved in brick; wagons move over it as though on wings. The wide meadows and cow pastures are interspersed with marvelous parks. The plains are not tiring to the eye here, which feasts rather on the ever new and ever prettier parks and buildings which, half hidden, look out from the shrubbery.

I passed by a sawmill which appeared very noteworthy to me. On three adjacent frames nine saw blades were placed. These could be adjusted closer or farther apart. The blades are about three feet long and little thicker than our frame saws. The three frames do not move together but rather one after another. Nine pieces are cut at the same time without its being necessary to move the log out of its position.

Utrecht is a large city adorned with many beautiful buildings, but not as pleasing as Arnhem. I noticed particularly the unpleasant odor everywhere due partly to the sulphurous peat bogs and partly to the canals, in which all sorts of refuse is thrown. The water of the canals was never renewed except by the rains.

In all Dutch church towers there are chimes, and you can usually see through the open steeple the whole space filled with these large and small bells. Through almost all streets canals flow. Next to them lie the workshops of artisans; on top of these are the streets, so that here, in the literal sense of the word, one tramples on the heads of the working class.

Every day three packetboats leave Utrecht for Amsterdam, eight hours away. They depart at six and ten o'clock in the morning and at two in the afternoon. These boats are fifty to sixty feet long and about ten to twelve feet wide and are divided into two rooms. In the front room a person pays a fare of 30 stüber and in the back one 20 stüber (20 stüber is equivalent to one Rhenish gulden). Even the second room is equipped with convenient chairs and benches, and each person on boarding was given a cushion by the cabin boy on which to sit. He judged by physiognomy whether a passenger was worth a velvet one or one made from ordinary cloth.

In the city these vessels are pulled by men from bridge to bridge. Outside of the city a horse is hitched to a very long, thin rope and trots along pulling the boat. If not much time is wasted in loading and unloading, it arrives in Amsterdam in five hours.

We Swiss still cannot imagine how indispensable tobacco has become to the Dutchman. Few minutes of the day pass without it. As soon as he gets out of bed he reaches for his long clay pipe. He smokes at tea or coffee, and in order to smoke some more he no doubt goes to bed later than he otherwise would. If one of these packetboats is carrying mostly men, everything is fenced in by pipes, and you cannot move to the left or right without causing disaster. A pot of burning peat stands in the middle, so that no one need do without that costly weed merely because of lack of fire.

It is surprising how the people here have defied nature, I might say, to gain a paradise. Both shores of this canal are truly magically beautiful. Along the shores of Lake Geneva and Lake Maggiore, it is Nature that has spread an immense, unsurpassed beauty and majesty and yet immeasurably inviting gentleness and warm appeal. On the canals of Utrecht, through his artifice man has been worthy of his master.

A ship is passing by loaded only with little barrels made of fir wood. What could they contain? It is water, nothing but spring water, which is shipped from Utrecht to Amsterdam and there sold for shining money. There I stood — apt student — and that was the trouble; I felt an incredible thirst. In spite of the dark brown color of the canal water, I tried to satisfy my thirst with it, but in vain. The passengers got out in order to refresh themselves at an inn; several drank milk. I ordered a glass also, but it cost more than liqueur does at home. I felt acutely the value of good water.

We arrived in Amsterdam, that colossally proud Amsterdam.[12] With its 300 windmills and 22,000 houses, it constitutes a little world by itself. A group of ragged fellows stood along the bank, offering to serve as porters or guides. They are a shameless pack. They wanted twelve stüber to guide me to Mr. Mandach. I offered half the amount. They complained that this was ridiculous, but before I had taken a hundred steps, two of them came running after me. Only by scolding could I get rid of one of them.

Entering the city itself is completely overwhelming. Each building seems surpassed by the next. In every street there is a canal. On both sides of the canals there are lanes and footpaths heavily shaded by trees. Hundreds and hundreds of big and little boats swarm in the canals under the refreshing shade. From hidden cages come the whistling of quail

[12] With the growth of commerce in early modern times, Amsterdam became a great seaport and one of the principal outlets of traffic along the Rhine. The maritime route for centuries crossed the Zuider Zee. The entrance to the harbor eventually silted up. Reshipment of goods was generally necessary, as indicated in the accounts of both Schweizer and Rütlinger. In 1824 a fifty-mile canal to the North Sea was constructed. Since then the route has been shortened to fifteen miles and greatly improved.

and the songs of nightingales, and astonishment is transformed into pleasant confusion.

You have to have been in a foreign country whose language you do not understand and in a situation like mine to understand the gratitude I feel here in far-off America every time I think of Amsterdam and the cherished names of Mandach and Isler. Even at my first visit I was received, not as a stranger needing advice and help, but rather as a friend. Mr. von Mandach completely set aside his own business to arrange the contract with Captain Niederholt. All went well, and I can get over upon fairly good terms.

June 27. Today I returned to Saart to get my wife and child, and to see to the unloading of my belongings, which were placed aboard a packetboat this evening. We were promised definitely that they would arrive in Utrecht in the morning and that they would be declared free of duty by the customs office.

June 28. This morning we packed up everything and took leave of our Skipper and his wife. Our esteem for his wife was richly increased by her many kindnesses to us in Cologne and by her constant friendliness, and we did not part without emotion.

By accident we missed the boat in Utrecht and had to walk to Amsterdam. It was oppressively hot, and it was late at night when we wearily got there. A well-dressed Hollander whom we had asked outside the city about the next road led us to Mr. von Mandach, at whose home we enjoyed a reception that revived body and soul. His worthy wife was really motherly in her care of us.

Today my belongings were loaded on a boat which leaves tonight for Texel. All other arrangements have been completed. The freight charge on our baggage was about four and a half per cent of its value on the average. Added to this were many duties that had to be paid on it, like customs inspection, sealing, passport verification, and other fees. I became quite frightened by all this, and, for the first time, regretted having burdened myself with so much baggage, as these expenditures stood in an unfortunate relationship to my supply of money. Only in the evening, in the last hours before departure, did we fully realize how much Mr. von Mandach, Mr. Isler, and other Swiss had done to dispel every anxiety. Quite overcome with so many emotions and experiences, we tumbled rather than walked onto the boat. As soon as we had composed ourselves a bit and the boat was about to leave, Mr. von Mandach and his wife boarded the boat once more, and we felt as though we were about to take leave of old friends.

June 29. We are now on the Zuider Zee and have already experienced a foreboding touch of seasickness. We had an adverse wind the whole night; the worst of this is that this is just the wind that our ocean vessel needs to clear the Texel channel. In any other wind this would be nearly impossible. A Jew who lives on Texel Island thought that Captain Niederholt, in a wind like this, will certainly clear port and sail without waiting for us.

The whole day we had an adverse wind and gloomy, rainy weather. Among the ship's crew are three Dutch sailors who have taken posts on an East Indian transport. They are rough but good-natured fellows who want to regale us sometimes with sugar, sometimes with coffee, punch, baked goods, and so on. But our appetite is gone.

June 30. Sure enough, this morning we got to Texel and just as surely Captain Niederholt had put out to sea last night. This is a sad state of affairs. Mr. Hoghland in Helder, to whom I had a letter, did not understand German. I sought out the Jew who had come along on today's boat and asked him to be my interpreter. I learned that no ship was going to the ports of Baltimore, Philadelphia, or New York for another three weeks. My baggage must be put under the royal transport seal if it cannot quickly be loaded on a boat destined for America.

July 1 to 4. After much scurrying around I negotiated a contract with an American, Captain Lord. We are to pay 250 Dutch florins (the Dutch florin or gulden is the same as the Rhenish) for transportation for the three of us, supplying our own food. We could pay 400 florins and receive the ship's meals. We chose to feed ourselves. On our six crates we are to pay 30 cents (45 kreuzer) per cubic foot. Tomorrow we board the boat. Our Captain seems to be a gloomy, unfriendly fellow, but we have no choice because within a period of four or five weeks not another ship is going to the United States. The week before over thirty boats are said to have put to sea from this port.[13]

[13] Personal and public records of transatlantic travel in that period confirm the prevalence of terrible conditions, particularly on board westward-bound ships. The congestion, filth, foul odors, disease, and lack of proper facilities for preparing and eating food often took a heavy toll of life and health. A substantial proportion of the immigrants were highly vulnerable to these conditions. European and American publics were shocked. Attempts of the United States government to pass regulatory legislation brought very little advantage for immigrants until the post-Civil War period. The same is true of similar efforts of other governments, like Great Britain and Hamburg. The two Swiss families were particularly fortu-

Our ship is called the *Xenophon*. It has three masts, and according to the assurances of Mr. Hoghland and Captain Schmidt, it is an excellent vessel. Its masts extend considerably higher than the others.*

July 4 to 26. The region around Texel is a sad, melancholy, sandy wasteland. Not a tree or bush gladdens the eye. Huge piles of sand are often blown together in seconds by the wind. The wind howls in the forest of masts, and the sea gulls screech wildly and greedily. Is it the insatiable lust for money or iron necessity that holds people here in this desolation?

Except for the two pilots and the ship's carpenter, our Captain has only black sailors. The cook is a surly old fellow who, with his greasy face and gray beard, is wonderful to behold. Otherwise they seem to be fairly good-natured people.

The sailor's way of life is very simple. In the morning each has about a half measure of tea and sea biscuits, at noon about two pounds of salted meat, cooked in sea water, and potatoes. On Tuesdays and Fridays, they get bacon and peas. In the evening, again, they receive the usual measure of tea and every Saturday half a glass of whiskey; and on Sundays instead of the potatoes a piece of corn pudding. About one pound of zwieback is given to each man per day. The pilot assured me that it was already over two years old, and that the Captain had a year's supply left. Also he assured me that the food on other ships was mostly better, but that the sailors here received ten dollars a month, while on other ships sailors generally received only eight or nine. Now we are happy that we can feed ourselves; we could not have adjusted easily to their manner of living.

The town of Helder lies about half an hour's distance from the harbor and is fairly large and well built. Mainly innkeepers, merchants, and artisans live here. The coiffure of the women looks almost like that of a horse. Many metal bangles and buckles are used, and they appear to serve to ward off bites and blows. How capriciously the goddess Fashion rules her handmaidens. In this place, heavy, rugged metal must enhance

nate in the facilities they were able to secure. The *Xenophon* had a crew of fourteen and a passenger list of five persons. The *Massasoit*, on which the Rütlinger family later took passage, had twelve crew members and carried twenty-five passengers. Ships of no greater tonnage not infrequently carried hundreds of passengers. Later, as efforts increased to improve prevailing conditions of travel, methods of exploiting the vulnerability of travelers also became more efficient.

* A more detailed account of the accommodations of this ship is given us by the wife of the author in a letter to her parents which appears as a supplement at the end of the journal. [c. k.]

beauty and in other places even gossamer and gauze are too thick and heavy.

Here and there you see the cheekbones of whales driven into the ground to serve as fence posts and gates. Behind the town of Helder there are two fences like this which are nineteen feet long. From this you can get some conception of the monstrous size which these animals often attain.

Until today I did not think that our Captain could laugh, but now he has convinced me very strongly to the contrary. Perhaps it is not unimportant that I tell you about the cause of it. Today I wanted to tighten up a little barrel which was leaking, and I tied it with a cord on the ship's ladder. When I came back about a quarter of an hour later, the cord was cut and my barrel was gone. The Captain came by at that point, and my little mishap, I think, really tore his shrunken midriff apart.

Here almost nothing but peat is burned; even the bakers do not use wood. At home we would have considered it impossible to bake bread with peat alone, while in this place they do not know of anything else.

The tea service is on the table most of the day. Lazy and self-satisfied, the females sit around it, rarely doing any work. It seems to me the German woman is superior to the Dutch in every respect.

We provided ourselves with staples for the sea journey; bacon, rice, peas, zwieback, potatoes, a little cheese, and a couple of crocks of beer we bought here. Our tireless friends, Mr. and Mrs. von Mandach, provided us with butter, coffee, tea, and brandy. A pound of bacon here costs nine stüber, a pound of rice two, a hundredweight of zwieback eighteen florins. Potatoes are very expensive and pitifully bad, like those namesakes of theirs that a few years ago intruded like mangy sheep into the herd of our delicious potatoes.

Near our ship sea nettles (*Horturia physalides*) may often be observed. Surprisingly enough, they are nice looking, sky-blue, violet, dark and light red, like moonflowers. They tempt the unsuspecting person to pick them, but when one touches them, covetous curiosity is rewarded with burning pain — a striking metaphor of vice.

July 16 to 19. The cargo of our ship has arrived. It consists of 250 barrels of Dutch brandy, and zinc and brass articles. Our Captain has gone to Amsterdam; now at last our departure approaches.

Since the cargo has arrived, the customs officials seal the middle and lower holds every night, and we sleep in the cabin. The reason why Dutch brandy is so rigorously guarded by the Dutch themselves is to ensure that the ship captains cannot smuggle any of it to the tavern keepers, since export brandy does not have nearly the duty on it as that consumed in the country.

Captain Schmidt, a Hollander, who lives here by the harbor and whom I visit occasionally, has told me now and then of the fate of many emigrants in the year 1817. About 1300 of them were packed on a single ship. After they had been at sea only a few days, they were dying by the dozens from lack of food, water, and fresh air. The Captain and his German partner considered and decided to turn the ship back again. Almost every person was sick. After several weeks' stay, part of them lying in hospitals, part staying on the open fields, and piles of them dying, on order from the Dutch government six hundred of the healthiest were chosen, and, under Captain Schmidt, put on board ship. The healthy father was torn from the sick mother and the weeping healthy mother from the whimpering, helpless child, probably never to see it again. I will spare my friends an account of what happened here. It is to Mr. Schmidt's honor that he, wherever possible, listened more to the voice of humanity in making decisions than to the dictates of harsh duty. Also one can believe that on the ship he must have kept exemplary order, since of the six hundred passengers who were brought on his ship in such terrible circumstances, not a hundred people died during the trip.

July 20. Today all is being made ready for departure. Everything is being tied on, nailed fast, and wedged in as though we were going to fly through the air or be hurled across. In the afternoon the sailors went on shore again. A few came back on the boat in the evening and practically beat each other to pieces. Blood welled freely from their faces. The pilot looked on calmly as though a suit were being brushed off and only held them back a little when they started to attack each other with iron bars. Beaten up as they were, they dragged themselves off again to another tavern.

Next to us is a ship named the *Rousseau*. His picture, drawn in a hurried manner, appears on the front of the ship. Just opposite this the unspoiled African sons of nature were beating each other almost in two. How often things coincide so strangely, and ideas can be associated.

July 21. During the night the Captain returned from Amsterdam. Early in the morning the Dutch pilot boat came to lead the ship out of the harbor. Only two sailors were on board; all the rest were still ashore in the taverns. Gradually they came stumbling along, blind drunk. I expected the Captain to punish them vigorously for this mischief, but he did not say a word. Rather he strolled up and down very calmly. He seemed to be calculating how he could most quickly dissipate the anger they have swallowed which is expressed in hatred and joy in destruction. Mr. Schmidt and a customs official came on board to say farewell. I asked them in amazement why the Captain did not punish this debauchery. Mr. Schmidt shrugged his shoulders and said: "Hard words never help anything; and if he permitted himself more than that, it could cost him a great deal in America." This, then, is American liberty? Is this worth leaving friends and homeland for? For this, then, Washington * and Franklin fought and worked. Yet our fathers also did not fight for the establishment of wild bacchanalias which are now being celebrated on the battlefields of St. Jacob and Stoss[14] and so on. Still, in spite of its misuse by the wicked, freedom always remains the most precious of earthly treasures.

> *Lass dich nicht irren des Pöbels Geschrei,*
> *Noch den Missbrauch rasender Toren.*

> Don't be fooled by the rabble's screams,
> Nor by the misdeeds of raving fools.

Saying goodbye to Schmidt and the good customs official really was painful to me. Despite our less than prosperous circumstances, they always treated us with friendliness and concern and showed us many courtesies. In our new life we will have many pleasant memories even of this sandy waste.

We expected to be going out to sea, but outside the harbor we again dropped anchor, even though the wind was very favorable. The sailors have again gone ashore to continue with their debauchery.

July 22. We are still near the harbor; the wind is not favorable. Today four more passengers came aboard, a young merchant from Lüttich with a servant, and two Frenchmen. One is a spoon-maker and the other a pot-mender or something like that. The first lives in the cabin, and the

---

* George Washington, North America's first citizen, general, and highest official, was born February 23, 1733, in Fairfax County, Virginia. He died on December 14, 1799, at the age of 67. For freedom, law, and the establishment of the United States, he deserves the eternal gratitude of his country. He was a great man. [C. K.]

[14] In 1405 an Austrian army was defeated in the approaches of the pass of Stoss. As the Austrian forces moved up a gorge to cross into Appenzell, the Swiss hurled rocks upon the attacking forces and routed them. A coalition of Swiss states defeated the Austrians at the battle of St. Jakob an der Sihl, in 1443. In 1444, 1200 Confederates attacked 40,000 French troops at St. Jakob an der Birs near Basel. They killed thousands before they were wiped out to the last man. News of this awakened a great surge of feeling for defense of the nation. See Valentin Gitermann, *Geschichte der Schweiz* (Thayngen, Schaffhausen: Augustin Verlag, 1941), pp. 64, 68–69.

others are with us in the hold. A goat and a cat were also added to our company.

July 23. Still near the harbor. Time is beginning to hang heavy. I stand by the hour on the deck and look down at the droppings of the starfish that have attached themselves by the thousands to the planks of the wharf.

July 24. Today we finally left with rather an unfavorable wind. Less than two hours passed before we were terribly seasick. One of the Frenchmen remained free of seasickness. On the twenty-fifth and twenty-sixth we were able to get up only with great difficulty. On the morning of the twenty-seventh a sailor came to tell us that we were very close to the English shore. As miserable as we felt, we dragged ourselves up on deck where we saw the high, white chalk cliffs and, soon after, Dover. We were, however, pushed by a powerful storm toward the French shore and came so close that we could distinguish streets and trees in Calais.

July 28. We are still being tossed around between Dover and Calais. The Captain would turn into one of these ports if it were not for the excessive costs due to the nuisance of the Prohibition Law. We are still continually seasick.

July 29. The storm has subsided, but we are not getting very far. We are very near the English coast. Pleasant grain and vegetable fields cover the plains; the heights are clothed with spruce. Here and there a lovely valley opens. Because of the beautiful view we have almost forgotten our seasickness. The ocean is swarming with boats. It is a singular sensation to be so near the country from which so much good but also so much evil has emerged.

July 30. We find ourselves just opposite the Isle of Wight. The wind has improved and this afternoon it was very good. We are sailing with sixteen sails, of which the smallest measures 200 and the largest 1000 square feet. With these, the wind can really be effective. The boat is truly an excellent vessel. It overtook some ten ships which came into sight today. It seems that it is not just the skill of even the best shipwright that makes a good sailing ship. Many small, almost unnoticeable factors are said to be decisive.

Today they uncorked another water barrel which has an unbearable smell and taste; the entire hold is filled with the stench. Doubtless the water has been along on several trips already. On top of that, we are not to help ourselves to water freely; it must be dispensed by the pilot. I let it be understood that we had not agreed to this. The pilot said that sufficient water would be distributed, but that it was necessary, because of the sailors, to put it under supervision. It seems that the Captain's physiognomy almost tells the truth.

July 31. Last night about nine o'clock a storm suddenly arose in the southwest. Quickly the sails were drawn in. Before they were half finished, it began to rain and hail furiously. Very few times in my life have I seen such lightning. The whole sky seemed to be a ring of burning pitch, but there was not much thunder to be heard. It was a dramatic sight to see the sailors in flashes of lightning, perched in the rigging like birds. The Captain did not leave the deck for a moment. By one o'clock the lightning and the storm were over and soon several sails were hoisted again.

There is no rest in the life of a sailor. I cannot understand how people are found for this calling. During good weather they relieve each other every four hours so that half of them rest while the other half work. But when there is stormy weather, generally all of them must remain on deck and face the storm and lightning. England is still in sight, for the wind is bad. We have encountered many ships.

August 1 to 5. Heavy storm without interruption. We became terribly seasick again and very weak. Up until the fourth it was with only great difficulty that we could leave our beds. The cook had to be persuaded with the brandy bottle to do us little favors, but the persuasion had to be renewed from time to time if we wanted to get any advantage out of it.

Anyone who goes on a sea trip, but does not want to provide his own board, should never neglect to bring along a little wine, beer, vinegar, as well as dried, tart fruits, prunes, sour cherries, whortleberries, and so forth. Usually thirst accompanies seasickness and is a result of it. With these things one suffers less and recovers more quickly. Some gelatin tablets would also be very good.

The more I think about it, the more I prefer boarding oneself. It must be very difficult after being seasick to get used to dried, salt meat and bacon again immediately without having anything else; the insipid tea, morning and night, must become unbearable to someone who is not used to it from childhood. Americans want nothing to do with soup, and the sailors and officers almost die laughing when they see us prepare our soup every day.

In preparing soup, fine noodles have an advantage because they need little time to cook. This is very important on a ship where there is only one kitchen. But a person who prepares his own food must see to it that good relations with the cook are maintained, especially if one does not

76

know any other passengers on board ship who could be of help during seasickness.

August 7 to 9. Powerful northwest winds and clear weather, but very cold. This and the tremendous number of sea fowl (I think they are the *Mergus meeranser*) make me believe that we are not far from the Orkneys and that because of the storms and the southwesterns we have been driven a bit too far north. We were told nothing about this by the Captain and pilots.

August 10 and 11. Fairly good north wind. The ship has been set on a west-southwest course. We put behind us five and a half nautical miles in an hour.

It is strange how man, faced with a lack of technical aids, develops a skill to artistic perfection, making use of the most insignificant things. This is the case when a sailor, using a contraption that any farmer could make in a few hours, weaves out of old, torn ropes others that would be hard to distinguish from new ones. The strands are twisted open, then the individual strands are tied, forming a barely discernible knot, combined with one another and twisted together again. They know how to mend a torn rope so that it is not noticeable, and also so that it can stand the greatest strain in the repaired section. I wish that my countrymen possessed this skill. It is true that rope makers would not do well then, but we Swiss sometimes can only assure our own existence at the expense of a neighbor's.

August 12. Completely becalmed and warm, clear weather.

August 13. Today was for me a day of horror and at the same time brought deepest gratitude to God. The sailors were bringing up hay for the goat from the lower hold. The trapdoors to the middle and lower holds lie directly under each other. While these were open, our child *
was playing on the main deck near the trapdoor. In the moment that I noticed this and cried out to her to go back, she fell into the lower hold almost thirty feet down, between barrels. I thought she had been dashed to pieces. By some marvel, she suffered no injury except for a bruise on her left shoulder. She had had a bucket in her hand, and during the fall her head got into it and was thus protected. If this had not happened, she would hardly have come out of the experience alive. Fortunately, her mother happened to be on the other side of the ship and knew nothing about this until the child had been brought back up to the deck.

August 14. Becalmed. Several hundred brownfish (*Delphinus pho-*

* A very lively, sensible, happy child, eight or nine years old. [C. K.]

77

caena) came swimming toward the ship today and without changing their course went on right under it. They were six feet long on the average.

August 15 and 16. A violent gale from the southwest. Now we understand well what purpose all the nailing down, clamping, and tying fast serve. Whatever stands free is thrown about the ship; if you chase after it, trying to catch it, the next thing you know you are on your back with your legs in the air.

We are again suffering a bit from seasickness; only the child is completely well and active. In an attempt to advance against the wind, the ship is maneuvered to receive the wind first from the left and then from the right side; this is called tacking. Tacking results in tremendous swaying of the ship, and the tilting sometimes leaves the railing on one side submerged in the sea while the other side is raised twenty-eight feet above the water. Even on this side the waves still beat over the deck. A damp, heavy fog covers us, and out of it a heavy rain falls intermittently. All this makes these days monotonous.

August 17. Northwest wind, and dry air again. Yesterday the walls were dripping from the heavy fog, but today all is dry. We are now making fair progress.

August 18. Little wind but very bright weather. Today we encountered four ships and in the north we saw one that was also going to America. It has been a long time since we have seen anything like this. There is something comforting about seeing another living thing besides ourselves. We are supposed to be about forty miles north of the Azores. My hope of seeing these lovely islands has gone down the drain.

This noon we saw the back of a whale. It was about twice the width of the ship. At a distance, another one spouted water into the air. It looks and sounds almost like a waterfall. Around three o'clock the wind was south-southwest; at once the Captain had several more sails run up, and we continued admirably until evening. Then, however, most of the sails had to be pulled in, because the wind was too strong and it appeared that we would have an unpleasant night of it.

August 19 and 20. The most horrible storm broke before evening on the eighteenth. A wave tore open a trap door on the main deck, and before it could be pushed shut everything was floating in water. A barrel of meat, which had been tied to a pillar with rather worn rope, tore loose. In a moment it was shattered in more than a hundred pieces, and bits of meat and wood flew around like timid birds from one corner to another. In the cabin and the kitchen everything was thrown down and broken too. Only toward morning were we able to clean up a bit. With little change this storm continued until the morning of the twentieth.

A violent storm is really a terrible sight. The roaring and raging of the waves and their dashing against the ship sound like the thunder of cannon. The crashing and creaking of the boat, the shouting, or rather, the bellowing of the crew, the clanking and racket of falling and breaking things, all this together is certainly something horrifying and thoroughly unpleasant for someone who is at sea for the first time. Not unwillingly, at this moment, pictures of a happier past come to mind to stretch us on the torture rack of regret.

August 21 to 23. Beautiful weather, but little wind.

August 24. The Captain is beginning to lock up the water supply, and he wishes to restrict our cooking to only once a day. I referred to the terms of the contract, by which he had granted us sufficient fuel and water. After much bickering he promised to give our family ten pounds of water daily. We suspected that the whole thing was a bit of rascality on the part of the pilot, who hoped to create a situation where people would give him tips to win his favor, and therefore kept repeating in the Captain's ear that we were using too much water. The Captain at any rate was fairly consistent in that he gave the other passengers their share of water too, though the two Frenchmen were well supplied with substitutes for the rationed water.

Emigrants cannot be too careful in making out their contract, so as not to be too restricted when at sea. They should specify a stipulated amount of water to be given each person and a discount on the fare if this is not received.

August 25 to 27. The wind is very favorable. Apparently we are near the Gulf of Florida because the sea is warmer than body temperature. But the weather is unpleasant, humid and murky. In one hour we put ten nautical miles behind us. The pace of the ship is fascinating. It cleaves the water with such force that the water swirls up ten to twelve feet high along the side of the ship. Man's skill is capable of much, astonishingly much, but how ineffectual it is against the forces of nature. In one day now we sail farther than we did previously in four. "With our strength nothing can be done," said the pithy Luther.

The dexterity of the sailors is revealed in every situation. Today one of them came into the hall to show us straw weaving. Out of the finely split leaves of a plant (*Typha*) he prepared a variety of attractive woven goods. Another was making himself shoes and still another a tailcoat.

79

As long as one industry is sufficient to maintain the inhabitants of a country, the greatest possible skill in this is indeed best, but when this source of wealth begins to fail, a people with multiple skills, even if not developed as highly, is much better off. With a multiplicity of skills, needs may readily be provided for which would otherwise drain off the last penny. A people who have learned to produce a wide variety of things for itself is, to my thinking, happier and also morally better than a people who must do without as many things as possible.

August 28. We are still having good wind and fog as thick as mashed potatoes. The sea is again much colder and looks greenish. Both of these things are indications, the sailors say, that we are approaching the New-foundland Banks. We see many sea gulls.

August 29. Very clear weather; no wind and a burning heat until toward evening. Schools of fish or dolphins are visible and a fierce storm has come up. It seems that certain species of fish know when a storm is coming. We are now on the Banks. From time to time the depth is plumbed with a sounding lead and the soil sticking to it is examined, by which they can tell if they are getting too close to the shallows and whether they are following the right course. We are to sail a course approximately in the middle of the Banks, because the most dangerous shallows lie on both sides. Many ships sailing from Europe to the United States take another course and do not come through the Newfoundland reef. They sail south to a latitude of about 24 degrees and the longitude of the Gulf of Florida. By taking this route they can make good use of the generally prevailing west and northwest winds. When they are in the longitude of the Gulf of Florida they are helped by the strong northward flow of the Gulf stream, even if there should be an adverse wind. Along this route the weather is supposed to be fair most of the time, while on the straight course over through the Banks there is generally foul weather and a great number of storms. But on the average the northern trip is made in less time.

August 30. This morning the southeast wind changed to the northwest so quickly that the sails could hardly be changed. It continued to blow quite forcefully all day. In the evening the wind changed just as quickly to the northeast.

Today the cat fell overboard. The Captain immediately lowered a lifeboat, but the poor foolish thing had already swallowed so much sea water that it could not be brought back to life. In losing her we lost quite an important member of our ship's company. As it was, in spite of the cat's watchfulness, rats had carried things off in broad daylight. To judge from the mischief that goes on every night, their numbers are legion.

August 31. Fairly good wind and clear weather. We are finding a great amount of some kind of moss today. With a harpoon on a rope, we were able to haul some up. It has endive-like leaves on which were numerous berry-shaped outgrowths, and on these we discovered many little white-yellowish creatures somewhat like very small lice. What a chain of these little creatures it would take to match the length of a whale!

September 1. Again adverse winds. We are going to have to endure several days more of the wet element than we formerly believed we would. The air is clear, and yet it is so sultry that it is almost unbearable in the hold. How must it be on a ship on which there are hundreds of passengers?

This evening in the southeast we saw a remarkable meteor, rather like the northern lights. From the exact point of the southeast a multitude of fiery rays shot out to the right. Their height could have made an angle of 60 to 70 degrees with the horizon. The phenomenon lasted about a quarter of an hour. The sailors could not remember having seen a similar spectacle in this part of the sky.

September 2. Somewhat better wind, also rain. In the evening we all thought we saw land to the northwest, but after a half hour the supposed land rose in the sky. It was a strip of clouds which for a long time afterwards maintained their outline.

September 3. A bright, pleasant day, but little wind. To the north a ship is visible which is also heading for the United States. A lovely sunset glow ended this day. The entire sky was covered with crisp little clouds which were incomparably illumed by the setting sun. The ocean seemed like a purple carpet. Beauty may be found anywhere in God's earth; no spot is completely without beauty. Until late at night we remained on deck and feasted our eyes unendingly on the starlight.

September 4. Again a pleasant day, but again little wind. For an hour this morning we sailed over an area of the sea which moved almost imperceptibly, while outside this definite area the ocean was rather agitated. All day long we encountered currents which came generally from the west and north and were almost shattering in force. Several times the Captain made tests to determine how much the ship was deflected by these currents. He did this by letting down a lifeboat from which an anchor was lowered and after twenty minutes the angle between the lifeboat and the ship was measured. There are said to be hidden rocks near here; this necessitates knowing the exact course of the ship.

81

Today we saw several snakelike creatures in the water. They were very attractive and multicolored. They were about as thick as a big thumb with a disproportionately large head. I cannot remember ever having heard of these creatures before.

The starlight shines here as it does at home only on the brightest winter nights. Venus and the Milky Way light up strips of the sea as though lanterns were shining above it. The murmur of the currents, now gentle, now loud, calls up thoughts of the rustling leaves and rippling brooks of our homeland.

September 5. Again a very bright day, but complete absence of wind. If there is even the faintest puff anywhere the Captain has the sails raised, only to have them lowered again shortly thereafter. We are still encountering currents; they create an unusual effect on an otherwise mirror-like sea. It looks as though we were seeing an inundated land from which the water was beginning to drain off.

In Helder and many times since then, I have heard the sailors sing the melody of "Let Life Be Joyful" and the Viennese cowherds' song, "Early in the Morning When I Get Up." There seems to be in this music a classic beauty that never ages and that finds its way over every border. I was also interested to hear that Ambühl's song, "I Am a Brown Swiss Maiden," has been translated into English and is a beloved folk song of the Americans. It pleases me not a little that such a monument has been built to my countryman in a faraway land.[15]

September 6. This morning we saw a great many fish again. In the afternoon we had another storm but it subsided by evening. Today we sailed over the smaller Banks.

September 7. A bright day and favorable wind. We made nine miles an hour. In the afternoon around four o'clock we spied a ship in the west and by seven o'clock that evening we had overtaken it. The Captains communicated by megaphone. The ship came from Liverpool and has already been 53 days at sea. After they had exchanged information about

[15] "Freut Euch des Lebens" ("Let Life Be Joyful") was written by Johann Martin Usteri of Zurich. The composer of "Bin ein braunes Schweizer Mädchen" ("I Am a Brown Swiss Maiden") was a fellow countryman, Johann Ludwig Ambühl (1750–1800). The latter song had first appeared in Ambühl's *Neue Schweizerlieder*, published in 1776. The cowherds' songs or *Kuhreihen* were popular songs sung especially by the young men who tended village herds in the Alps during the summer. Singing these songs was sometimes forbidden by officers of Swiss mercenary forces because of the acute *mal de pays* caused by nostalgic songs. The "killing homesickness" was described by doctors attached to Swiss mercenary forces abroad. See E. J. Hobsbawm, *The Age of Revolution, 1789–1848* (London: Weidenfeld and Nicolson, 1962), p. 137.

many things, they said farewell to one another and our ship sailed proudly on.

It is very important for a passenger to get on a ship which is a good sailer. Besides taking you where you are going sooner, it also has the advantage of rocking less.

Today in many parts of my native land, but probably not in all, Prayer Day is being celebrated. — O Fatherland, O Fatherland, how harmony has left you! Must every grain of sand be a stumbling block? Must virtue flee with prosperity? How will mutual love and trust ever manifest itself again when there is discord over trivialities? How my breast would swell with pride if, in a distant country, I learned that harmony had once again been established.*

Never as fervently as today did we reflect upon all the good things that God has wrought for us this year. Far from our homeland, in that notorious Holland, He allowed us to find friends and benefactors. Without being able to work, we have enough to eat at sea to satisfy our hunger, while at home often, despite hard work, we could hardly provide ourselves with scanty fare. Marvelously He has turned aside ever-present danger. Indeed, the Lord has truly done great things for us!

September 8. Another pleasant day, but no wind. At noon we saw many fish, about an arm's length in size. The sailors tried to catch them with hooks but none wished to bite. After these had disappeared, a tremendous school of very large fish swam by, moving from the south. As far as the eye could see, the ocean resembled a cutover forest where only the stumps remained standing. Often they formed something resembling a bridge twenty to thirty feet wide. They gravitated northward, as though they had mutually bound themselves to emigrate together. In the evening, about nine o'clock, a tremendous fish appeared very near to the ship. It followed us for almost an hour. It was not easy to see it well in the twilight, but the sailors said it was a shark.

Everything is being made ready for our arrival in port. The decks are being washed and scrubbed, the railings and masts freshly painted, the flags repaired, the mended sails taken down, and new ones hoisted. One day of good wind ought to bring us to the long sought land. I find

* Not everything is what it appears. Concerning Swiss unity we will believe and hope for more than appearance seems to indicate. But can the native land of a noble patriot be angered because he wishes all citizens, without regard to creed, to gather together on one day before the God of love??? It is, indeed, one fatherland which unites all in equal love and freedom, and one God who has protected, saved, and blessed this native land throughout so many centuries. [c. k.]

something very unpleasant about landing in New York. Probably there is much old English pride and manners there and not much sympathy for foreigners.

September 9. Heavy gale from the southwest. The ship is constantly tacking and is making but little progress. Once in a while a ship is sighted; we have overtaken three of them.

In the beginning, we just could not understand why the sailors always laughed during a heavy storm and made so little of it. Now the play of the waves gives us pleasure too, and we can laugh with them when a wave unexpectedly breaks over the ship and thoroughly soaks some of the people. This honor fell to us twice today. It is really something worth seeing when the sea is turbulent; the water cannot be seen any more, for it has been beaten to a foam. If you imagine that you are standing on a mountain in Switzerland which affords a view of numerous glaciers and snowy peaks, and then that these are suddenly thrown one upon another, then you have some idea of the ocean in storm. Much more is added to this spectacle by night because of the phosphorescence of the water. Every wave seems to gush forth sparks of fire which are extinguished very slowly.

September 10. The storm continues, still on the open sea and no land in sight. The Captain climbed up to the crow's nest several times today and looked about quite puzzled. Judging by the big steps he takes and the great quantities of tobacco he chews, he is a bit irked.

I do not believe that the Captain has spoken a hundred words during the entire trip with anyone except when he had to give orders, and he certainly never did that with two words if one was enough to make himself understood.

September 11. Today at noon we actually sighted land to the northwest; some thought it was Long Island, some the area around Albany. If the wind improves a bit, we are supposed to make harbor tonight.

September 12. A terrible gale raged last night. The big sail on the middle mast could not be pulled in fast enough in the darkness. Wham! The storm snapped the mast, together with its metal sheath, as though it were a matchstick, although it was three feet around and held with thick iron bars. The Captain now tried to turn back to the open sea, and this morning land had vanished again. In the evening we sighted land again. The Captain took it to be the area around New York, and ordered the men to navigate the ship in that direction, as far as the storm permitted.

Today a new mast had to be made in spite of the heavy rain and the storm. The carpenter had to tie himself to a rope until the holes for the pulley were bored.

The sailors scrubbed out their cabin and with great jubilation threw into the sea their dirty bedding and the greater part of their clothing, which was certainly no longer very spruce.

September 13. It seems that the land we sighted yesterday lay below New York, because in the night, as we were approaching the coast, he had the ship bear to the southwest. Today again there is no land to be seen. Our patience is quite taxed. We remain on deck until late at night hoping to spy out land, but in vain.

September 14. It was still before dawn when the servant, H. Z., got us out of bed to see the land we have yearned for, not very far away. It was the coast of New Jersey, not far from the harbor. In veritable bridal array the land rose before us. We could now hear the breaking of the surf against the forested shore and the rustling of the morning wind in the tips of the tall oaks. Pleasant, half-hidden dwellings peeked through the bushes. Quickly they slipped from view, and even prettier ones greeted us. Lovely hills appeared before us with woods, fields, and herds in pleasing, colorful confusion. Innumerable ships and boats rocked and swarmed around us like colorful butterflies on a mild spring day. A handsome schooner is moving toward us. It is a pilot. Cautiously at some distance he inquires about the health of the ship's company. Now he is being pulled up. He is a pleasant young man who greets the new arrivals with a sincere handshake.

The sea narrows into a slender tongue. Two hills with numerous buildings form the gateposts of the harbor. Hundreds of fire pits threaten death and destruction to him who wantonly seeks to violate this refuge of freedom. But what do I see? A new world appears before my eyes. An ocean in miniature lies behind these posts, and along the shores lie little cities, marvelous buildings, estates, and islands. To the left of the harbor is the hospital, nestled against a hill. This alone could count as quite a little city. From there right now a sloop is bringing the doctor who is to inspect our ship. Farther on lie the ships that are in quarantine. There must be more than forty of them. We can sail right to the city. The view of New York City opens before us and it is enchanting. As in a dream, new things crowd before our eyes and vanish just as quickly. There, in an inlet, a column of coal-black smoke whirling to the sky; it is the smoke of a steamboat, which now roars toward us without sails. We are sailing past attractive forts and barracks.[16] Our ship anchors down at the end of the city and now probably a fairly prosaic part of my diary will begin.

September 15. Yesterday, right after the arrival of the ship, an official from the customs house came on board to seal up the cargo. In his presence, we had to take out of our crates what we needed for the next few days.

Today I delivered the letters of introduction which I had received from Mr. von Mandach and Mr. Isler. I found Mr. de Rham[17] a completely honest and pleasing man who tended to my affairs with genuine eagerness. Here again I felt the influence of my noble Amsterdam friend very strongly. I cannot praise Mr. Schmidt, the Prussian commercial consul, in the same way. The cold reception and dismissal which I received there would not have alienated me if he had not promised his active assistance to every countryman coming here, as was made known by a published letter of his which he had addressed to Mr. Maier Gonzenbach in St. Gallen. I would have preferred to omit this remark if it were not for the fact that many a Swiss, believing in this letter, would in the end find himself misled. I, myself, know many fellow countrymen who think they can rely on Schmidt's offer.

I asked everywhere today about a room so that we could do our own cooking while we were here, but thus far I have not found anything. We will probably have to go to a boardinghouse.

Today I learned that Captain Niederholt had taken no more than 46 days to reach New York from Holland. He took the southern route, making use of the Gulf stream.

As soon as an American ship has entered the harbor, the sailors are paid off. If they find service on a ship about to pull out, then they husband their money fairly well, generally speaking. If they do not get a job right

[16] The system of fortifications surrounding New York City was extended during the War of 1812 until the area "bristled with fortifications." See Martha Lamb, *History of the City of New York* (New York and Chicago: A. S. Barnes & Co., 1877), Vol. II, pt. 2, pp. 660–661.

[17] Henry C. de Rham was an eminent banker and importer in New York City. He came to the United States around 1807 and was serving as Swiss consul at the time Schweizer and Rütlinger came to America. He was associated with a group of Swiss immigrant merchants including Iselin, de Luze, Merle d'Aubigne and d'Ivernois. Henry de Rham was, according to Scoville, "one of the finest men in the city and county of New York." He was part of one of the most distinguished literary circles of his generation, one which included his friend Albert Gallatin. See J. A. Scoville, *The Old Merchants of New York City* (New York: John Lovell, 1889), pp. 216, 327–329; also John Austin Stevens, *Albert Gallatin* (Boston and New York: Houghton Mifflin, 1898), p. 367.

away, they go through the greatest part of their pay in taverns in a short time.

September 20 to October 10. When you want to get your belongings from the ship, you go with the inventory of your possessions to the customs house. There it is decided if they must be brought to the customs house or if they can be inspected on the ship. If you have very little, or if you have no new things, the latter happens. As in European customs houses, there is a good deal of arbitrariness here. It is a good thing if you have packed separately all new articles intended for resale and can show an accurate bill of sale for them. It is even better if you do not have to have the things inspected in the customs house. I was not so fortunate, and I did not come out of it too well. Without the forceful intercession of Mr. de Rham it certainly would have gone worse. On printed books we had to pay fifteen per cent, on cotton articles twenty-five per cent, and the same for linen articles.

I was told I could be optimistic about selling my Bibles here if I would wait until the Bible Society meets in eight or ten days. Everyone advised me to sell the Bibles in New York at any price, because money is scarce in the country and last year a handsome German Bible had been published in Lancaster. Subscriptions had been taken in all states, and in spite of that there still were two thousand copies left unsold. We moved in with a German innkeeper named Ulmer who, however, treats his fellow countrymen anything but fairly.

I am more convinced with every passing day that immigrants with little money do not do well to invest their money in commodities. The English flood everything with wool, cotton, iron, steel, and brass articles. The Dutch bring linens. On top of that the American merchants want to make at least fifty per cent profit. If an immigrant has to turn his things into money quickly, he is almost always in a bad position. Besides that, people in Germany know the taste and fashion of Americans too little to be able to select things that will attract buyers. A knifesmith, W., from Strasbourg, arrived with a fairly large quantity of his wares and hoped for a quick market and high profit. He had definitely heard that a table knife cost up to three fourths of a dollar and an ordinary fork cost up to forty or sixty cents. He was indeed not a little taken aback when he found that they could not be sold at any price. He went about the country with them, back and forth. They are still unsold, and he is a poor man. All of his knives were too pointed, and the forks too blunt. The knife serves the American as a fork as well, and therefore it must be broad in front and rounded off. The fork must be like a carving fork, with only two long, strong prongs, because the American uses it only to hold the meat or to keep it firm. The Americans have a proverb: "You don't just have to teach Germans how to work, you have to teach them how to eat too." Certainly if speed is the highest art here, then they are complete masters. As soon as food is set on the table they fall upon it like wolves on an unguarded herd. With the knife in the right hand, they cut and bring vegetables and sometimes meat as well to their mouths. With the fork in the left hand, they deliver meat without interruption to the teeth. In rending and gulping down they have a proficiency which would not shame Mr. Isegrim.[18]

Another German last year brought several crates of tobacco pipes because he had heard that a very ordinary one cost up to one and a quarter dollars. That is actually true, but in all of New York you probably would not find twenty people who smoke anything but cigars, and that is the way it is supposed to be everywhere. "Smoking a pipe is too much trouble. We have other things to do than to spend our time stuffing and cleaning a pipe," an American told me today laconically.

A Prussian brought axes with him because he had read, in a travel account by a learned man, that a wood axe costs three dollars here. But the learned man had forgotten to mention that axes here are shaped entirely differently than in most parts of Germany, and that they can clearly be used much more advantageously. My good Prussian had to sell his axes as old iron. The axes here are about eight to ten inches high and five inches wide and their greatest thickness is one and a half inches. The handle goes through at half height. The axe-head doesn't bow out but is wedge-shaped. It is a combination axe, wedge, and sledgehammer. What an accomplished woodchopper can do with this instrument! There are some among them who can chop and split five and a half cords of wood a day, including stacking them.

Things didn't go much better for a man from Baden who brought saws. The big tree saws no one bought, since they are rarely used here. All big timber is chopped. For cutting wood into small pieces for cooking or heating, frame saws are used. The frame saws which this man

[18] Isegrim or Isengrim the Wolf and Reynard the Fox were central characters in the cycle of animal stories that seem to have been created in the twelfth century in the border region between France and Flanders. In the popular fabliaux, Reynard the Fox achieves advantage over such rivals as Isengrim the Wolf and Bruin the Bear. In popular parlance, an "Isengrim" was a person who was considered sullen, dour, or gluttonous. See Jakob Grimm and Wilhelm Grimm, *Deutsches Wörterbuch* (Leipzig: S. Hirzel, 1877), p. 2181.

brought along, however, did not fit into the ordinary saw frames used here. They are not made for turning saws. Where a turning saw is needed a plain push saw similar to our hole saw is used. I must admit the superiority of their frame saws. They are not especially thin, but are of excellent material and are well made. The teeth are also sharpened a bit on the flat side. The saw therefore can do a great deal of cutting without wearing the teeth very much. A sawyer can cut a cord of oak or hickory wood four feet long in two hours, although each log must be cut twice. It would be difficult for two men back home to do this work in half a day. In general, Americans have a tremendous dexterity at their work, and their tools assist them admirably in this.

There seems to be a position for me in Mahattanville,[19] two hours from New York. I must wait, however, for the final decision until a superior official, who is now forty miles away from here, returns. Today Mr. Eddy[20] and Pastor Schäfer accompanied me there. It is a hospital for the insane.[21] Next to it are several hundred acres of land and a botanical garden. The main building is not quite finished yet. It is probably the largest building in the state of New York. Numerous corridors lead underground into cement-walled places where the ill can stroll and get fresh air without being out of the overseers' view. Up on the roof is a gallery which affords an almost unlimited view. Like a sea, the majestic Hudson flows between the flatlands and the hills. Ships swarm on its smooth surface. Far in the distance it disappears in the mountains which are veiled by a blue haze. Many rivers and canals cut through like threads of silver; to the right is the great plain towards Albany.

Today we went over to Long Island. A steamboat and a rudder boat pulled by horses go back and forth continually.[22] It makes you shudder

[19] Manhattanville (Schweizer apparently didn't hear it quite right), at the north end of Manhattan Island, is today a part of New York. At that time, the city covered only the southern tip of the island.

[20] Thomas Eddy was a New York philanthropist who spent his life in advancing numerous benevolent enterprises. He founded the first free school in New York. He was a leader in efforts to modernize the penal code and improve the penal institutions. Eddy led in efforts to establish programs of crime prevention and took part in founding the Society for the Reformation of Juvenile Delinquents. Along wth DeWitt Clinton and others he planned the establishment of the Bloomingdale Asylum. He was much interested in the treatment of the mentally ill and corresponded with persons active in this field all over the world. See Lamb, *op. cit.*, p. 518. He was one of the commissioners appointed to explore the whole route for inland navigation from the Hudson River to Lake Ontario and Lake Erie (*ibid.*, p. 579).

[21] This was the Bloomingdale Asylum, a private hospital for the insane, opened in New York City in 1821.

[22] Until 1810 barges with oars and boats impelled by horse power were the only means of ferrying. The horse boats had a wheel in the center propelled by a hori-

to board such a glory-wagon of the human spirit for the first time. The American steamboats generally have two or three boilers, because in this way the danger of an explosion is greatly reduced. Splendid rooms with paintings and mirrors hung on the walls, and floors covered with Turkish carpets greet the passengers. At a touch light as a feather, the boat roars away.

As we got off on the other side, a pair of beautifully built windmills caught our attention. We went up to the wings and found that the shutters were all made of cast iron, but so exactly were they fitted into one another that even a faint wind turned them rapidly. From there we went along a corn field that stood like a little forest. My wife kept insisting that most of the stalks were over twelve feet tall. We pulled out a few of the biggest and found that they were over fourteen feet in length. Yet the ground seemed poorly cultivated and badly fertilized. Not far from there we found several water mills built on a little inlet of the ocean; they were in full operation. In the beginning we just could not understand where so many waterfalls came from so near the ocean. The tide, it seems, rises three and four feet here; at high tide a kind of bay is closed off from the ocean by a sluice and grinding is done as the tide ebbs. So the puzzle was solved.

Where we went we found a great deal of fruit, especially apples, often lying half a foot deep under the trees. Cows and pigs availed themselves of it. We were troubled by this wanton waste; we scolded about the laziness and carelessness this reflected, but soon thereafter we modified our harsh judgment. An elderly man met us, addressed us in German, and spent a long time with us. I asked him, then, the reason for the waste of fruit and the careless cultivation of the land.

"Don't reproach the Americans for laziness or carelessness," he said. "You will soon discover that we are more industrious than any German people, but we have too much to do. A farmer with two hundred acres is not a big farmer. He keeps few hired hands because daily wages are still high, even though there are more unemployed and less money than there used to be. Now is the time of the corn harvest and the sowing. Where can he find time to gather fruit? Besides this, in our manner of living, fruit is not regarded as essential to our table. We would rather

zontal treadmill worked by horses. Such boats used in New York in this period were capable of carrying as many as 550 passengers in addition to carriages and horses. After 1810 steam ferryboats were increasingly used. See William L. Store, *History of New York City* (New York: Virtue & Yorston, 1872), p. 356, and Lamb, *op. cit.*, p. 518.

have a piece of beef and are more satisfied by it. We always have enough for cider. On the market, people would not buy it in quantity. If our cows and pigs eat it, then at least use is made of it. As to the cultivation of our fields, don't pass judgment until after you have been here a few years. Neatest and cleanest isn't always best. If we can produce enough, the appearance is unimportant. An acre of wheat yields on the average 24 bushels at 62 pounds market weight, an acre of corn 36 bushels. The result justifies our methods. And furthermore, the yield of our fields has increased for forty years, while according to what I hear yours has been decreasing." The old man might not have been completely wrong in his way of looking at these things.

Finally he said this to us: "It is certain that many times you will regret the step you made. It will be astonishingly difficult to find suitable employment. It may well be that you will have to sacrifice your last cent and the last decent rag from your body before you achieve some kind of livelihood for yourself. But don't be discouraged; you are, after all, in a fortunate land. In five years you would not want to return. If you should find yourself without bread or a job today, you would not have to go begging, for you could find the kind of care in a poorhouse that many a farmer over in Germany doesn't have. So again, remember what I say, America is a fortunate land!" We thanked the old man for his instruction, and, bitter as it was, we tucked it away.

It was already dark when we returned to the hill in front of which the harbor lies. A marvelous spectacle unfolded before our eyes. A large expanse of the harbor was lighted by four columns of flames that swirled to the sky. Streams of sparks were hurled toward the sky. It was four steamboats from whose smokestacks the illumination ascended. The marvel of this scene was heightened when we observed the fires glide ceremoniously over the water and heard the thundering of their rudders.[23]

It is oppressively hot, and the ungodly mosquitoes make it even more oppressive. These pests are usually most irritating at night. August and September are supposed to be the time when they are worst; areas far from rivers are supposedly free from them. It is remarkable that another pest which in Europe so often is the trial of our days and the plague of our nights, and the extermination of which occupies millions of fingers, seems to be unknown here. Certainly I have not seen or felt a single one.

[23] Steamboats were such an awe-inspiring sight, especially at night, that sailors unaccustomed to them were known to flee below deck in terror or jump overboard. One New York farmer ran home to tell his wife he had seen "the devil on his way to Albany in a sawmill." Lamb, *op. cit.*, p. 532.

Almost every night a fire alarm is heard.[24] The first time I took to my legs in a hurry. In the largest street, not far from the museum, a house was burning. A crowd of curious people gathered around it, the men smoking their cigars unconcernedly. Several constables took care that no one got too close. The firemen were chatting. It seemed to me that they were waiting for the fire to reach out to the entire neighborhood so that it would be more worth the trouble of putting out. All at once came a strong gust of wind, and with inconceivable fury the fire spread to another house where liqueurs and brandy were stored. Now, however, the hoses were put to such good use that within eight minutes' time not one burning coal was to be seen. For the first time I had the opportunity to see the exemplary fire-fighting methods. Many neighboring houses were hung with wet cloths; everything, I think, was saved from the three houses, and yet very few people had been engaged in the enterprise.

There are several fire insurance companies in New York. As soon as a constable or anyone else notices a fire the storm bell is rung. (To announce church services it is only struck on one side.) Every member of the fire company of the insurance company involved hurries to his post.[25] When the threatened place is near the sea, a pump is used and hoses are attached to deliver water to the fire engines. In addition to this, drinking water, which can be found along every street, can be used by the fire engines. If the danger appears great, the bells of other churches are tolled. Whatever is saved of household wares and what remains of the building belongs to the insurance company. That is why you see the owner or tenant of a burning house standing leisurely by and calmly watching the fire after he has rescued his own person.

The water from the pumping fountains in New York is bad, but on the other hand you can get good water everywhere. There is a water pipe from Mahattanville to the city which supplies abundant good water. A steam engine pumps it to such a height in a building that from there it can be piped to all parts of the city.

[24] Alexander Hamilton reported that during his residence in New York City twenty-four hours never passed without a fire alarm. In the period in which Schweizer visited New York, it was estimated that firemen were called out perhaps five hundred times a year. See Stone, *op. cit.*, p. 512.

[25] In each ward of the city volunteer companies were organized; it was considered an honor to belong. By 1825 there were 1347 such firemen in New York City with forty-two hand-drawn engines with pumps and ladders at their disposal. There was a horse-drawn wagon with ten thousand feet of hose. Steam fire engines were introduced in London in 1832 with great gain of efficiency. This innovation was resisted in New York City for thirty more years despite disastrous fires. See Stone, *op. cit.*, p. 584.

In a store I found agricultural machinery, among which a turning plow, a machine to sow corn, beans, and other things, a machine to take kernels of corn off the cob, and a spelt huller were distinguished by their unusual simplicity and practicality.

It is impossible for Europeans to imagine rightly the activity and energy, or rather the reality and life, of America. It is the dream of a high fever made real. One hour you exult in the good fortune of becoming a citizen of this happy land under such a just and wise constitution and government, being able to live among such unprejudiced, moral, and educated people; the next hour you would like to flee to an uninhabited desert. The principle of an eternal anarchy is reflected in the Constitution. The laws seem to benefit only scoundrels. The people seem to be a mob of vagabonds, haphazardly come together, from whom all feeling for tradition, order, and propriety has vanished. You no longer find a pleasing, gentle education, but only materialistic self-interest.

You step into a workshop and find a fine, pleasing, well-educated shoemaker or tailor, one who could indeed pass for a personage in Europe who had completed several schools. You come into the house of a prominent citizen, who has perhaps a million dollars; the rooms are fitted with the most costly furnishings and the floors, beginning by the front door, are covered with Turkish rugs. Mother and daughter sit on sofas made of mahogany or ebony, the upholstery supported by steel coils; they dress themselves in clothing which would not shame a princess, and you are greeted with the words, "Well, whaddaya think of this country? You got a wife and child?" If a person is given a polite invitation to dinner, it is offered with the formula, "Well, canya eat with us?"

When you go down a street you see attractive houses to the left and right; wherever a door opens a gorgeously dressed person emerges. But then you come to the street where mostly Negroes live; horrible faces wound about with kerchiefs meet you; everything indicates the deepest degradation. I stepped into a room today to inquire about someone. An unbearable stench almost made me recoil. I wanted to find out what the cause of it was. In the corner of the room lay half a quarter of meat from which the family, when hungry, cut slices. Complete with the new inhabitants that crawl all over them, the slices are roasted a bit in the fireplace and devoured. The son cut a slice off and assured me that it tasted very good. This was an Irish family that thus lived and feasted like New Zealanders.

A law states that the tenant gets free rent if the house burns down during his occupancy. "How considerate and humane!" says one in praise of America. "What an accursed school for arson!" screams another. As a result of this provision twenty or thirty houses are often set on fire in one night.

"It is better to allow ninety-nine guilty persons to go free than to convict an innocent man" is the fundamental principle of American justice. "How protective and liberal! How worthy of a free, enlightened people!" says neighbor A, who by an unjust judgment was deprived of honor and fortune and driven from home and country here to this foreign part of the world. "It certainly is an excellent principle, perfectly adapted to raising ninety-nine thieves to one honest man," counters neighbor B, gnashing his teeth because some rogue has just robbed him of several hundred dollars, and has known how to find refuge in the letter of the law, like some bandit finding protection in the cliffs of the Apennines.

"What kind of a miserable, pitiful police force do you have in Europe? In the midst of the most populated lands, robber bands are organized which often carry on their activities for years before they are finally cleaned up. The citizens of the cities in which they are entrenched tremble before them. Yet your streets swarm with mounted police and gendarmes, like a carcass with flies, and every half hour a traveler has to endure an inquisition and carry pockets full of passes and passports if he doesn't want to be locked up. On the other hand, here highway robbery is as rare as a comet, and a theft or any trick like that doesn't go unsolved three weeks. The planter in the most remote woods lives as securely as the mayor in his council chamber does in your country. Yet in the whole United States we don't have any mounted police, and our constables don't waste a penny on things not related to their main job. No one asks the traveler for a passport from New Orleans to Plattsburg and from Washington to the South Sea."

"Yes," says a European, who has been done out of his inheritance by too much faith and trust, "your robbers don't have to lurk in the forests and break through stone fences and walls. They prefer to open boxes and coffers in broad daylight and assume wrongful possession of them by means of judges and lawyers. And that every American is as much of a policeman as an old police chief in our country doesn't deserve such special praise."

That's the way one feels at the start in America. At least I did; and I am stubborn and proud enough to believe that every unprejudiced stranger would also feel the same way. It seems as though a capricious genie had chopped up all possible good and bad together in a concoction and poured it over America.*

It is true that high daily wages are paid in America, and it is also true that there are many unemployed as well. Even now an ordinary day-laborer is paid one half to three quarters of a dollar a day with board, but what has not been realized in Europe until now is that the day-laborer here works twice as much as one in Switzerland. Even at the most ordinary labor, the worker has a highly perfected skill. An American wood-cutter or woodchopper would be admired in Switzerland and Germany as much as a mechanic or painter or musician is. The newly emigrated German or Swiss doesn't have this dexterity in the beginning and is therefore hired only when no one better is to be found. The American farmer is not so poor that he has to be that careful with a half dollar. He would rather pay that wage to a skilled laborer than give board to an unskilled one.

Still you must not imagine the unemployed to be in pitiful circumstances as the unemployed certainly are in Germany. An unemployed person does not need to suffer hunger. In the past several years the Germans seem to have lost their good reputation, but the farmer is still hospitable toward every stranger. Much worse off are the people who have not yet paid their passage. Almost always they are indentured to appallingly harsh masters. Ordinarily only a farmer buys an indentured servant (this is what the people are called who must serve for their passage money) who because of rough treatment of his help cannot get day-laborers or hired hands. He treats his indentured servant harshly, so that he can get back the price of passage in the shortest time possible. If he perishes because of it, the master is not blamed. Often the servant is beaten like a slave. However, the servant may be given his freedom if he can prove mistreatment in court with legal witnesses. But this is difficult. You must not have such an idealistic concept of the American love of justice as to think that a poor indentured servant can so easily bring suit against his master.

The state of New York is laying out a canal which will have a very

* We agree heartily in this with our honest countryman. It must be difficult for a European to describe and evaluate because of this. It takes more time to judge quite without prejudice the indigenous, traditional phenomena of another hemisphere. "Who says America is warm, healthy, wet, low, fertile, is right; and another who says the opposite is also right, especially for other seasons and other areas. It is the same with peoples: all kinds of people are found in all zones of a whole hemisphere." Herder's *Ideen z. Phil. d. Gesch. d. Menschh.* [C. K.]

important effect upon trade and will greatly raise the value of land in the western part of this state and in the state of Pennsylvania. Lake Erie, Lake Ontario, and other smaller lakes in this area will be connected with the Hudson. The whole enterprise will be finished in two years at the most. Even now steamers regularly travel five hundred miles every week. A large part of northwest Pennsylvania is accessible because of rivers that flow into these lakes. In a short time trade with the Indians can be extraordinarily expanded, considering how simple connecting Lake Huron and Lake Michigan with Lake Ontario would be, and considering how much of the Indian population still lives around these lakes.

In the last few days an Indian tribe arrived here to receive their annual payment for relinquished land. It seems to me the description of their beautiful physique, noble bearing, and similar things has been much exaggerated. Their coal-black, tufted hair, and their fixed stare give them a loathsome appearance. I have observed them many times running through the streets, stooped, their heads pushed down onto their shoulders, with clubs held in their hands.

At present the American farmers are complaining greatly about the low price of flour and the consequent lack of money and wish for nothing more passionately than for war in Europe. A hundredweight of flour at present costs two dollars (a dollar is the equivalent of two and a half Rhenish gulden and has 100 cents or 90 pence). A pound of bread costs three cents, a pound of beef five to eight cents, pork five to six cents, butter fourteen to eighteen cents, and a bushel of corn forty-five to fifty cents.

Meat is not properly utilized. It is priced according to its appearance. No meat from the head reaches the butcher shop, and rib parts are sold cheaply. Today an innkeeper's wife complained that she had been cheated by a farmer over a leg of mutton. He had sewed on a number of pieces of fat which did not belong there. I was amazed at this kind of deception, which is very rare in Switzerland. I was told that this is quite common, especially in summertime when fat has a lower price than meat.

Today a pig was run over in the street. Without doing a thing about it, the driver rode away laughing. I inquired if he did not have to make compensation, and I was told no. The law cannot forbid anyone to run his pigs in the streets, but when they are run over, or killed upon entering anyone's yard, no one can be held responsible for it. Also, when a person is knocked down by a vehicle in the street he cannot hold the driver liable. That is why the pedestrian travels on the raised brick-paved footpaths on either side of the road.

Apparently nothing will come of our plan to sell our Bibles in New York. Furthermore, the position in the hospital in Mahattanville is not to be open until spring. Well, we are quite willing to resign ourselves to what may come. Fortunately America is large. Tomorrow we leave for Philadelphia.

October 11. Yesterday at noon we boarded a sloop going as far as South Amboy in New Jersey. From there we traveled in a stagecoach to Bordentown on the Delaware, and from there we took a steamboat down the river to Philadelphia. This whole trip from New York to Philadelphia with this arrangement costs a person three dollars. Each person is allowed to take thirty pounds of baggage along. The distance between these two cities is about a hundred miles. There is a similar arrangement by way of New Brunswick and Trenton to Philadelphia; this, though, costs each person two dollars more.

The weather was rainy and stormy. We had hardly been traveling an hour before there were both ridiculous and nauseating occurrences among the passengers. We experienced not the mildest discomfort. We were not a little delighted to have accustomed ourselves so well to sea travel. At three o'clock we arrived at South Amboy; the stagecoach was waiting and twenty people were packed into it. It was suffocatingly hot and cramped. We would much rather have gone on foot, if only it had been a decent road, but the wheels often sank to their axles in the mud. Finally, in one such puddle, the axle broke in two. Everything had to be unloaded, or rather, thrown into the mud. Late at night we arrived at an inn. The wagon had to be repaired. Some went to bed and others sat around the brandy bottle. We and the one other German passenger among us lay down on the ground next to our trunks. At four o'clock the horses were hitched again, and we drove off at a lively pace. In the afternoon at four o'clock we arrived in Bordentown.

The area between South Amboy and Bordentown is not at all pleasing. The low-lying areas are swampy and the higher places are sandy and rocky. The forests consist mostly of red and white oak and hickory (*Juglans alba*). In the swamp persimmons are found in abundance. On the higher lands red cedars (*Juniperus virginia*) and several varieties of wild grape are found. There was one blue kind that did not taste bad at all. Most of the area seems to be scantily populated. Often you drive miles before coming to a plantation. In the west the land is supposed to be more heavily populated as well as healthier and more fertile.

Every day a steamer goes from Philadelphia up the Delaware as far as

97

Trenton and back again. It takes New York passengers, those coming by way of New Brunswick as well as those who use the South Amboy line, to Philadelphia. These steamboats are about the size of an average merchant ship and have three stacks next to one another. They are fired with ordinary Scotch pine. The balancing girder is about twenty inches on the high side and about fourteen inches on the wide side, and about thirty-six feet long. Yet the gigantic strength of the steam plays with it as with a feather quill. What a fearsome power if it should shake off the fetters of man's control.

There is hardly anything more beautiful imaginable than the shores of the Delaware; one estate is more splendid than another. A hundred years ago savages still lived here in the darkness of the impenetrable forests; now there are gardens and expensive buildings in the Grecian style crowded together. What a mighty creator is freedom! No horde of useless officials wrested these houses from the blood of their countrymen and is consuming their marrow here. No, most of the holdings belong to plain farmers, other ordinary citizens, and merchants from the city, who live here for a time in summer. Such farm holdings are rarely found in Switzerland and Germany. I like to mention the good wherever I find it, only I cannot bear it when people make an absolute paradise out of America and try to raise its inhabitants to the status of angels.

Because of our late disembarkation, we arrived very late in Philadelphia. Nevertheless, there still was much activity in the streets. We stayed overnight with an old German lady, Mrs. Gunther, who keeps a boarding-house.

October 12. I had already written from Cologne, and also from New York, to Mr. M. to whom I had letters of introduction. I had asked him to seek out any kind of a job for us. Today I went to him. He received me pleasantly and was very friendly; he insisted that we move into the inn in which he had lodgings. He had not been able to arrange a job for us, but he promised to see about getting letters of introduction or recommendations by means of which I might find a position in the country as a teacher.

This afternoon I met a Quaker from Germantown whom I had previously met in New York. He immediately took me to another Quaker who spoke German so that he could make himself understood. He offered to take us in next winter, if we did not find a suitable position. At the same time, he invited us to visit him tomorrow and to see if we would like it there because he had to know our decision then.

October 24. On the thirteenth we went to the Quaker, Reuben Haines, in Germantown.[26] The man greeted us in a very friendly way and offered, if we wished to stay with him, to entrust us with the supervision of his garden in the spring. In the winter, however, he could not promise us a salary, but then there would also be little work to do. We would instruct one another in German and English, and I was promised friendly treatment. Since I had no other prospects and since in Philadelphia everyone who knew about it wished me luck in entering the service of this respected man, I did not hesitate to accept this offer. Furthermore, everyone advised me not to go to the western states. What drew me to him even more was a cabinet full of mineralogical specimens and a fine plant collection.

The first day that we arrived we discovered that we had not chosen a good place. A wild ruffian by the name of Garique, who was employed as foreman, treated us harshly and unfairly. (Reuben Haines was rarely at home and seemed to allow Garique to do as he saw fit.) From early morning until late at night he worked us without interruption, so that we hardly had time to eat in peace the meager food left over from his table, which was given us in the kitchen. He himself did not do a thing all day long. I soon decided to leave this place at the end of the week and travel on. Moreover, the prospect of selling my Bibles in Germantown or Philadelphia had evaporated. I asked Pastor B. and Doctor H. to give Reuben Haines my reasons for not being able or willing to remain, but the gentlemen would not extend this courtesy to a stranger, although otherwise they had shown me much friendliness. There was nothing I could do but write Reuben Haines a note in German and request his servants to give it to him upon his return home. And so at eight o'clock in the evening of the twenty-first, after our day's work was done, we started out on the road to Philadelphia.

In fairness to the other servants and the old mother of Reuben Haines, I must say that their behavior on this evening really moved me. Everybody cried; the old mother had her arms around first one then another of us and asked us to stay until Reuben Haines came home. A Negro threw himself down before us, and by means of signs and broken German gave us to understand that he would not get up until we had assured him

[26] Reuben Haines was a wealthy merchant who began his career as a clerk in the Philadelphia store of Garrigues and Marshall. He retired to Germantown where he lived in "Wyck," one of Germantown's historic mansions. Haines was active in community affairs and devoted much of his leisure to study. See Willis P. Hazard, *Annals of Philadelphia in the Olden Time* (Philadelphia: E. S. Stuart, 1877), p. 414, and E. Digby Baltzell, *Philadelphia Gentlemen: The Making of a National Upper Class* (Glencoe, Ill.: Free Press, 1958), p. 199.

that we had no hatred toward him. The unfeeling, Pharaonic despot Garique and his family clenched their teeth. The contemptible behavior of this fellow so embittered me that, in spite of everything, I could not have remained another night.

On Monday morning, I went to the Quaker, Cook, the man who had taken me to Reuben Haines, in order to tell him the reasons for my action. I had hardly opened the door to his office when he met me with these words: "My dear Schweizer, I already know everything. I am so sorry things turned out this way. Reuben Haines returned home the very hour you left and wrote to me yesterday morning about it already.

"He instructed me to inform you that he had dismissed Garique and his family, and that they had to move out today, and that he would discuss things with you under much better conditions if you wanted to try it once more."

I was somewhat undecided, and if my bones had not ached so I might have tried my luck in Germantown once more. But I stuck to my decision.

In fairness to Quakers generally, I must remark that this Cook rendered us no insignificant services after this incident. I have related this experience in such detail to show into what situations poor immigrants often get and what a dire fate almost always awaits those who cannot even pay their passage across the ocean.

Germantown is a pleasing little city. It would be difficult to find one like it in Germany. It has only one street, but that is several miles long. Every house has its land right next to it, which is why the town is so extended. There is hardly a single bad house in it. Along the street are footpaths shaded by poplars and willows. Germantown was settled entirely by Germans, but now there are few people who understand German. It is said that the two German churches are hardly attended at all.

In Germantown we had to help husk corn and put it in the barn. Here the ears of corn are left in piles until they are eaten by the pigs. A small part is used for the household. Even in this simple operation the Americans have great dexterity. In three motions the cob is husked and piled on the floor. In the first step, the leaf covering is split open with a sharp wooden stick firmly tied to the middle finger and the ring finger of the right hand. In the second motion, the cob is snapped out in such a way that the entire husk including the leaves remains on the stalk, so that it can serve as winter fodder for the cattle which are driven to these fields. In the third step, the cobs are thrown into heaps that are started at intervals.

100

The corn in the area is topped close to the uppermost spadix. The earth is heaped up around each plant, which is not always done, to be sure. After the heaping, pumpkin seeds are sown between the rows. On one acre, so cultivated, the average yield is said to be 36 bushels of corn and up to a hundredweight of pumpkins. An acre is 45,000 English square feet.

The pumpkins are fed to the horses and pigs. At twelve o'clock noon, the horses are unhitched, several pumpkins smashed open with the foot, and thrown to the horses. At twelve-thirty they are already hitched up again. With a load or without, the horses always have to go at a brisk pace. They are never unhitched before seven in the evening, and by five-thirty in the morning they again stand before the wagon. Despite all this rigorous treatment the horses have a good appearance.

How well the corn grows with only an average amount of cultivation is indicated by noting how many ears are found with twenty-two rows of kernels and fifty kernels to a row. On every stalk three or four ears are left. Three or four stalks always grow side by side, which is also detrimental to the size of the ear.

It always seems to me that agriculture here is still in its infancy. It may be that I am too hasty in my judgment. Systematic crop rotation is reported to be rare among farmers, and if it is practiced by one farmer or another, the manner of rotation will vary in each case. They all seek to produce the greatest variety of grain possible. Corn, rye, wheat, oats, buckwheat, and clover are generally planted all the time, but in all possible varieties. Feeding in the barn is unknown; the clover is grazed or fed in the pasture.

Barely half the straw is cut. In Long Island, we saw oats being cut and mowed, and this work is another example of American speed. The harvesters stand about six feet apart so that each one has a strip of land six feet wide in front of him. Then he spreads his legs far apart, so that without moving to the side he can reach the outermost part of his strip with the sickle. As he puts his left foot forward, he cuts with one stroke the right half of his strip, lets it drop, puts his right foot forward, and cuts the left side in the same way. Their sickles are about once again as large as ours, less circular, and cut a more eccentric swath. A good harvester is supposed to be able to harvest an acre in one day, and a mower is expected to mow three acres. A binder binds three acres, tying the bundles himself, and gathering them together. The latter task is not much trouble, because there is not more in one sheaf than that which can be held with

101

both hands, that is, the amount cut in one swath of the sickle. As soon as it is cut, the grain is immediately tied, hauled away, and usually set in stacks next to the barn. This explains why the day-laborer receives a dollar a day and also how a farmer can cultivate three to four hundred acres.

Yellow fever broke out in Philadelphia this summer. Through good regulations it was prevented from spreading out beyond a few streets along the Delaware.

Philadelphia, like New York, is supplied with good water from a considerable distance. A steam engine outside the city pumps it up to such a height that it can be piped everywhere.

Today there was a report in a newspaper that an American brig arrived in New York after making the journey from Liverpool in England to New York in sixteen days.

October 28. Mr. M. provided us with letters of introduction from Dr. H. to people in Lancaster, Yorktown, and Harrisburg. He himself gave us two for use in Lancaster that might lead to a position in a school or some other employment. Mr. Cook also gave us several. He very earnestly recommended that we adopt the practice of Americans who travel on foot and avoid staying at inns but rather turn in and find lodging with the first good planter.

So on the morning of the twenty-fifth we left Philadelphia. Mr. M. accompanied us for a stretch and promised to take delivery of the goods which I had shipped by sloop from New York and to store them.

The paved road from Philadelphia to Lancaster is well maintained and leads through a pleasant area. At noon, according to our advice, we stopped at the home of a planter named Rudolf. He was German but had come here at a very early age and had several plantations. The house in which he lived stood on a hill. In Germany you would almost take it for the seat of a count, but here we were informed by herds, you could almost say the uncountable number, of cattle, pigs, sheep, horses, all mixed together as in the garden of our first parents, that a farmer lived here. He received us in a very friendly manner and immediately had the table set and served us with liberal, patriarchal hospitality, and invited us to spend the night with him. We thanked him for his offer but continued on for some miles.

Even though this style of travel is customary here for the pedestrian, at first it is very difficult to accept. Some inner feeling, either prejudice or pride, rebels against it; it seems to brand a person as a beggar. Also,

102

it must be learned, as I found out later; a person must ask, but he must be neither cringing nor aggressive. It must be requested with confidence as something to be expected, but not demanded brazenly and greedily. The planter considers hospitality as sacred, but he will not allow any unpleasantness to be engendered in practicing it. Anyway, this evening we could not persuade ourselves to practice this art further, in spite of our good instructions, and so we turned in at an inn. The innkeeper spoke German. "You're German, aren't you? Did you just come to this country? You must not stop at an innkeeper's, you must go to the farmers and save your money; you can surely make good use of it." Now, I thought, no innkeeper is ever going to lecture me about this again; I'll try to remember it the first time.

In the morning, we left early and had our breakfast at an Anabaptist's named Zog. We inquired of him as to the whereabouts of the colony of Anabaptists under the leadership of Augsburger. He informed us that they had settled several miles above Cincinnati.* Zog had a magnificent plantation; the buildings grouped together formed a little village. At the moment they were busily engaged in cooking a fruit butter.

In every household a large amount of apple butter is cooked. They boil down the best apple cider to half, then apple slices are added in the desired quantity and cooked to mush. Everything is then mixed together with constant stirring until it is thick, then spices are added. Often you see forty or fifty such pots of butter in a pantry, and some of it is put on the table of a farmer at every meal. If it is made of good apples, and carefully prepared, I would prefer it to cherry butter.

This morning we had breakfast at an Anabaptist's, noon dinner at a Quaker's, and supper and lodging at a Presbyterian's, at whose home we arrived very late. Unfortunately, no one could speak a word of German in the household. In spite of this, we were received hospitably. The lady had our bedroom heated and was so diligent and concerned for her

* Christian Augsburger, an Anabaptist from Alsace, who at the behest of his community went to America in 1818. He informed himself concerning the country, particularly the area around the Ohio, in order to be able to give accurate information as to the advantage of emigrating to that region. He wrote his people a letter, a copy of which was received by Schweizer in Basel. Schweizer passed it on to one of his friends, and it was thereafter read by many and was found to be very important and valuable, especially for those desiring to emigrate. This man, at the entreaty of his friends, returned to become their leader. About 400 Anabaptists gathered together under his leadership and embarked from Havre de Grâce in May 1819. In spite of Schweizer's numerous inquiries, until now only the most absurd reports of their perishing reached us. We see, therefore, that there are people enough who take great pains to prevent the emigration of others by means of false reports. [C. K.]

guests that a German observer would have taken us for long lost friends, not people from another part of the world who had stopped here for the first time and probably for the last as well.

Considering how in recent years immigrants through all kinds of escapades have injured the reputation of their kind, there is an amazing amount of good-natured hospitality in the American planter and his family. Because of this virtue, it is only fair to be patient with their less attractive qualities.

It is a unanimous conviction of the Americans that since the French Revolution the immigrating Germans, and since 1800 the Swiss, have changed greatly for the worse. Earlier they could be trusted with anything, the Swiss contending with the Germans for highest honors. A German or Swiss hired man or maid generally received double the pay of an immigrant from any other country. Since that time, however, they have excelled other national groups in thievery, cheating, laziness, and drunkenness. What a sad observation! Has the entire German population deteriorated? Or does a different class emigrate now?* Whoever wanted to take the trouble could without much difficulty gather material for a universal chronicle of crooked tricks which are attributed to German immigrants.

I cannot describe what a bitter, poignant experience it is to hear these facts about the people to whom one belongs. Often it is only a lack of sensitivity without any intent to offend, but frequently there is a pleasure in inflicting pain, a nationalistic pride, which is the source of this willingness to tell these stories.† It is really an error to think that immigrants are received with open arms or that the American government will provide such great advantages to them. A great many wish that immigration could be restricted to those people who would be accepted anywhere, to those with money, or at least to decent people. We do have a tremendously huge continent with sparsely settled areas, the American says, but since the Revolutionary War our population has doubled every twenty years, without counting immigrants. Judging from available evidence, this population trend is being sustained. What an ungodly mass of people we will have in a hundred years! Does not the seed of our political disruption lie right here? At present a hothead can find a place to let off steam in some sparsely populated area, but if he could no longer escape to such a place, then his activity would become detrimental to society.

* To accept the first would be rash and severe. It would be easier to understand the second. [c. k.]

† Very true!! [c. k.]

Propositions have been made to start a colony of free blacks in Sierra Leone in Africa, in order to move them away gradually. Every black who decides to go there will receive free transportation and will be provided for there also, but the venture is not making progress. The blacks like it too well in America to allow themselves to be talked out of it in this way. Furthermore, there have been no glowing reports of conditions there received from the first transports that were sent.[27]

These days a penetrating, cold, northwest wind has been blowing, and though it has subsided now, we had frost for the first time. They say that it probably snowed in the mountains, but it is warm here again. From time to time we encounter tremendous herds of cattle, mostly two-year-old gelded oxen which are being driven to the coastal cities from the states of Ohio and Kentucky. The animals are middle-sized but rather fat. Money from the sale is used for the purchase of merchandise.

Not far from Saudersburg we went into a farm to drink water. Immediately the farmer's wife brought a pitcher of milk and some cake, begged us to sit down to rest, and constantly lamented that we could not speak English.

I must admit that this hospitable characteristic is extremely dear to me and quite honestly not just for the sake of its advantage. A gift of a dollar would not give me half the pleasure that a meal does.

There is something heartwarming and patriarchal in hospitality that is reminiscent of the golden age. In truth, Moses knew how to describe this custom. How diligently he instructed Abraham to practice this duty! How he urged him always to think of nothing but the strangers who were his guests! In short, this custom compensates me richly for the unpleasant things which a journey into a foreign land involves. Naturally this custom must not be expected in a city, or in every house along the highway where the roguery of immigrants has made it wither away.

We were rather tired when we finally noted by the 60th milestone that we were approaching Lancaster.* We stayed at the inn called The King

[27] The American Colonization Society was organized in Washington in 1817 for the purpose of transporting Negroes to Africa. Some supporters were motivated by humanitarian concern; other supporters looked upon the project as a way of eliminating objectionable free Negroes. The first group to be sent to Africa arrived in 1821 on the coast of what became Liberia. Only about 6000 were sent to Africa between 1821 and 1867. Its financial support came from private donations and credits voted by southern legislatures; the society failed to get the financial aid requested from the Congress. The heat, humidity, snakes, and the hostility of Africans did little to encourage American Negroes to seek settlement there.

* Lancaster is, therefore, approximately 60 English miles inland from Philadelphia. [C. K.]

of Prussia, where once again we found a true landmark of American hospitality.

From now on for a while my diary will stop, and instead I will give my friends what I find in the cluttered chamber of my memory. Many times something will be mixed into my account which has appeared two or three times before, but you well know, indeed, how difficult it is for me to do this perfectly.

After I had delivered my letters of introduction here, I found again that for the present not a thornbush, not to mention a grapevine or fig tree, was waiting to give me shade or shelter. The prospect of searching for shelter across the mountains yet this autumn was generally considered an extremely risky undertaking. I thought the smartest thing to do was to rent a room in order to put my wife and child under a roof in a less expensive place, and then go to Yorktown and the other places to which I had been directed. This trip had the important result of convincing me that in Saint Penn's Paradise there was nothing for me to do other than perhaps to stand in front of the abyss and watch that no one else fell in. That would have been a herculean task and a very thankless one besides, because whoever wants to come will not be deterred even by a flaming sword.

Now it occurred to me that selling my Bibles, while it perhaps would not bring much profit, would at least dispel boredom and acquaint me with the country and the people among whom I traveled. It was quite difficult for me, and the burden at first seemed to tire and oppress not only my body but my soul as well. Yet gradually I accustomed myself to my new job; although it brought me no resounding reward, it did bring me many important experiences which in time to come can prove useful to me or someone else. Without being presumptuous, I think that I can say that I know the way of life in America as well as many who have lived here half a dozen years.

My friends perhaps expect here a definitive judgment of America. I think I owe them this, but I cannot give it without apprehension, being misunderstood, and being accused of glaring contradictions. What I say here of Pennsylvania can, I think, with few exceptions be said of the other states.

Pennsylvania is a very fertile land; few areas of Germany or Switzerland would give such a high yield for such superficial cultivation — with the exception of oats and barley — but this fertile land is not as healthy as Germany. A whole host of rheumatic complaints and a multitude of

108

putrid nerve fevers have acquired their citizenship too. However, they rarely elevate themselves into very serious illnesses.

It is not to be disputed that the American farmer and worker live much more happily than the German or Swiss. Of the innumerable oppressions which unfortunately rest upon these classes in Germany — and I include Switzerland as well — the American knows nothing. There are no monopolies * — except that bestowed on the inventor of a thing for a certain time — no guilds, no qualifications of residence; nothing, absolutely nothing, restricts him from the free and unencumbered use of his strength and ability. The taxes that even the richest farmer pays hardly amount to as much as he spends for the tobacco he smokes. The farmer is mostly a little prince, who cannot understand that anywhere in the world there are people of his calling who do not have meat on their table every day. A person who tries to make him believe that some cannot even get their share of the daily bread is considered an unmitigated liar. The worker is less well off, but still the lack of the necessities of life is something unknown to him.

On what level of spiritual and moral culture the people stand I do not venture to discuss in full now. To do this one must have an accurate knowledge of English, which is now the ruling language and will become increasingly dominant.

It seems to me that the general character of the people, of the northern provinces particularly, is patterned after that of the so-called Yankees.† It has often been asserted that the American people have no national character and that only after centuries will one be formed. It is certain, however, that it has pretty well been formed already. At least up to the present I do not find it particularly pleasant.

The American is not lacking in brains or talent for serious study, but rather in easily gained means of developing these further, and especially in the desire or rather in a general incentive to do so. So far the way for a scholar does not seem to be a shining one. As officials, people with practical ability are always preferred, even if they are less learned. And their institutions of learning must be conducted in a fairly republican manner, that is, a teacher must work for the many. Consequently not many learned people are employed here. Still it must be said in praise of

* Exclusive privilege to trade or sell, or the right given by the state to trade or manufacture exclusively. [C. K.]

† This is the name given to the first settlers, whose ancestors came from Ireland. [C. K.]

these schools that they are not, as they are here and there in Europe, hothouses for the development of crudity and sloth.

I think it can be maintained that America is still behind Europe in spiritual culture, but it will not stay that way for a hundred years. In literature, art, and music, however, it will be a hundred years or longer before they reach the rank of Europeans. Not light but warmth is lacking. Their sanguine temperament seems to be passed on to the immigrants. The most intolerant sects, which in Europe would have dealt out sword and fire to dissenters, become fairly quiet here after a few years – indifferent, I might say. Here we have the measuring stick according to which the religious and moral condition of the people can, to some extent, be judged. They do little that is evil, because they feel little temptation, and they achieve little good other than that which is the result of habit. If one were to apply pressure all volition would be completely lost.

This autumn a new governor was elected in Pennsylvania. It is unbelievable what a tremendous interest the people take in such an election. Several weeks before, the hired man in the stable, the wife and the maid in the kitchen, the farmer behind the plow, the merchant behind the counter, all can speak of nothing else. Poor laborers often bet a year's salary on whether the Federal or the Democratic party will win.* Each party attacks the other unmercifully in the newspapers and the so-called handbills. The smallest mistake of an opposing candidate whom they wish to defeat is depicted in an exaggerated manner. If the treasurer should make a mistake of accepting bad notes, involving only a few dollars, harsh criticism is directed against the governor. Such an incident can be so magnified and so sharply attacked by the opposing party that instead of the usual nine years in office he would now, after only three years, be put out of office by a large majority vote.[28]

* It is well known that the inhabitants of the North American States have for a long time been divided into two parties: an oligarchic one which restricts freedom, and a truly democratic, republican one, which latter is by far the largest. These two in their political beliefs are often diametrically opposed to one another, as for example in the French Revolutionary Wars. [c. k.]

[28] Partisanship in state politics was acute at this time in Pennsylvania. In 1817 William Findlay began a term as governor which was marked by much political discord. The Republican governor was at odds continually with his political opposition, which controlled both houses of the legislature. His official conduct was subject to investigation. In the 1821–1822 session of the legislature, however, Findlay was chosen United States senator. General Joseph Hiester, an officer of the Revolution who had been defeated by Findlay in 1817, became governor in December 1820. Recalling the severe attacks made upon Findlay, Hiester in his inaugural address tried to set the level of his administration above the narrowness of contemporary partisanship: "I trust that if any errors shall be committed, they will not be charge-

As soon as the election is over, however, you hear nothing more about it. Some days pass before a new topic sets tongues into motion again.

Similar situations prove that the people watch over their rights carefully. Here even a Napoleon would not find it so easy to step on the necks of the people. Nor is any party so devoted to its candidates that it would tolerate their encroachment on any legal or customary rights. As soon as the new governor, Hiester, was elected, he was informed quite clearly by the newspapers of his own party exactly what was expected of him, what bad practices were to be done away with, what officials were to receive advancement, what enterprises were to be supported, and so on. It was also bluntly explained to him that he was expected to take a reduction in salary and thus give evidence of his patriotism. This loudly expressed voice of the people was most certainly heard, and the salaries of most of the officials were lowered substantially.

The newspapers here are universally popular reading material. I often found them in the most remote plantations, and a great many are published. For example, Lancaster is a city of 6700 inhabitants, and seven newspapers are published here. These numerous dailies, in addition to political news, make the American familiar with new discoveries and improvements, and they awaken his participation in his government and country. At every opportunity the advantages over any other government and country are pointed out. Often they speak out rather bitterly concerning general or specific misdeeds, and in this respect they are not without value. On the other hand, they close the way to books. The farmer is spoiled by them as by novels, and everything seems boring and dry which is not a newspaper.

In order to give an example of the tone of American newspapers, I offer here an article from the *Readinger Postbothe*: [29]

MARKET PRICES
But not of flour, grain, and Magdalene-water

Christian charity: Very rare and not to be found on the market.
Credit: Dead since the Count when so many swore themselves out of jail.

able to intention. They will not proceed from a willful neglect of duty on my part, nor from any want of devotion to the best interests of our country. Such errors, I may justly hope, will meet with indulgence from an enlightened and liberal people . . . Considering myself as elected by the people of this Commonwealth, and not by any particular denomination of persons, I shall endeavor to deserve the name of chief magistrate of Pennsylvania, and to avoid the disgraceful appellation of the Governor of a party." William H. Egle, *An Illustrated History of the Commonwealth of Pennsylvania* (Harrisburg: DeWitt Goodrich, 1876), pp. 242–243.

[29] This was a German-language newspaper published in Reading, Pennsylvania.

Friendship: Often requested, but cannot be bought without money.
Gossip: Abundantly available without cost.
Promises: Dirt cheap.
Pride: The market is overloaded.
Stupidity: Very general.
False oaths: 25¢ apiece and many more on hand.
Gratitude: Completely out of style.
Good reputation: Very rare; 200 will easily be sold for 500 to 800 dollars, to be used up weekly.
Honesty: Of no value.
Churchgoers: Very few to be found.
Love: Only found in children.
Marriage: Almost contraband merchandise.
Lazybones: Like Continental dollars, 75 for one good one.
Party spirit: Almost expired; however, becoming more animated as the 10th of October approaches.
Religious and political sects: A heavy load of them, but few Christians and bloody few patriots.
Spiritual refreshment: Rapid decline.
Work: A great deal for judges and lawyers.
Government jobs: Most of them filled twice.
Votes for sheriff: Of much value and in much demand.

Such articles are not rare.* Some attention is given to important trials and judicial decisions. On the whole the major issues of public opinion are more discussed than in Europe. This makes the officials a little more careful.

The newspapers are crucial in another important matter. They are a means of discovering where lost cattle are. Since in summer cattle never enter the barn and the farmer looks after only the milk cows and not always even after them, it can often happen that a cow can wander miles away. Whoever finds a strange cow on his land is required to give notice of it in the newspaper. After a certain period of time, if the owner is not found, the animal is forfeited to the man who printed the announcement.

Cattle raising is a fairly important branch of agriculture in Pennsylvania. Frequently I ask farmers how many head of cattle they have and receive this answer: "I honestly can't say. I haven't been into the bush for a long time. I may have lost several head or also gained a few calves. I think there must be between thirty and forty."

Milk cows and work horses are usually fed with clover. Calves and

*What reader is not appreciative of this example of American journalism?! [C. K.]

112

cows about to calve are driven into the woods and are often entrusted to Mother Nature for months at a time.

Most farmers do not put their cattle into barns even during the winter. At most they are sheltered in a shed only in bad weather, even though winter weather after New Year's is generally strenuous. With this indifferent care, you could not expect a strong, handsome strain. They are medium-sized. Some time ago I read in a newspaper that a farmer in Warwick Township had a calf that weighed 180 pounds at eight weeks, and it was considered something extraordinary. The milk production also is not great. This does not concern the farmer very much; he uses the milk mostly for sows. Cheese is rarely prepared with the exception of a sour, soft cheese (cottage cheese) which in summer must not be absent from any table. This is prepared in the following manner: curdled milk is set near the fire until the whey separates, then the curds are hung up in a cloth until the whey is completely separated. It is then mixed in a bowl with sweet cream. This cheese cannot be older than three days, if it is to please the American taste.*

Nothing astonishes the Germans as much as the gorgeous houses of the farmers. In Germany the most beautiful houses are in the cities; here, however, just as beautiful, or more beautiful, houses are found in the country while on the other hand many shabby little houses are found in the rural villages. Often you think you see before you a little village, and it turns out to be only the buildings belonging to a single farmer. You still can find, here and there, a poor log cabin built by the father or grandfather of the present owner when he first settled there; next to it stands a fairly good wooden house into which the first settler moved after six or eight years; the son no longer found this satisfactory after a time, and a house of brick or fieldstone was constructed in Greek style. In the other two houses live the families of ordinary day-laborers, to whom the farmer has given several acres of land to cultivate and to provide pasture for a few cows and pigs. Next to these buildings, there are usually a barn, a washhouse, and a large stone building used to dry meat, a smokehouse.

It is no small task to cure the meat demanded by a farm family. A big family often slaughters from fourteen to twenty pigs and three to four head of cattle. To a German this seems rather gluttonous.

In America you hear as much complaint about bad times, unemploy-

* Such a cheese would certainly please Europeans as well. [c. k.]

ment, and lack of money as in Europe.[30] The farmer can no longer sell his products at the former high prices, maintains fewer hired hands, uses craftsmen no more than is absolutely necessary, while as a luxury he formerly used them more. The wage earner and the craftsman will not reduce their style of living and complain of wants that they have created for themselves. The farmer complains about things which are not available. Two accounts will make this clearer.

Several days ago a farmer came to my friend, Mr. D. Endress, and asked him if he did not want to buy a wagonload of wood. The weather was terrible and the roads seemed to be bottomless.

"Well, for heaven's sake, why do you come to the city with wood in this horrible weather?" asked Mr. Endress.

"Indeed, if I didn't need a few dollars I certainly wouldn't have driven here," answered the farmer.

"I'm sure that isn't true. I would bet on it that you don't just have one or two hundred dollars lying in the house."

"Yes," answered the farmer a bit annoyed, "but who would be so profligate as to touch his silver dollars?"

If the farmer had been paid for his wood in silver instead of bank notes, he would certainly have added it to his other silver and would have driven to the city with a second load. A few days later Mr. Endress learned that this farmer had received 400 silver dollars for fattened cattle the previous week and had carefully stored up the money.

From these stories you might conclude that bank notes have far less value and that banks must have poor credit, but that is not true. The tradesman and merchant prefer bank notes over silver, but the farmer prefers to save silver because he feels more secure with it. The reason why a farmer does not spend his money is that when he needs money and can provide sufficient security for it, a bank is quite willing to grant it to him. In addition to this, banks have priority over other creditors, and therefore it is foolish to loan money to anyone seeking to borrow from a private person.

[30] Note de Tocqueville's observation: "In America I saw the freest and most enlightened men placed in the happiest circumstances that the world affords; [yet] it seemed to me as if a cloud habitually hung upon their brow, and I thought them serious and almost sad, even in their pleasures. The chief reason for this contrast is that the former [the peasants in Europe] do not think of the ills they endure, while the latter [the Americans] are forever brooding over advantages they do not possess. It is strange to see with what feverish ardor the Americans pursue their own welfare, and to watch the vague dread that constantly torments them lest they should not have chosen the shortest path which may lead to it." Alexis de Tocqueville, *Democracy in America* (New York: Vintage Books, 1954), Vol. 2, p. 144.

On my selling trips, I came upon the poor hut of a daily laborer who at the time was busy beating flax. Eight half-grown children loitered about the house. More to get into conversation with these people than out of any hope of selling something to them, I asked if they would like to buy a Bible.

"Yes! We've wanted to buy one for a long time, but we rarely get to the city, and now we haven't a cent in the house and don't know how to get one either. We only get our wages in supplies such as flax, hemp, and similar things, and now no one wants to buy. But you must stay for dinner this noon; you will, won't you?"

"Oh, yes, I will." But how amazed I was. Instead of the meager meal I expected there were sausages, ham, a guinea hen, cabbage and salad, butter, white bread, jam, and an apple pie on the table.

You must help yourself as best you can when you are poor and have so many children, the wife said. When the children are older they plan to go up the Susquehanna where cheap land still may be bought. Here they had only eight acres and this was hardly enough to feed their three cows and eight pigs.

After dinner I was entreated to wait; they wanted to try to borrow the money someplace. After about half an hour, the man came back with the necessary money to buy the Bible. This, then, is American need and poverty!

I could relate innumerable anecdotes of this kind. There are a few more I cannot help telling, because they also illustrate the hospitable atmosphere and the peculiar poverty of this country.

On that spur of the mountains which extends from Cumberland between the counties of York and Lebanon toward Berks, I lost my way on a road that led from the area of the plantations deep into the woods. The sun had long set when I came upon a log cabin and asked for a night's lodging. Fever was raging in this isolated area, and the home owner was sorry that I would have to sleep on the bench, since four of his family were in bed with the fever and needed the bedding. It was sultry weather and a very unpleasant odor came from under the door. I decided it was better to go on, and I excused myself for disturbing them. Three miles beyond, the man said, I would come upon a house, and he described the direction. I found the hut readily, and a light was still burning in it. I knocked, and instead of first asking who was there a stooped old man opened the door.

"May I spend the night with you?" I asked.

115

"Oh, yes," he answered. "You're so late. Did you lose your way?"

As much as I tried to prevent it, his wife had to get up out of bed, make coffee, heat a piece of chicken, and get butter and preserves. I had to tell them about the ocean voyage and Switzerland until late into the night. He said that he came here with his parents from the Palatinate when he was eight years old. He was indentured to pay for his passage. After he was free he worked as a hired hand for a long time and saved up a considerable bit of money. A German had tricked him out of it by telling him that he would buy a plantation for him with the money. Under cover of night and fog, he ran away and left his wife and child in the lurch. After some time, he learned that the fellow had died of fever in New Orleans. After this experience he served a few more years, and with part of the money he earned he bought the freedom of an Irish girl and married her. With the rest of the money he had purchased forty acres of this stony land. They had lived fifty years on this very spot. No one had wanted to buy this stony land from them, and so they had always remained poor because they were never able to undertake anything bigger. Their children died, and so they had to do all the work themselves. He had just passed his 87th year and his wife her 76th.

In the morning he showed me all around his land. More than sixty of the most beautiful fruit trees repaid the old man for his care. With the stones he had built a wall around his land. Four cows, six sheep, and eight pigs nourished themselves and him from this land, and supplied him with clothes, coffee, sugar, and tobacco through barter. The sprightly old man accompanied me over two miles and invited me to visit again, if I should ever come to this area.

"If a German hadn't betrayed me, perhaps I would be a planter," he said very sincerely. "But nonetheless I'm as pleased as a child whenever I see a German again."

Late one evening I arrived in Berks county after crossing the Schuylkill by ferry. Although it was already very late, I wanted to continue another mile and a half to a place where a man from Baden, whom I had met in New York, was supposed to be living. It was a very cold December night. Before I reached my destination, I became so cold and weary that I knocked at the first house I came to, in order to warm myself a little. A stocking-weaver lived here who absolutely would not let me go on any farther. Several neighbors sat around the fire. After the stocking-weaver had inquired about the trade and origin of his guest, one of the men began to discourse something like this:

116

"Yes, yes, it is no easy matter to get into a profession in America. They are always saying in Europe how much a day-laborer and an artisan earn here, but they don't realize how little the farmer uses them, how the master is only a bungler here. I am a bookbinder by profession, and as a journeyman in Germany I saved up a considerable sum of money. Then I wanted to go to America to make my money grow. I came to Philadelphia four years ago. My savings had diminished considerably, because that crook of a Captain I had took me and his twenty other passengers to Spain, and by treating us miserably forced us to sign on another boat. Thus two thirds of our fare, which we had to pay in advance in Havre de Grâce, was lost.

"In Philadelphia I couldn't find work, although I offered to work for several bookbinders for my board. During all this searching, I went through all my money, and on top of that in order to get my last two meals I had to leave in hock my handsomest vest. Not knowing where to go, I walked down King Street and out of the city. I was so lost in thought, I didn't even see the Schuylkill bridge until the man in charge asked me for the toll, but alas! I didn't have a cent left in my pocket. Not caring whether I lived or died, I sat down on the ground. A Quaker who was then passing by asked me, 'Are you sick?'

" 'No, things aren't going so well for me.' I answered, and told him my situation.

" 'If you lose your courage, then you will indeed be lost. Here is the bridge fare; more I will not give you. Learn to help yourself. Take this thought with you on your way: He who looks back whimpering, in America, may well turn into a pillar of salt,' said the man, and left me.

"I crept over the bridge and dragged myself up the road. It was getting toward evening, and I was tormented by hunger and thirst. Now, for the first time in my life, I would have to beg. This seared my soul. I convinced myself, however, and approached a house and asked for shelter. 'You look suspicious to me. I've been robbed many times already. But you can stay in the barn,' the farmer said. This was too much humiliation for me.

" 'You don't have to give me anything,' I said, angrily, and hurried out of the door. Several hundred feet from the house I threw myself under a tree and stayed there until morning. Then I left the road and took a footpath into the woods.

" 'You must be going the wrong way,' a voice cried out to me. It was a woodcutter; I had not seen him, though he was quite near.

" 'Every road leads me the wrong way; don't worry about me,' I answered him.

" 'Oh, come on, sit down. We'll have a little drink of whiskey,' the man said laughing.

"I don't know if it was his laughter or his invitation which made my rancor vanish. I sat down with him. He brought out some whiskey, meat, and bread, and urged me to eat. In answer to his questions, I told him my plight. He laughed and said, 'You don't know how to adjust to a bad situation at all. Stay with me today. I work by the day, and my quarters aren't far from here in the woods. In an hour we will go home.'

"I accepted his invitation. The man and his family occupied a small log cabin. His two sons were making a pile of charcoal and another pile was already burning. I enjoyed being with these good-natured people so much that I stayed eight days more with them and helped chop wood and make charcoal. These people almost laughed themselves sick when, in the beginning, I could hardly raise the axe and couldn't hit the wood. The man, in addition, taught me many good things and tried to stuff some American self-reliance and enterprise into me.

"Then I went to Baltimore. At the charcoal-maker's I had learned the art of foraging. No longer did I stop at a farmer's without some purpose in mind. In Baltimore I was offered work, but only on a percentage basis, and I would have had to have my own tools. No one would give me credit. 'We've been misled by Germans too many times,' was the reply I met everywhere. I was advised to go to Pittsburgh. I went, but my shoes and socks gave notice and left my service.

"Where to get money? I heard, in one town, that their minister had died. I went to some of the church directors and told them that I was going, as a missionary preacher, to the western states, but in order not to leave a single opportunity unused, I would like to preach in their church next Sunday. My request was readily accepted. I studied until my head smoked and preached a powerful sermon on Sunday. After the service the farmers gathered around me and told me they had never heard such a sermon, and that I absolutely had to become their preacher. I didn't trust the whole thing, and so I claimed a higher duty. 'Well,' they said, 'if you absolutely won't stay with us, we will get together something for you for today.' Said and done. This caper brought in fifteen dollars.

"Then I bought myself shoes and socks and wandered on to Pittsburgh and down as far as Chillicothe, but found work nowhere; I went back to Pennsylvania, and now I am — a charcoal-burner.' "

118

"And you don't have cause to complain," the woman of the house interrupted. "Consider yourself fortunate."

"Yes, I must say that I wouldn't want to become a bookbinder or a preacher again," he answered.

"I have changed occupations, too," another began. "My wife and I were basket-weavers in Europe. To come here we had to be indentured for half of our passage. I was separated from my wife and child and handed over to a veritable Satan, deep in Kentucky. My wife and child remained in Pennsylvania. As soon as my period of indentured service was over, I returned there. My wife was not yet free. The basket-weaving brought in very little. I could sell them for a good price, but I couldn't sell enough of them. I write a legible hand and during my service learned English. So, the winter before last, I got a position teaching school and was able to buy the release of my wife and child. Now we live fairly comfortably, and I would certainly not trade jobs with a basket-weaver."

"I am a native-born American, and all my life I have taken great pains, and made so little progress that if I were to buy a Bible from this man, I would have to borrow the money from one of you," began the stocking-weaver. "What could we do with a lot of land, I always asked my wife. We can't work it alone, and day-laborers are too expensive. Once our children are grown we certainly will be able to buy land. So we stayed with our ten acres and earned a pretty sum weaving stockings.

"One day I decided I would like to put my horse in the barn; I put my money in the bank in C—— and bought 640 acres of land in that highly praised state of Ohio as so many other fools have. What happened to the bank you know. The establishment of the Union Bank [31] gave it the

---

[31] In the case of *McCulloch v. Maryland*, John Marshall delivered the opinion he had written for the unanimous Supreme Court position with regard to the constitutional issues involved. The historic decision of March 6, 1819, held that the Congress had the right to establish the Bank of the United States, that the Bank had power to establish branches in the several states, and that the levying of taxes against these branches by the states was unconstitutional. The decision is regarded as a landmark in the development of federal power and as having saved the federal government from being taxed to death by state governments. Ohio ignored this decision, regarding the case as feigned. The state government attempted to collect its prohibitory tax of 1818 and, further, seized $100,000 from a branch of the Bank as payment of the tax. The decision of the Supreme Court in the cases of *Osborn v. The Bank of the United States*, in 1824, upheld the position advanced by the Bank. Marshall referred back to the principle established in *McCulloch v. Maryland*. The Osborn case settled the issue conclusively. The importance of the cases in constitutional development is indisputable, although the Bank later succumbed to Andrew Jackson's maneuvers to block its rechartering. See Harold J. Plous and Gordon E. Baker, "McCulloch v. Maryland: Right Principle, Wrong Case," *Stanford Law Review*, Vol. 9, no. 4, July 1957, pp. 710–730.

deathblow. My money was lost. Just when the second payment was to be made on the property, the value of all products fell by half, and the value of the land in Ohio fell to a quarter of what it had been. No one wanted to move to the highly praised land any more. I was lucky to have lost only the first payment. Now I can weave a hundred pairs of stockings before I see one dollar. Everybody wants to pay only in kind. You too, Jack, would rather let your dollars rust before a laborer would get a penny from you, and all of you rich misers are the same."

Gray old Jack, who up until now had kept his silence, stuck a fresh cigar in his mouth, smilingly stroked his chin, and said to the stocking-weaver, "John, in order that the stranger should not have unnecessary sympathy for you, I must tell him that only your stinginess has brought you to this. You were afraid to buy a piece of bushland on which you could have kept a couple of hired hands, and you would have had to work three or four years before you could have sold a bushel of wheat. The daily earning of two dollars in cash was too tempting for you to give up for a later reward. Then we were able to get six to eight per cent for our money in the banks in addition to other benefits. That wasn't enough for you. You wanted to make twelve to twenty per cent, so you signed four or five times as many notes as your cash warranted. Because of this greediness to make everything yield a profit, you drove up the price of land unreasonably. It was high time that the government through the establishment of the Union Bank made it necessary for you to redeem some of your notes. That you could no longer make it, that the people were ruined by it, was not the government's fault, nor the fault of changing circumstances. Only greed was the cause. And why did you buy land at this time? Precisely because, as you said, hundreds and hundreds of fools thought that this madness of buying land would increase with each year, and that a hundred pounds of flour would always continue to be worth eight dollars.

"Nevertheless it isn't so bad in America that you have to pay for your missteps with need and deprivation. None of the farmers or artisans who lost their fortunes through their speculations in the last two years ate one chicken less. And even in this period of scarce money of which you complain, your table is as well covered as mine. That I, and many others as well, hold our money fairly intact necessarily springs from the fact that we didn't want to earn anything with it. Seeking profit you lost yours. But in order that you won't call me a miser for a second time, I say to you that if you would like to buy all the man's Bibles, you may get the money from me."

Now there was a pause. The stocking-weaver was the first to start laughing and the others joined in very heartily.

"But now I'd like to tell a little more about my life," old Jack began again, "so that the young man here won't think that luck rained dollars through my roof.

"My parents were poor day-laborers in Cumberland county. I helped work by the day until I was eighteen years old. Then my parents and I decided that it would be better if I could learn the shoemaker's trade.

"A distant relative of my father's, who practiced this trade, took me on for three years. He was a very stern master who rarely let me sleep over four hours, but outside of that he was very good to me. A Quaker not far from us engaged a German girl as an indentured servant. From the minute I saw the girl all my thoughts were of her. It wasn't long before we were making hundreds of plans for our future life. The years of service seemed an eternity to us, and it was decided that I should make an attempt to negotiate for my freedom with my master.

"One day when I was alone at threshing time with my master, and he was in a very good mood, I began like this, 'Master, I would so like to be free.'

" 'You free? I think you are a fool. You have almost two more years to serve, and from where would you get money to buy yourself out?' he asked.

" 'Well, you could do it easily if you wanted to.'

" 'Yes, if I wanted to,' he said slowly, putting down the flail. 'But why do you want to be free?' he continued.

" 'I would so like to get married,' I answered.

" 'You! Marry! Become free! What female has put that bug in your ear?'

" 'Which one do you think? Bale, who is an indentured servant at Gerber's,' I replied stuttering.

" 'Jack, you are such a fool,' he said. 'Bale has even longer to serve than you.'

"After a while he continued, 'Listen, Jack, because you have so much confidence in me, and because I know Bale to be an honest, capable girl, I will go with you now to Gerber and talk to him about your situation.' We went. 'You can wait in front of the house until I've talked to Gerber.' I was hot and cold as I stood in front of that house. Soon the old people

121

in the living room began to laugh loudly. Then I was invited in and Bale too.

"The old people promised to give us our freedom for 100 dollars, which we were to pay after one year, and at the same time to provide us with five acres of land at six dollars. We thought heaven had been handed to us as a gift. Quickly we went to the preacher to be married and the next morning began housekeeping in a log cabin with one broken pot which had been left there. Truly our neighbors helped a great deal. At first I made shoes for wages, then I bought leather. Bale spun and knitted. After two years we had our debts paid off. We sold our five acres of land for 100 dollars and I still had a good supply of leather and one cow and six pigs.

"Then we bought 80 acres of uncleared land situated not far from the Lehigh. The excellent building material we cut ourselves, dragged it to the river, and took it to Castor. This enterprise completely paid for the land. We remained here for six years. Then we sold the land for 2000 dollars.*

"Then we could indeed undertake something. We bought a plantation of 320 acres of which twenty acres were cleared and on which stood a house and barn. The land lay along the Susquehanna and I found that a sawmill could readily be started there, and there was no lack of good lumber. This brought in many a good dollar, and God rewarded our hard work. We stayed there almost thirty years. Many people settled in the neighborhood. I thought the land had reached the peak of its value, and I sold everything.

"I could then buy plantations for three of my sons and provide well for myself. And if I should die today or tomorrow, my other children know where they can settle.†

"People are always complaining about the present time, and from my earliest days I've heard the same complaint. I know of times when flour was worth far less and merchandise was much more expensive.

"Even thirty years ago, immigrants sometimes wandered around in confusion for four or five months without work or income. I have a tidy little fortune, but there have been many times in my life when I didn't see money for months. I wasn't any poorer because of this, and because I now keep a little money on hand doesn't mean that my guinea hens

* Almost 5000 imperial florins. [c. k.]
† Can live in a good, well-ordered manner. [c. k.]

taste any better than yours. I am of the opinion that the present time is the best for people with little money.

"Land and provisions are cheap. You learn to budget money, and I have often observed in my life that people who came to settle in the so-called bad times worked themselves up the quickest. That is how it was with the smith, R., in L———. He came to this country at a time when things were much cheaper than now. He had about 150 dollars left which he lost partly by being cheated and partly because he used it up, since he couldn't find work. I can still remember very well how he went around in L——— with worn-out shoes and was willing to work just for food, and how B. gave him a job breaking rocks, because this was the only work he could find. He forged his first horseshoe out of an old tong on a rock. B. saw that it was usable, and provided him with a small anvil on which to make horseshoes. From time to time a neighbor gave him a few cents when he did work for him. Now he has a plantation which, just between us, is worth 10,000 dollars and he sells sixteen to twenty head of cattle every year. The bad times taught him how to save.

"Tailor B. came to this country in the so-called good times. He got work quickly and had a good income. It would have been easy for him to set aside his two dollars every day, but he hasn't even been able to own his land free and clear to this day, and all because he never learned how to handle a shilling."

"It isn't easy, however," said the stocking-weaver, "to get a start when people come here without money, because no one gives them an opportunity to earn anything or hires them. The Germans and Swiss particularly encounter this. They are considered by most Americans as a curse. The German societies which have occasionally been organized make the poor immigrant's adjustment more difficult rather than better, when they offer him help. They try to get him out of the cities as fast as possible."

"Yes," said Jack, "earlier, when I said that the present time isn't so bad for the poor, I didn't mean to include the poor German immigrants of the last two years among them. It is true that the Germans, and especially the Swiss, have surprisingly lost during the last few years the good reputation they once enjoyed. People try to avoid even giving them something to eat, let alone giving them a job. Naturally this affects the innocent along with the guilty. In spite of this few have starved, and, in populated areas, none.

"If a poor German manages to struggle through a year diligently and honestly, he will again have the trust which they all had thirty years ago.

123

Then he rarely lacks necessary subsistence. I am almost certain that the person who has to accept the first job that comes along that will furnish him food, no matter what the conditions are, often for inhuman work, is better off for it than the one who brings along several hundred dollars. Generally this is taken from him anyway by crooks among his own countrymen in swindles involving land in unpopulated or unhealthy areas or land which cannot be cultivated.

"Thousands have come to grief this way. How many hundreds did that damned C. in B—— swindle in this manner? How he cheated M. who came to this country a year ago with 4000 dollars! As soon as he figured out that M. still had money, he offered him land for sale. M. wanted to be very cautious and wanted to inspect the land first. C. went with him personally and showed him the land. M. considered himself fortunate to get such excellent land, returned with C., made the purchase properly and moved on the land with his family. How surprised he was to find that C. had assigned him entirely different land than he had seen the time before — worthless land on which food for even a dog couldn't be raised!"

"What could he do? He had no witnesses. The bill of sale itself did not support his position, because the number and boundaries described were those of the land to which he was now forced to move. C. knew that he would be confused by the survey with respect to specific number and boundaries. M. went hungry and tormented himself until his remaining money was dissipated. Last fall he came to M——town sick; his wife and eight children became sick, too. If the German society hadn't taken care of him, he probably would have perished in poverty up there.

"How badly R., A., and G. treated the groups they assembled over there and led to America! As they all tell without exception, they were already cheated in Holland by the leaders of the group. In America the leaders all but revealed their neat little schemes themselves. The immigrants separated. Those who no longer had any money could go wherever they pleased, and the others, who still had money and faith enough to continue on, lost both in the western states.

"In these instances neither the circumstances of the time nor the Americans can be blamed. The Germans don't gain anything to their credit in this. Perhaps these evils that now burden German immigrants will result in their government becoming increasingly concerned about the kind of people to whom their citizens leaving for this country entrust themselves, and what kind of fate awaits them."

124

In the morning my stocking-weaver bought a Bible and, sure enough, got the money to pay for it from Jack.

In the mountains that extend through Pennsylvania you can find wild grapes almost everywhere. So far I have seen six varieties, and there are said to be more. Often several big trees are entwined by one large grapevine as though woven together by a spider web. Several bear very tasty grapes. Even in December I found completely dry grapes still hanging on the vines. They say the grapes are not as good every year as they were this year, since in the dark woods they often do not ripen enough. This year, however, because of the extraordinary heat they ripened readily.

When the foreign demand for flour is no longer so insistent, the vineyards will be cultivated as they are in Germany. The success of the domestic grapes which are occasionally planted has shown the potential sufficiently. In the mountains of York county about forty years ago a planter family established a small vineyard. I saw several of the vines still remaining. A woman whose father had made this attempt assured me that it would have been very successful but all of the neighbors laughed at her father so much for wasting his time on such an occupation that he finally became disgusted with the enterprise. The American still has to get accustomed to middling wine; even the Spanish and French wines he often mixes with sugar and whiskey.

The drive to complete every job as soon as possible is everywhere evident. It is a general characteristic.

Flax and hemp are generally broken on a breaking-frame. The worker stands by the hand breaking-frame so that it is to his right and the part that opens is facing him. There is a handle attached to the upper part of the breaker; he raises it and beats down with it. This position is really the most natural. The operator can swing the material under the breaker much more quickly and more easily than in the method we use at home. An operator of a breaker is supposed to be able to break forty pounds of hemp and thirty pounds of flax in one day.

The scutching of hemp and flax is usually done with a very simple machine. Four swingles are attached to a wheel which is about four feet in diameter. The wheel is set in motion with the foot. The scutcher can be adjusted, moved closer to or farther from the operator. A person with such equipment is able to scutch sixteen to twenty pounds of flax in one day, they say.

The making of whiskey must be carried on just as skillfully. Each boiler should normally be drawn off every hour and be filled again. A chain which during the transfer of the liquid is pulled around on the bottom of the boiler prevents burning. The vapor first enters the pre-warmer, condenses there in part, and drops down into the boiler lid which is equipped with a groove. The spirits come out of the pre-warmer into a cooling vat with snake-like pipes and are first condensed there. Most of the whiskey has a very bad taste, however. Could it be because of the materials used, corn, rye, or does it lie in the method of preparation?

A shoemaker in Philadelphia last year received a patent for inventing a way of making shoes without sewing. The sole and the top of the shoe are nailed together with two rows of wooden nails. For these nails the wood of sugar maple is used. First it is softened by boiling, then dried again as thoroughly as possible. As long as a shred of sole or top remains, every shoe holds together watertight. In the first year, the inventor of this Peak shoe was said to have kept from sixty to seventy journeymen busy. Now he has sold the right to many shoemakers.

The finest women's shoes of Moroccan leather, as well as the shoes and boots of wagon drivers, can be made equally well. There are many shoemakers who can finish three pairs of Peak shoes in one day.

Among all agricultural products the potato is the most expensive and the worst tasting. They are not much better than our so-called pig potatoes, and yet a bushel costs half a dollar and sometimes even more. It is more because of the lack of a good variety than the fault of the land. The farmers plant few; their cultivation takes too much work, they generally explain.

In all possible ways the American mills surpass all others of their kind. Rye flour is almost as white as the so-called wheat flour in Basel, and a little whiter than the choice flour of Toggenburg. The best wheat flour, which is known by the name superfine, looks like starch or spelt, and yet out of one bushel of wheat — 62 English pounds — 45 pounds of superfine or 52 pounds of medium fine flour are ground. The medium fine is still almost as white as Toggenburger white flour. Never is more than one kind ground from the fruit of the grain; the rest all goes to bran.* In the newer mills the flour is taken to the upper stories from the bins in sacks by means of mechanical power.

Unmilled grain is rarely sold. After threshing the farmer drives his grain to the mill. The miller must then pack the flour, if it is to be sold

---

* It would have been desirable if the author had examined more closely the reason for the unusually white flour to determine if it lay in the grain more than in the milling, or if it could lie equally in both. [c. k.]

to port cities, in 200-pound barrels. If it is to be sold in the inland cities, it is put into sacks of 100 or 150 English pounds. The farmer doesn't concern himself with it further until he takes it to market. Here such efficiency reigns that there is never the slightest cheating either in weight or quality. The merchant in New Orleans orders a couple of thousand barrels of flour from Pittsburgh or Philadelphia with all the assurance he would have if each barrel had been presented to him for inspection.*

It is very inconvenient to visit the market in the inland cities. As soon as day breaks, the market opens, and one hour after sunrise it is already over. The farmer holds firmly to this practice. He does not want to waste time from work because of the market. If the buyer does not like it, he can just wait until the next market is held.

The farmers sell their produce from their wagons; no stands are set up except for the meat counters. A market master goes about everywhere and examines the weight of butter and other small products. If the butter is overweight it is cut and thrown back in the seller's basket. If it is underweight it is confiscated, auctioned off, and the proceeds go to the county.

It seems to me the Americans have adopted many of the customs of the English and Dutch. Cleanliness is carried so far in some things that it becomes almost a vice. Every week the houses are scrubbed from top to bottom and not just with water and sand but with soap. The most miserable log cabin in the deepest woods is scrubbed at least once a week and freshly whitewashed. The outhouses are set several hundred feet from the houses, and the revulsion against the excrement so highly esteemed in many places in the Netherlands and Switzerland is carried to such ridiculous lengths here that a farmer who sold a great many vegetables in Lancaster suddenly lost all his customers because a rumor went around that he used human excrement as fertilizer on his land. He could not even sell his butter. People spoke with revulsion about the man as if he had committed incest.

Since the care of the kitchen takes up considerable time on American farms, and the washing and scrubbing not any less, you never see a female working in the fields, with the exception, perhaps, of an indentured servant. In the house, however, they take care of everything pertaining to the domestic economy, for example, making candles, boiling soap, preparing starch, canning berries, fruit, and cucumbers, baking, spinning, sewing, and milking the cows.

* A fine character trait of the Americans! [c. K.]

127

Recently I went to Columbia, which lies on the Susquehanna River. It happened to be Sunday. All of a sudden I heard behind me in the woods a great deal of noise from laughter and shouting and the trampling of horses' hooves. I had barely turned around when a group of girls and young men on horseback went by at a sharp gallop. A while later a group of men and women came along at a slower pace. They were Mennonites riding to church. I passed by the church later; it lay in the middle of the woods. Over two hundred horses were tied to the trees. In America, in the country, there are hardly any churchgoers but rather churchriders. Even if the church is only a half hour away, they get on a horse to receive admonition and learning. To be sure, in fairness, I must say that the planters often have six to eight miles to go to the nearest church.

If several planters have settled in an area which is very far from a church, they usually get together to build a meetinghouse. Then they arrange with a preacher, according to the circumstances, to give them a sermon every two or three weeks. There are preachers who serve eight to ten such communities. If such a community grows or has several generous members, they take on a catechizer who must instruct the children. Then perhaps they get a helper, a deacon, and gradually they build a church and select their own minister.

The daughters of well-to-do people in our country study a little music to improve themselves, but instead of this, here the young American girl learns to ride well. There is much jealousy concerning this among them. It is an interesting spectacle to the Germans to see a group of farmers' daughters fly past at a fast gallop on their beautiful horses, wearing satin clothes, Indian shawls, and a high feather plume on their straw hats. It does, however, make a very unfavorable impression to find that such a queen of Amazons can barely spell. To be sure, gradually a more genteel and useful education and manners will find a home here.

This winter they are working diligently on the connection between the Susquehanna and the Schuylkill. This undertaking is very important for the northwestern part of Pennsylvania and generally for all areas above Harrisburg which are near the Susquehanna. They can bring their products by water to Baltimore and Philadelphia; the latter city will benefit considerably from this. They are talking very seriously of connecting the Susquehanna with the new canal being constructed in New York State from Lake Erie to the Hudson. The state of New York has reportedly made a very excellent preliminary offer to the state of Pennsylvania. If this should happen, the land in this area will be more sought after, in a relatively short time, than that in the neighborhood of New York and Philadelphia. It combines almost all desired advantages.

Products will then have outlets to numerous areas, and Montreal in Canada will become just as good a market for many articles as Baltimore, Philadelphia, and New York, and just as easy to reach. It has the general reputation of being the soundest land in America. It has the fertile soil which only the western states can have and the most pleasant location in the whole United States, according to the unanimous testimony of all travelers.

Should not these areas from Erie and Ontario to Laurel Hill and the Blue Mountains deserve the attention of Swiss emigrants as much as the western states? There cattle raising, agriculture, and fruit production would be the easiest to combine because the resulting produce could then be readily marketed. Bee culture in these areas would also be a significant activity. The honey from the Lake counties * is by far preferred to any other available honey. Hundreds and thousands of immigrants have been led, partly by a lack of knowledge on their part and partly because of exaggerated praise, to migrate to the western states and bury themselves in that endless western interior. Here there is no inland market available at all, and the nearest seaport is New Orleans, 1200 miles away. For three quarters of the year no one dares to approach this city except a complete fool because of the fear of being struck down by yellow fever. The superabundance of produce weighs heavily upon the inhabitant of the western states and makes him poor. A proof of this opinion is given in the address of the President of the United States at the last session of the Congress. In explaining to the Congress the condition of the nation's finances, he said, "There are almost 22 million dollars in forfeited debts for land, which cannot be collected unless many thousands of hardworking citizens are to be ruined, for it is at present impossible for them to turn their produce into money. I therefore entreat the members of the Congress to think of means by which this standing deficit can be covered in some other way." [32]

* The lake country or the area of the five large inland seas of which Erie and Ontario are the closest and are situated about 150 hours' distance from the ocean. [C. K.]

[32] Schweizer has rendered a rough paraphrase of a portion of President James Monroe's Fourth Annual Message to the Congress, November 14, 1820. The actual text is as follows: "It is proper to add that there is now due to the Treasury for the sale of public lands $22,996,545. In bringing this subject to view I consider it my duty to submit to Congress whether it may not be advisable to extend to the purchasers of these lands, in consideration of the unfavorable change which has

129

Perhaps this is the place where my friends would ask me the question that has so often been asked before and so variously answered: "Is it generally advisable, or only under certain circumstances, to come to America? Is it advisable for all or only for certain people?" Even though I have come to know the greater part of Pennsylvania, I would not dare to answer this question conclusively. Yet I think that my views are fairly accurate, and no one would be much misled because of them.

As long as a government or some other organization of honest men does not direct and control immigration it will remain a risk for every immigrant. The possible misfortunes are so numerous and the immigrant knows too little to avoid them; all he knows is the remote hope of a better fate that seems to lead him to this decision. How many lost their fortunes before leaving Dutch or French seaports or were cheated out of them by nefarious sea captains or inhumanly treated! When they reached America, they often had to indenture themselves to cruel masters and lost their health and life before they saw the dawn of the long-anticipated day of freedom. Many who brought money to America lost it all because they were unfamiliar with the language and the laws, or because of the cunning crooks who preyed particularly upon the new immigrants either as they disembarked in seaport towns or when they purchased land. Even Americans are often cheated when buying land from private individuals. Many immigrants became victims of the unhealthy regions in which they settled because they lacked knowledge or were misled by the cheapness of the land. Many more became victims of privation and overexertion in isolated areas where the nearest neighbor lived ten or twelve miles away. Often a family was simply not capable of clearing two acres of land in a year and living all that while on crushed corn as their only food in sickness and in health.

Certainly people in Europe hear frequently about all the difficulties with which immigrants must often contend. It is often quite obvious that the person giving the account wants to present only one side of the story. He wants to convince the oppressed farmer or artisan, who despite his best efforts can hardly get enough potatoes for his children and from whose nursing child the hardhearted bill-collector would tear away the last good

occurred since the sales, a reasonable indulgence. It is known that the purchases were made when the price of every article had risen to its greatest height, and that the installments are becoming due at a period of great depression. It is presumed that some plan may be devised by the wisdom of Congress compatible with the public interest, which would afford great relief to these purchasers." James D. Richardson, *A Compilation of the Messages and Papers of the Presidents* (Washington, D.C.: Bureau of National Literature, 1913), Vol. I, p. 643.

pillow, that he would never find things so good anywhere else and that his desire to emigrate is merely curiosity and frivolity. When, I say, when you can notice that the teller is not concerned with giving brotherly warning or friendly enlightenment to one whose thoughts are occupied with emigration, but is rather giving vent to bitter anger because the worms under his feet are trying to turn, such an account, to be sure, does not serve to banish the desire to emigrate. Rather it makes you believe that even the truth about it must also be a lie.

Often in public journals the most disgusting tales are told to the detriment of America, which every schoolboy knows to be fabrications. I do not know what the purpose of this is. If they want to raise the sensible desire to emigrate to an emigration-mania, they have picked the right means. If they wish to give warning to an incautious emigrant, they must "give clear wine," as the saying is, and tell the whole truth. They need not deny the advantages which America has over so many other countries, perhaps over all the countries on earth. But they must also point out how much the immigrant risks and suffers, how many bitter humiliations he has to tolerate, how many great sacrifices he must make before he can enjoy these advantages! How many cannot in their whole lifetime achieve their goals, but must, like Moses, be satisfied if they can only see Canaan and know that their children will achieve the success they wanted.

Would not many of the potential and actual mishaps be avoided if a government or organization were to control and direct immigration? This question can be answered in the affirmative with great certainty. If such a society, under the direction of an expert, honest man, were to buy land, they could all be far more certain that the land was fertile, well located, and had a clear title. This is rarely possible for the individual immigrant, with little money, to determine. Furthermore, if the society were to turn over to experts the direction of the whole trip, beginning at home and including booking passage, and if possible provisioning the ship, the cost of travel would be cut to less than half of what individual immigrants must now spend. If ten or twenty families settle together, they will be far less vulnerable to the many mishaps and deprivations which await the isolated settler. But for the sake of the welfare of both the individuals and the group, it would be necessary to make such arrangements that each member would find it in his interest to settle wherever the society decided, as it often happens that immigrants with money are robbed blind by unscrupulous land speculators. If nothing more were done for

131

immigrants than to make it compulsory for from twenty to forty families to settle together and stay together for two years, one could guarantee that they would prosper. After this period of time, they would not want to move. Should a few want to, the value of their land would already have at least doubled.

How very quickly prosperity is advanced by cooperative effort has been proved by the Harmonites, that is, the sect which the Württemberger Rapp established.[33] Several years ago he came to America with some of his countrymen. Using the wiles of a fanatic, he became the leader of his visionary countrymen. He knew how to take care of their money, and in this way made them stay with him. He bought land in the area of Pittsburgh, divided it equally among his followers, and drew up a religious covenant according to which no individual could sell his land. After four years or so, he sold all the land held by the society for more than ten times the amount of purchase, and with the money he bought land along the Wabash. A good businessman, who stayed there a few days last fall, assured me that the land of the colony could be sold any day for five million dollars and that the cash held by the group controlled by Rapp had already risen to over half a million dollars.

Every decent, intelligent man, of course, detests the self-gratifying, crafty religious fanatic who sets himself up as an absolute despot over a group of people in the midst of a free land under the guise of a religious organization. Nevertheless he has indicated the solution of the problem: *how and in what manner a colony in America must be established if the leader and the colonists are to profit by it.* Furthermore, he has proved

[33] In 1805 a German communitarian sect which had migrated from southern Germany settled in Harmony in Beaver County, Pennsylvania, at the head of the Ohio Valley. The Harmonite movement had developed in Germany, as did a number of other sects of the time, in an atmosphere of religious unrest and dissatisfaction which was particularly focused upon the established churches. The Harmony Society in America was led by Father George Rapp from Württemberg. The Harmonites or Rappites moved, after several years, to a new community farther west, New Harmony, in Indiana along the Wabash River. Although the new settlements were successful, the Society in 1824–1825 sold its property to Robert Owen, who had been interested in the progress of the colony for over a decade. He initiated at New Harmony a secular form of communitarianism. The Harmony Society relocated in Economy on the Ohio River in Pennsylvania, within fifteen miles of their original settlement. Their communal life in this settlement attracted widespread interest and attention in America and in Europe. It was one of the most successful communities of this kind, and it prospered until the rapid growth of industrialization later in the century made such economic units as the communitarians established increasingly obsolete. See Arthur E. Bestor, Jr., *Backwoods Utopias: The Sectarian and Owenite Phases of Communitarian Socialism in America, 1663–1829* (Philadelphia: University of Pennsylvania Press, 1950), pp. 34–35, 100n.

that in America, too, agriculture and manufacture can be combined. They make a cloth from the wool they grow that sells for ten dollars for a bolt two and a half yards wide. The leather which they tan themselves and the shoes which they also manufacture are said to be much in demand from New Orleans to Pittsburgh. The wine they make is preferred by discriminating Americans, and Europeans as well, to Madeira. It would be sad indeed to believe that such cooperation can be achieved only by visionaries.* One would think that there are less harmful methods of obtaining it. Apart from religion, if a certain theocratic or hierarchic organization is necessary, I would rather borrow it from the Moravians than from Rapp.

If a fairly large group of families settled down together certainly many artisans would be found among them, including cotton-weavers, embroiderers, makers of spinning machines, spinners, and so on. They could count on being able to practice their trade to advantage, in time, especially because these articles now have an import tax of twenty-five per cent which will soon be raised half as much again, or perhaps importation may be completely forbidden.

In the beginning, to be sure, they will have to accept other work. But without a planned, cooperative settlement a cotton-weaver is much worse off than in his native land, until he has learned a new trade. The worst off are accountants and clerks in stores; actually, everyone who earns a living with the pen considers himself betrayed by the lowly prospects. Farm families with small children and no money are also not in a good position. A family like this was offered in indenture in the newspapers for several weeks last fall. As I learned later they were separated from one another by over 200 miles. The father and one child went to the Blue Mountains and the mother, with two children, was taken to Virginia by a planter.

I think milliners would fare the best, and I think also that women who can embroider and sew well would soon find profitable employment. Among craftsmen, the first I would advise to come would be smiths, locksmiths, and shoemakers. The articles they make bring rather good prices. An axe costs two to three dollars; a door lock of iron with latch and only one bolt costs the same amount; a pair of ordinary boots six to eight dollars; a pair of shoes two to four dollars. The materials would cost about as much as in Switzerland. I think I have already mentioned that the

* Should they really be called this?? If we can believe other accounts, then the author has expressed himself too harshly. [C. K.]

leather here is worse than in Switzerland. Perhaps a tannery would not be a bad enterprise, because I am convinced that the tanners treat the leather too quickly and too superficially. Cowhides cost eight to twelve cents a pound and sole leather from thirty to fifty cents a pound.

When I say that this or that artisan would have an advantage in getting along, no one must expect to find a job in the first city he comes upon. Americans are not much induced by cheaper wages to employ immigrants nor by lower prices to buy from them. A foreigner must first make acquaintances before he gets customers, but once he has them he doesn't have to worry much about someone next to him working for less. There seems to be a connection between this characteristic and the fact that now, when everyone is complaining about unemployment and the lack of money, the artisan would rather leave a city than lower his prices to meet competition.

Land prices in the western states have dropped considerably. Twelve miles west of New Lancaster there would be plenty of land for sale at a dollar and a half and eight miles from New Vivis at one dollar per acre.

Acquaintances who have seen the land praise it as very fertile, healthy, and well watered. In Pennsylvania land is considerably more expensive. About 300 miles from here, not far from the Susquehanna, land is for sale at three dollars an acre. This must be paid for within five years. The society, however, offers sufficient security to make possession assured. Farther up in the lake counties in the states of Pennsylvania and New York there is still a good deal of land for sale but not under five dollars an acre.

People with a little money are much better off buying land of which several acres have already been cleared and on which there is a dwelling house. Here they can grow their own requirements at once. They can set to clearing remaining land with better results since wood cannot be cleared away immediately to gain room for planting. You can understand how densely the trees often grow in the forests by the fact that a sawmill belonging to my friend D. E., not far from Buffalo, could only clear four acres in four years even though eighty pieces twenty feet long were sawed every day. Both of these things must seem incredible to a Swiss. I must add, however, that on these four acres trees of the pine family grew, and these generally grow more densely than deciduous trees.

As you go northwest in Pennsylvania the needle-bearing trees are more plentiful. So far I have not seen any of our red and white pine anywhere, but many other varieties, some of which, like the Weymouth spruce and

134

the hemlock (*Rinusstrobus* and *P. canadensis*), frequently grow to tremendous size.

From Philadelphia to Harrisburg you rarely see a sugar maple, but after that they are plentiful. Much more widespread is the magnolia family. On the shores of the Susquehanna I often found twenty to thirty *Magnolia grandiflora* and *tripetala* next to each other. Only four miles from Lancaster the *Lamus sassafras* and the *Lamus benzoin* are fairly common. The *Lamus sassafras* reaches the size of the mightiest oak. The farmers often have their cider barrels and water barrels made of this wood, because it gives the beverage a pleasant additional flavor. The *Gleditschia* varieties are also fairly common near Lancaster. The *Gleditschia inermis* is often planted in front of houses, because it gives such dense shade. Posts which go into the ground are made from the wood of *Gleditschia triacanthos*. They insist that in fifty years such a post will be as fresh as one newly hewn. The pods of these two varieties taste something like honey; they are called honey locusts in English. The foliage drops before the pods do, and it looks very unusual to see such a leafless tree hung with pods half an ell long.

Brooms are made from the wood of young hickory trees and from an oak which I cannot identify. A piece of wood is split, then with a knife thin strips are cut the full length but not quite through. When the broom has the desired thickness and the handle the desired thinness the strips are bent down over the handle and bound together. One of these brooms can outlast four made of birch rods. Still another kind of broom is made of the panicles of the *Browalia demissa* and *elata*. Almost every farmer plants from eighty to a hundred bushes for this purpose. Six or eight panicles are woven around a handle. This makes a broom in which the fineness of a brush made of boars' bristles is combined with even greater durability.

In America there is little difficulty in moving to another state; just so, the American makes little of changing his residence or making a trip of several hundred miles or living away from his family for several years. These are trivialities the decision for which can be made in an hour. I must tell my friends a few examples of this, which I have observed myself.

Mr. S. in New York took me to a friend's house one evening. The friend is over sixty years of age although he still has two daughters who are about eighteen years old. After we had discussed all sorts of things, S. said in a very casual voice, "I hear you're leaving here and moving to L——, is that true?" "Yes," answered the friend, "I have a plantation there and the tenant has given me so much trouble the past two years with his rent payments that I'm going to settle this matter and move there myself. I can rent my house in the city more readily and then I'm rid of this trouble." I asked the daughters if it was easy for them to leave New York. "Yes, it will be all right to move that far and Papa won't go far away at his age." I asked the old man how far it is to L——. He was already chatting about something completely different with S. "Oh, it's only a hundred miles from here!"

A young man in Lancaster, a tailor by trade, got married two months ago. He has an attractive and good wife; he loves her and is just as deeply loved by her. They lived very close to us. "Peggy [Margaretha]," he said to her the other evening at dinner, "I just can't stand the miserable business situation here any longer. There are as many tailors in Lancaster as horses. Today Lawyer H. came back from Lexington. He thinks it would be much better for a tailor in Lexington than it is here. I think I'll start for there in the morning. I'll borrow a horse to go as far as Pittsburgh and send it back with the stagecoach. Then I will go on down the Ohio. What do you think? I'll be back in six or eight weeks, but if I find something for us I'll write to you. You can have an auction of the household things. Keep the big spread * and the shears and follow me." "Oh, I think what you say is right," said Peggy. "Still you should stay until the day after tomorrow so I can get your clothes in order." Then nothing more was said about it.

Today I happened by the door. My tailor was just mounting his horse. Peggy fastened the saddlebags more tightly. "Are you really serious?" I asked. "Yes, I want to see once for myself how it is out there [in the western states]. Goodbye, neighbor! Goodbye, Peggy!" "Goodbye, William!" Peggy said as she cheerfully and dutifully shook his hand. "William, please let the horse trot; you ride better that way!" Peggy called after him as he turned the corner and was lost to her sight.

On a bright, beautiful November day, I crossed the area around Frederickstown with my bundle of goods. Under the upper balcony of a fine, large house sat an old planter. "Come sit with me for a while," the man called. After we had chatted a while, an elegantly dressed man rode into the yard, dismounted at the stable, removed the saddlebags and approached the porch. "Good evening, father," said the young man. "Oh, it's you! Good evening, Stephen. Your coming is quite unexpected,"

* A bedspread of gaily colored wool, generally very artistically woven. The most important gala article of an American household. [Note by the author.]

137

answered the old man. "Yes," continued the younger man, "there hasn't been much to do the last few weeks because of the turmoil and since a boat was going to Baltimore I thought I'd like to see what you and Mamma are doing." "Mamma is in the kitchen; come, let's go into the living room," said the old man.

I wanted to leave so I would not be in the way during the overflow of motherly love, but the old man said I had to come in and that his son had things to tell us. "Mamma!" he called from the living room to the kitchen. "Come on in, Stephen is here!" Then the mother entered. "Welcome, Stephen! My, how handsome and tall you've grown! I wouldn't have known you if your father hadn't said who you were. I think it's now a little over four years since we've seen you. To be sure, I had completely forgotten how you looked," said the mother and went back into the kitchen.

"You've built a very nice house and barn," Stephen said to his father. "Yes, did you notice? It cost me some twenty thousand dollars, but it's much nicer than the old one, isn't it?" "Take a look in the barn and see the place." Stephen went, and then the old man related that four years ago Stephen took 2000 barrels of flour to Santo Domingo where he sold it very profitably. Since then he has gone to the East Indies twice. "He gets a bit homesick, but otherwise he's a fine boy," he continued. "And of all the six boys he is our favorite." Stephen returned and related very laconically, but well and clearly, how Christophe had died and the revolution had broken out.[34] Then Mamma opened the kitchen door and called, "Speak louder so I can hear too!"

Not much more fuss is made over marriage than over leaving and returning. To a German there seems to be an exaggerated freedom and independence, or should I say looseness and impetuousness, involved. If a single fellow sees a girl he likes, he waits for an opportunity to grab her hand. If she squeezes his hand, then he is invited to visit her. He goes as often as he likes without worrying about the opinions of either set of parents. If he has a job or is able to establish a business, the wedding finery is immediately acquired. In the quiet of the night they drive to the justice of the peace or to the preacher and in four minutes they are united. Then they drive several miles farther to a tavern, have a gay time, and return home before daybreak.

In the morning they go back to their work and often the parents do

[34] Henri Christophe (1767–1820), King of Haiti, committed suicide when a revolt against his dictatorial rule on the island broke out.

not find out about the marriage of their children for several weeks. Only then do they begin to think of establishing their own household. Of course there are exceptions to this rule; in many marriages arrangements are more formal. The farmer's son who expects a plantation from his father as a wedding gift, and the daughter who would not care to miss having her household furnishings, and perhaps a dozen cows, are a bit more concerned about the wishes of their parents. Nonetheless, parental authority is now, and continues to be, in a miserable state. In truth, in the nursing child there can already be seen the selfish, bullheaded adult. I do not always want to be uncharitable when I am not certain of the outcome or the reasons for these things, but I can assert that this situation exists generally, nourished by the willfulness of the children, and greatly restricts the advance of learning and urbanity.

Recently I heard that the German society of Lancaster has drawn up a resolution to send a warning to Germany concerning ill-planned emigration. This is to be published in the newspapers. Only farm families who are able to bring several hundred dollars into this country are advised to come. For artisans emigration is not recommended.

I have expressed my opinion about this before, and I would not take back what I previously said even though, in the light of the decision of the Lancaster German society, it will seem wrong to many people. I will repeat the opinion I earlier expressed: *Unless a government or a private organization makes a complete study of the local situation, and directs the transportation overseas as well as the settlement, emigration will continue to be a risk for every person.* There is only this difference, one may risk more than another, or rather, some have more to lose than others. A farmer who can bring several hundred dollars here is considered at home a respected man of property, and here he is in danger of becoming a beggar. On the other hand, many who paid their fare with great difficulty already had the beggar's stick behind the door at home. Such a person thinks that he can meet nothing worse than the poverty and deprivation he already knows. In some respects he is right. He must, however, realize that in a totally strange country poverty is more oppressive than it is in his native land. To be sure, many a poor man achieves a better life for himself here. But many lost more than their lives here, as when a man's wife and child had to be separated from him by several hundred miles and on his deathbed his dimming eyes search in vain for his loved ones and no loving hand closes his eyes.

Most Americans agree that under efficient leadership a colony would be successful here, but they cannot undertake something like this themselves. They lack the most important things required: enough familiarity with the people to make a wise selection, and an accurate knowledge of the way of life and characteristics of Europeans. Also, the immigrant who still has a little money will not allow himself to be dictated to, but wants rather to make his own decisions; and it is dangerous to become involved with those who do not bring any money.

Several colonization attempts have been made, and almost all of them have failed, some because they did not take necessary precautions, some because the leaders of the colony were motivated by base self-interest. In my travels I have met many families whose relatives in Switzerland and Germany probably believe that they are members of this or that colony which was advertised in public journals with great pomp but never organized. I would like to give vent to my indignation here, though it may be better to remain silent.

In all the newspapers now there is much discussion about the need for domestic manufacture and the raising of import taxes. That may become necessary in a few years. The state of Pennsylvania alone this past year imported more than 54 million dollars' worth of manufactured articles. This is still balanced by exports, but it is believed that they will be much less this year. Is the time not approaching when there will be more incentives for European manufacturing workers to emigrate than for those that pursue agriculture? But it must never be forgotten that now and in the future families of manufacturers who come individually will rarely be successful. Since it can be assumed that the products exported from Pennsylvania are mostly agricultural products, and of these primarily flour and meat — cheese and whiskey are often imported — you can get an idea of the overabundance of these products. As the population grows, production increases. "If it continues like this, in a few years we will have to throw our flour into the sea," a farmer said recently as he came home from Philadelphia, very depressed. A large number of manufacturing workers would have to be transplanted here before they could consume the surplus.

It is strange that Americans have so little feeling for beautiful gardens. At least in architecture they have some feeling for beautiful design. The reason, I believe, is not flattering to the popular character. Little genial sympathy, no sense of the poetry of life, only a speculative philosophy of life exists here. That is why painters, poets, musicians are as rare here as the nightingale, but the country swarms with lawyers and jurists as

Egypt swarmed with locusts in the days of the Pharaohs. If it is true that land and climate determine a people's character, then it is a pity that the Spaniards were not transplanted here several hundred years ago lock, stock, and barrel. Perhaps then guinea hens and pigs would have been roasted on woodpiles instead of heretics.

Since Christmas there has been much cold weather here and considerable snow. Once the Reaumur thermometer fell to twenty and a half degrees below zero. The Delaware was no longer navigable and the Susquehanna was so completely frozen that wagons could be driven over it. Apparently it has not been this cold for many years. In spite of this great cold the livestock is driven out for the whole day; the pigs remain in their open enclosures and the poultry find their night quarters in the trees as in summertime. In Switzerland domestic animals would perish with this careless kind of husbandry.[35] I would hardly have believed that habit could be so effective with animals!

People believe that when wild animals come down from higher areas it is a sign that cold weather will continue. This belief proved true this winter. During very mild, beautiful weather in December, a panther was seen in the area of Marietta, ten miles from here; occasionally wolves were seen, and a wildcat was discovered not far from Philadelphia.

German nut trees generally will not do well here. Even if the trees grow, they very rarely bear fruit. The different varieties of hickory trees, on the contrary, produce extraordinarily well. Both in the lowlands and in the mountains there are whole forests of them. Rarely does a late frost harm them. The walnut trees (*Juglans regia* and *oblonga*) grow on very rich soil. Would not the hickory trees do well in Swiss forests, too? It would be worth the trouble to make numerous experiments. The trees grow quickly. The nut has a very good-tasting kernel and is rich in oil. The wood is by far the best of all deciduous or non-deciduous trees for firewood. Just green from the tree it burns well, and heats almost as well

[35] Later, other Swiss immigrants were similarly struck by the contrast between Swiss and American agricultural practices noted by Schweizer (see also p. 226), Rütlinger, Buechler, and others in the early decades of the century. Writing in 1886, Paul Schenk expressed the determination of the Swiss colonists in Kentucky to feed and shelter their cattle properly in Swiss fashion instead of entrusting them as the Americans did to the natural elements. See Paul Schenk, *Die Kolonie Bernstadt in Laurel Co. am Beginne ihres sechsten Lebensjahres* (Frankfort, Ky., 1886); Paul Schenk, *The Colony Bernstadt in Laurel County, Kentucky, at the Beginning of its Sixth Year*, translated from the Swiss in 1939 by S. A. Mory, Sr. (London, Ky., The Sentinel Echo, 1940). Schenk's work is cited in Guy S. Metraux, "Social Aspects of Swiss Immigration into the United States in the Nineteenth Century" (unpublished Ph.D. dissertation, Yale University, 1949), p. 47.

as coal. While a cord of oak costs three dollars, hickory brings five or six dollars, and still most people prefer to buy it. I am going to enclose for my friends several kinds of nuts, and I would be very happy if experiments were made with their planting.

With the planting of *Browalia demissa*, seeds of which I have enclosed, I must note that they are planted in mounds like corn. As soon as the panicle has formed the kernels, sometimes even before they are formed, the panicle is snapped off so that in maturing the bush will not be so spread out but will grow closely together.

The news has just arrived that the branch or daughter-bank of the Bank of the United States in Cincinnati has closed and that all their loans amounting to 2,280,000 dollars have been legally called in. The citizens here who own land in that area were very dismayed to hear this because land values probably will decrease there even more.

In most states the Bank of the United States has established a branch. The state of Ohio assesses a tax against its banks, including the branch of the Bank of the United States, which was assessed 100,000 dollars. The bank protested against this and proclaimed that it would pay taxes only to the United States but never to an individual state, since it was not a private corporation. The government of Ohio would not desist. A suit was instituted before the Circuit Court, but in the meantime the bank suddenly closed and called in its loans. Considering the lack of money in the state of Ohio this might well ruin a few hundred farmers.

I think that a diary without dates is a checkered thing, a kind of harlequin costume. I have not seen my scribbling for fifteen days and have just returned from a trip to the upper areas of the Susquehanna. So I will add to the bank situation a little description of the life of colonists in a completely wild area.

I have often heard of the extraordinary self-reliance of the Yankees who were the first settlers, and I did not want to pass up the opportunity to see this pioneer life for myself. Around Wilkes-Barre I learned that a Yankee had moved last spring to a place nine miles away. Someone described the way to me which led through a tremendous forest of maple and nut trees. Here and there in the midst of a clearing a small log cabin was seen which, however, was always inhabited by ragged Irishmen. A small log cabin which had a front porch led me to believe that my hero lived there. A woman was busy milking a cow and seemed very surprised when I came toward her. I asked about lodging for the night. She did not want to agree immediately but said I should wait until her husband came home. The woman spoke excellent German, and I soon dispelled her apprehensions. In the meantime the man came home, but to my dismay he could speak little German. In spite of this, he was very hospitable and I spent a thoroughly enjoyable, happy day with these people.

The man came from Massachusetts, the woman from Rhode Island, both of well-to-do families. They had married last winter, and on the advice of a relative, who eight years ago had settled sixteen miles away, they moved out here in the spring and bought 160 acres of land. After they had paid off the first quarter of the sale price, they had only two dollars left. Their household goods consisted of a wool blanket, a musket, an axe, and an iron pot. With the two dollars they bought two young pigs and a pound of gunpowder. In the first two days, the man trapped two badgers and eight opossums. They dried their meat to live on while getting established. Then the man went out to fell logs for building material. Meanwhile the woman went out to get clay to plaster her future house. Then they had gone to get their two nearest neighbors, who lived four miles away from them, to help make the house. The following day they had already moved into their house. They had no seed of any kind, however, so the man went twelve miles away and, by hiring himself out by the day, earned wheat and potatoes. In the meantime, the wife stripped bark from trees and gathered moss for their bed and gathered together foliage and burned it. Then wheat and corn were sown between the stripped trees and the seed harrowed into the soil with the branch of a tree. The man again worked by the day to acquire some of the necessities. The wife did without bread for four weeks, but she herself supplied an occasional roast with the musket. So they fought through the first summer. Now, however, they have two slaughtered pigs, a cow and four young pigs, twenty to thirty bushels of corn, a fine-looking acre of wheat behind the little house, and as many potatoes, beans, and peas as they need to last them all winter. "We even planted ourselves pots and pans," the wife said, laughing. It was true. She had made them out of gourds.

In the morning she showed me a supply of various pelts, among which were many muskrats. "These will provide us with the means of making our farming more productive next spring. Soon my husband will go to the nearest city where he can sell them," she said. "All this," she added with noble pride, "only Yankees can do. The other Americans and the Germans lack either the physical strength or the strength of character or both to determine to do something and then carry it out.

"We are learning to enjoy life, but we also have the strength to renounce pleasure, not just when necessity demands it, but often indeed by choice in order to exercise our strength and to show that we are Yankees."

As long as I have been in America, I have never heard a woman talk like that, and every step she took convinced me that she could not only talk, she could act as well. I admired her aloud, but she modestly turned aside my praise. "You have just known the females in Pennsylvania; among dwarfs it is easy to be a giant," she said. "If you knew many Yankee women, you would find that I am not worthy of tying their shoes."

I was assured by many reliable friends that it is often the case with Yankees that a young couple, even if they come from wealthy families, will, after their wedding, move into the wilderness with a very meager dowry, make their land arable, work by the day for wages, sell their cleared land, and then move farther into the wilderness. Husband and wife compete in hard work and self-denial. But once they have become prosperous, suddenly the door is opened wide to the finer pleasures. An attractive house in the Greek style is built and beautifully furnished, books and musical instruments are acquired, and the hard life of the settler sinks into oblivion as in the river Lethe.*

The German supposedly cannot take as good care of himself when he dares to venture into the dark forest. I will tell another little addition to the above which Mr. E., a very trustworthy man, told me.

Several years ago Mr. E. bought a man and woman from Germany for the price of their passage. They served him faithfully and well for three years, so that after this time had passed he advanced them the money to buy 160 acres of land in an unsettled part of New Jersey.

The people did not do well at all, however, and E. had to help them out several different times. Despite the need they suffered they did not want to leave their place which had become dear to them. Then something happened which changed their lot quite suddenly.

Mr. E., accompanied by his son, stopped to see them one evening. The good people were as delighted as children who had found their father again after a long separation. Their only concern was providing properly for their guests. "Never mind," E. said to them. "I will eat with you what you have if only you will cook a little fresh meat for my delicate son, since he can't tolerate smoked meat."

* A river in Hades the water of which makes the souls of the dead who drink it forget everything they suffered on earth. [c. k.]

144

"Oh," said the wife, "if that is all that is missing we can help. We just got fresh meat. It's the first we have had in a long time, however. We can't shoot any wild game because I think it has all moved away," she said and with that fell silent.

E. said to them, "I can certainly see that you aren't doing well on this place. I am going to buy a plantation in this area where about one quarter of the land is cleared and then you can become my tenants as soon as you have sold your land here. Can you tell me of such a plantation?" "Oh, you couldn't have come at a better time," answered Jacob. "Just now a few miles from here a plantation like the one you are looking for is being offered for sale. It is the best one in the county, and very inexpensive, but it must be paid for in cash. But it would be difficult for me to become your tenant, as I don't know anyone who would buy my land."

"Let's leave that for now," said E. "When the time comes a way will be found. Tomorrow you come with me to the place and show me the plantation."

In the meantime supper was ready and everyone sat down at the table. "Here we have fresh meat," said the lady as she uncovered a bowl.

"Oh, you caught an eel," said E. As he placed a piece before his son it seemed to him that it had such a raw skin and he added, "Didn't you skin it? It looks so scaly." "Oh, that isn't an eel," the woman answered. "Those are pieces of a rattlesnake. Jacob chopped off the poor creature's head this morning."

Instinctively E. drew away from the table and pulled the plate away from his son who was about to fall to. "Good Lord," he cried, "how did you get to the point where you would eat such creatures?"

"Just try it once," said the wife. "There's really nothing so good as rattlesnake meat. In the beginning we ate a great deal of it. A Yankee showed us how to catch and kill them so that they won't get mean and bite themselves. Now we don't get them any more. This one has had a nest under the front door these past two years and we've made it tame. When Jacob whistled she came into the room and we fed her. Oh, we loved her so much, but every time she rattled we met either with good luck or bad luck. Once she rattled as both our cows died. Then again she rattled a few days before the farm was to be foreclosed when we couldn't make the second payment and you so unexpectedly advanced us money again. Last fall she rattled two evenings in a row and after that both of our children died. The other night she began to rattle terribly again. 'Oh, God! What lies before us?' I said to Jacob. 'Why don't you

145

kill her? We don't want to know anything about the future.' So in the morning he lured her out and chopped off her head with the axe. The poor creature came out so willingly."

Mr. E. couldn't decide to allow his son to eat any of the meat of the highly praised prophet. But he sat down at the table again and watched, not without horror, as the people devoured the fresh meat and left the smoked pork untouched.

In the morning Jacob went with him to see the plantation they had discussed and found that it really was very good and cheap. In order to be quite certain, however, he gathered information from other farmers about the land. All of them said it was the best plantation in the area but not everyone could buy it because it had to be paid for in cash. E. made the purchase complete and went home again with Jacob, who could speak of nothing but the beautiful plantation and wished for no greater good on earth than to be a tenant on it.

"Now, folks," E. began, "I must explain about the plantation I bought today. Several days ago a letter came for you from Germany with an enclosure of 700 dollars which came to you from an inheritance. The letter and money were addressed to the German society in Philadelphia and they gave me the assignment of bringing these both to you. I didn't want to put the money in your hand for fear that you might spend it unwisely or would be cheated out of it. I have deducted my claims on you, because you can pay now. The plantation is paid for and there is enough left even to improve your position."

For a long time the people stood there dumbfounded, unable to say a word. "Lord Jesus! The rattlesnake — if only we hadn't killed it!" the woman finally screamed.

For four more years these people lived happily and contentedly on this plantation. Then in a short time both died. Since they had no children the plantation was publicly sold for 4500 dollars. Two crooks who go to Germany from time to time and are still pursuing their usual activities were able to acquire the inheritance from the relatives for 500 dollars, and so could stick 4000 dollars in their pocket all at once.

Almost too late I realize that it is high time that I close my diary. May no one, because of me, be persuaded or dissuaded to emigrate if he no longer can find peace at home. I want to raise as few desires and crush as few hopes as possible. I wish only to supply information in order to guide desires and hopes more wisely.

146

Millions of people can still find an honest livelihood here if intelligence and honesty guide them on their way. Thousands and thousands of immigrants, relying only on themselves, have suffered need for a long time. People who can't or won't earn a livelihood by their hands are better off staying in the old world. For such people America is a desert and its inhabitants not their friends. Political and religious zealots also are not always comfortable. They feel like someone in a warm bed when cold water is dashed over his ears. No one will add oil to their flames. Only he whose miserable bit of bread is made bitter with sorrow and need, who can work and has the strength to do without for a while, will sooner or later feel happy and see sorrow and need vanish, even though he does not acquire any shining kingdoms.

I no longer wish I were back, even if I have to earn my bread forever with axe and spade. Much of what a man feels about the good or bad experienced here depends upon what kind of lot he left behind.*

Go forth, you pages, to my friends to whom you are dedicated. May you find them all alive, in a bright happy life. These people, whom I carry in my heart, will receive you with love and forbearance and will discount your errors. And if you reach there happily do not greet just my friends but greet everyone who reads you, and also the mountains and the valley, the cliff and the wood, the spring and the waterfall, the rushing brook, and all the sacred places that nature and friendship consecrate for me.

But not just to these, no, to everything which is part of my homeland bring a sincere, simple greeting.

JOHANNES SCHWEIZER

Note BY PASTOR KRANICH

THIS is as far as the diary of our honest American Swiss extends. Certainly every reader has accompanied him appreciatively and with warm interest, especially his many friends from this area. A tear of compassion came to many an eye as our noble-spirited friend made his moving farewells to the unforgettable homeland, to the mountains and valleys, springs and rivers and lakes. Always looking back to the cherished ob-

* Everything truly does depend, however, on the kind of attitude with which one accepts his lot and bears it, and trusting in God reconciles himself to it. "Qui fit, Maecenas, ut nemo, quam sibi sortem seu Ratio dederit, seu Fors objecerit, illa contentus vivat? laudet diversa sequentes? etc." HORACE, Sat. I. [C. K.]

jects he was leaving, he seemed to be inquiring if they would like to accompany him to the new world. Many a heart beat faster when the dear wanderer pressed them to his heart in tender memory. Many were happy to hear of the course of his fate and his adventures on land and sea, until he was in the harbor of his second homeland to which a mysterious magnet drew him. His comprehensive comments on various countries, products, agriculture, industry, and the customs of the people have given pleasure to many. One may find here also much material for contemplation as well as useful instruction for the heart. Whatever our wanderer recounted flowed out of his innermost convictions, as is clearly evident from the manner of his narrating. Even though he may have been in error here and there, his account, nevertheless, bears the stamp of truth. We all make errors, but each in his own way. Perhaps, too, if the author occasionally may not have drawn the American character with complete accuracy, his portrayal, nonetheless, presents a valid picture. His friends know him well and unanimously affirm that the foundation of his being is honesty.

But this dear countryman of ours was not alone on the long trek into the Promised Land. Accompanying him was a tender wife and a beloved little daughter nine years of age. What were their thoughts and experiences? Indeed, we are aware that the female sex observes many small things, as we call them, which would completely escape the male. In order to satisfy the curiosity of our readers as much as we are able in this respect also, we are appending an extract of a letter written in Lancaster, Pennsylvania, by the wife of the author of the book to her parents. We are presenting it almost exactly as it was written by her. Only occasionally did we correct the spelling or clarify the meaning of a word.

Letter FROM MRS. SCHWEIZER

DEARLY BELOVED PARENTS,

Now at last we are in the America of which we talked in such detail. And for the first time, I write to you from this very important part of the world which has now become my homeland.

Joy and gratitude to God fill my heart for His protection from many dangers on our journey; sadness and heartache come with thoughts of the immeasurable seas and lands which separate me from my beloved family and other faithful friends and from the beloved homeland. All these things flood my soul in such quick succession that I am not capable of giving you anything but a weak representation of all this!! Only rarely do I allow a small ray of hope of seeing you to again brighten my soul. Unfortunately, the hope is quickly extinguished, and I feel that it is only deceptive. Nevertheless, I am not allowing my spirits to sink. The hope of reunion is balm to my soul, even if it can only become a reality in the next world.

Dear Father, to my great pleasure, you fulfilled my request for an early letter which I addressed to you in my last letter from Texel. It was the happiest hour of my life when we received your first letter in America. Tears of joy ran down my cheeks. Ah, but the thought of how much time must pass before we can exchange letters disturbed me powerfully. Your letter of November 1820 we received in May 1821 after six months in transit. And this letter of mine, when if ever will you receive it? Only God knows.

I take it as my first duty to answer your urgent questions. How did I fare on the sea journey with the black sailors in red shirts whom I described to you in my letter from Helder? On the whole I can reply, very well. They showed us much partiality and consideration. For a drink of brandy, they would have jumped into the ocean for us in a minute. Also I can assure you that the friendship of the sailors, especially the cook and hands, is of more importance to a passenger than even that of the Captain. Even though a ship's crew is generally described as raw and wild, I must say on behalf of ours that here, too, there are exceptions. The Negroes, of whom there were ten on board, are a good-natured, grateful people. Their friendship provided us with many a measure of water and the best meat to be found on the ship and often in such over-abundance that we did not know what to do with it. Since we fed ourselves, we were not entitled to any food at all according to the contract.

But my goodness! What an experience a sea trip is, especially for people who never got off the saltbox! * Our trip was a reasonably good one, but it still took 51 days. If we did not have to endure danger and privation as well, and only had to be separated for 51 days by the endless sea from the many details of God's beloved earth, it would still be natural to feel an overwhelming desire for land. Indeed, we often had pleasant

* This is a Swiss dialectal expression suggesting a person who has never left his home. [C. K.]

days. When we had good, clear weather and fair winds it was really a delight to the heart to see such a palace as our ship was sail along its course. I wished then in vain that you, my loved ones, could just for an hour share this pleasure. But it was quite a different matter when the storm winds blew. We had to grab on to the first substantial thing available and not venture to move. The worst of it to me was the fact that I got seasick with almost every storm. My beloved husband was in its clutches only a few times and our child only for a few days. Even though seasickness is an annoying and burdensome thing, particularly because of where it takes up its residence, still it does not endanger life in the least. If no other illness accompanies it, no one ever dies from it. It consists mostly of these things: One always has a desire to vomit and feels dizzy and very thirsty. At the same time there is a strong revulsion to most foods. I could not bear the smell of coffee, tea, or sugar. Although the sailors had very convenient quarters of their own, they often came into the hold where we were quartered to pass the time of day and work on their rigging. Then there was endless laughter whenever I tried to get out of bed and tumbled back into the bed like a drunk. The young gentleman in the cabin, a compassionate merchant from Lüttich, sent his servant with a bottle of the finest wine for me several times. This was truly like a medicine and by this means I was again restored to health. Dried and cooked whortleberries, of which I am very fond, are also supposed to be a very effective cure for seasickness. Oh, dear Mother, how often have I wished for just a little handful of your supply of these berries, but all I could do was wish!

Besides, I really believe the seasickness was a veritable health cure for me. I am much healthier in America than on the other side, and my usual headaches appear much more rarely.

The extraordinary rarity of this occasion and my new enthusiasm concerning our boat increase my desire to give you, my dear parents, a little description of it. Under the name of *Xenophon* it is famous as an extraordinarily fast ship. It has three masts which rise almost to the heavens. On one of the masts waves the American red, white, and blue flag. On the rigging, which resembles a spider-web, hang over twenty sails. The deck is surrounded by a railing three feet high so that no one can fall overboard; on this deck forty to fifty people can stroll comfortably without bothering each other. At the front and back, on both ends of the boat, were the cabins of the captain and the sailors, and between these was the space for the passengers. All three were below the deck on one

150

floor. The deck was 66 feet long and 30 feet wide, in which space a great number of passengers would have sufficient room. We five passengers were able to make ourselves very comfortable. Under these rooms was the hold for freight and merchandise. Because of the danger of fire, the kitchen was on the deck, firmly held in place. However, if through carelessness a fire should occur, the kichen, fire and all, could quickly enough be tossed into the sea. Also in the kitchen stood a square cast-iron vat that was divided in two parts; in one part salted meat was cooked in sea water, in the other fresh water was boiled for tea. A fire was kept burning under the vat. Also an oven was provided. Potatoes were tied in a sack and hung in the boiling water until they were done. If the passengers had their own cooking utensils, they could use these facilities at their convenience. In Texel we had purchased a copper coffeepot that served us well. In general, providing food for yourself is much recommended to everyone who is able to do it. If my dear husband and I had had the usual ship's fare, I am sure we would not have survived; besides, providing for yourself is much less expensive.

I was never afraid except during the first few days and when we had some thunderstorms. The thought frightened me that if lightning should strike the boat, most of whose cargo was brandy, we would all be done for.

In other ways, a sea voyage is not as dangerous as you think at home; rather, as Augsburger says: "It is more troublesome than dangerous." Anyone who is seized by a desire to go to America should not be frightened off by the sea voyage. As time goes on, it becomes increasingly rare that a ship goes down.

We believe, dear Father, that your admonition has been proved valid over and over again: the departure from friends and homeland and the arrival in America are more momentous to the emigrant than the whole journey itself. You saw it from the right perspective. Only those who have experienced it can appreciate what it means to leave forever your parents, brothers and sisters, and so many other dear friends, and your country, and never hope to see them again. And settling here? If a person has little money or few possessions, he is often forced by necessity to settle in the wrong place. Even if he does have these means, it is not seldom that he is led to the wrong place by brazen cheats and so made unhappy.*

* He who has ears to hear, let him hear! Such sincere advice deserves to be heeded by those who desire to emigrate. [C. K.]

I had felt this wish so often, "Oh, if only we could *fly* to America!" But I must say now that no sane person should make this wish if only he has a little money for his journey, because the many hardships of the trip and even the expense are richly compensated for by the pleasures of innumerable sights and experiences of all kinds. Especially for young people, I consider it well worth the trouble and cost to make the trip to America, even if the reason for it is simply to enrich and broaden their knowledge. Furthermore, a person becomes freer from prejudgment and more understanding of other peoples.* I would not have gained much if my one-time wish had been granted. Nonetheless, we longed very much to reach our new homeland, and I am not able to describe in words our joy and the emotions which flooded my soul at the first sight of the mainland. The day of our arrival in America will be a holy feast for us all the years of our life. It is not only the day of our liberation from the dangers of the sea, but also the day of our introduction to the new homeland where an important segment of our life and our fortune begins.

Should anyone among my dear ones sooner or later decide to travel to America this information may prove valuable: He should provide himself with these provisions above all — noodles, rice, good hardtack (the ordinary kind becomes repulsive to a person), sugar, cakes of gelatin, which can be prepared in advance since they are so expensive in Holland, dried prunes, raisins, and whortleberries. Then several bottles of good wine and brandy; vinegar could also be useful. If he has these basic provisions, selection of the rest may simply be a matter of taste or practicality. He must insist on being able to cook at least once each day. He should promise to tip the cook and servants at the time of arrival, and now and then he should give the sailors a swig of brandy whether the captain and first mate grimace at this or not; this will be of great advantage to the emigrant. As far as linens are concerned, either bring so much that they need never be washed while at sea or else use only two garments and alternate washing them. Sea water eats through washables. Still, one should have a fresh change of clothing every four or five days. A person should not keep himself too warm, should wash frequently with fresh water, and should go on deck in the fresh air as often as the weather permits; all this is a protection against illness.

My dear ones, since I love doing it so much, allow me to speak a few

* What a pertinent observation from a completely uneducated woman! How receptive is the unjaded female mind to learning and to salutary impressions of the outside world! [C. K.]

words more about the cities of New York and Philadelphia, which are noteworthy in every respect. When we reached the harbor of New York where we disembarked there were many things to excite our wonder. In a marvelous setting, a naturally created bay, almost invisible from the ocean, forms the harbor of New York. At the time of our arrival over a thousand ships lay at anchor, their masts forming a large forest; among them were several marvelously luxurious steamboats. Oh, dear Father, if just for an hour I could present one of these to you for your admiration, I would give anything I have. New York itself is a very large city; many of its streets are 82 feet wide. Philadelphia is even larger and more attractive, with its immense streets laid out straight as a string. Hardly a city on the face of the earth is like this one. Just imagine what an impression such a spectacle must make upon people who are venturing out for the first time into the wide world! But the things which I saw to admire in these two cities are so numerous that you would get sick of my telling you about them.

Now I am coming to a different chapter. One after the other of you has asked with sincere curiosity, "Well, how are things with you in America? How do you like the country, the people, the habits, the customs, and the way of life? How can you get accustomed to all these things?" I will admit to you that now I cannot yet answer these questions to your satisfaction. All beginnings are difficult; should it not, then, be difficult to settle down in a completely new world? Truly everything in America is new, the land, the people, the cities and towns, the manners, the way of life — all of these, everything is different from Europe. Considering all these aspects, including unpleasant ones, which admittedly appear and are experienced by the newcomer, and considering further the painful memory of the irrevocable absence of beloved parents, family, and friends — how would it be possible to say in all good conscience that it's nice to be in such a situation?! Yet I am not letting my spirits fall. America is, and I think it will remain, a godly land which pleases me more every day, even though most of the people in my neighborhood appeal to me less and less.

We are not yet permanently settled; our home here is only a temporary one. After an eight-day stop in Philadelphia, at the advice of some good people we traveled on to Lancaster in the state of Pennsylvania. This area is about thirty hours away from Philadelphia. It has a population of about 6700 inhabitants, of whom one fourth are freed Negro slaves. There are ten churches and in each of these a special kind of religious doctrine is preached: Reformed, Lutheran in the German and English languages, Catholic, Quaker, Moravian Brethren, and various sects of Methodists.

The inhabitants are famous as the most prosperous in all of North America, but not as the best mannered. My dear husband rented a house here which consists of a living room, kitchen, and bedroom at the price of $40 or 100 florins for one year. This city is built in a completely different manner than are German cities. Every house has a large garden with berry and vegetable patches and an orchard. Usually the upper classes lease their gardens to the lower classes either for half of the year's harvest or for a moderate sum of money. We have actually taken one of these gardens into our life; on it stand over thirty of the most beautiful fruit trees.

If you could look over Lancaster from a height you would think that only a forest lay below, because thousands, really thousands, of the most beautiful fruit trees of every conceivable kind grow there side by side.

The churches of the city surpass each other in beauty and splendor. One of these churches is more like a tasteful casino than a church. They are attractive from the outside and inside they are decorated with arches, great magnificent crystal or golden chandeliers, Turkish rugs, and always the most beautiful draperies. In most of them there is an organ. But we miss one thing in these churches. Ah, the heavenly sound of ringing bells! Nowhere do we hear this sound; instead of bells, in each steeple there hang two miserable tinklers not worthy of the name "bell."

Weddings and baptisms are held not in the church but in the parsonage. The christening of children can take place without witnesses, in the presence only of the parents. Every Sunday I attend services in one of the churches, and each time I am seized with homesickness when I reach out for my beloved family. Instead of hearing a pleasing, harmonious chorale, in which at home I joined so wholeheartedly, I can hear only a one-part clamor. Later, when I return home, I try to calm myself with Gellert's songs,[36] but the wound of separation is more or less torn open again.

[36] Christian Fürchtegott Gellert (1715–1769) wrote some of the most beloved religious poems of eighteenth-century Germany. No single work of that period was more used by composers of Protestant hymns than his *Geistliche Oden und Lieder*, first published in Leipzig in 1757. See Max Friedlaender, *Das deutsche Lied im 18. Jahrhundert: Quellen und Studien* (Hildesheim: Georg Olms Verlagsbuchhandlung, 1962), Vol. II, p. 55.

A great balm for me in my dark hours is the bright, happy disposition of our child. How happy she is to be living in America I can hardly begin to tell you. Everything pleases her, even the English language, which disgusts me, and she is already fairly adept at its use. She chats with the women of Lancaster for hours, and I cannot understand a word of the conversation. Everyone marvels at her quick comprehension as well as at her brown cheeks, which are unusual in Lancaster. A prominent woman asked us to let her adopt the child, but upon our protesting, she was satisfied with our leaving the little one in her charge several hours each day. Every evening now she comes home loaded down with presents. Nevertheless, because of concern over the child's rearing, I would not like to remain in Lancaster. It seems to me that immorality is too prevalent here. It is precisely for that reason that I have not felt like making many acquaintances. This increases my boredom intensely and makes staying in Lancaster more difficult. However, we have had the good fortune to form a friendship which is very important to us, that of Dr. Endress, minister of the Lutheran church, and his dear wife and family, and also the friendship of a Mr. Jüngling and his wife from Hesse-Cassel, who, to our great disappointment, have returned to their homeland. These two worthy families have already shown us much kindness. Without them I, at least, would have been living in the midst of a city yet isolated from human society.

If a human being is grateful for any blessing of Providence, it is for the satisfaction of true friendship. Because of this I often try to fulfill this duty to God.

To this moment we have not suffered the least want, even though our cash assets were almost completely melted by the costly journey and the expense of taking along far too many things — which now we neither want nor can sell. Nevertheless, this winter we have enjoyed more meat, fruit, baked goods, and other necessary staples than we had on the other side, even in the most favorable circumstances, during the last two years before we emigrated.

We have always had the good fortune on our journey to be accepted in strange lands in a friendly way, and very often we were invited to spend the night without any cost to us. We even received, from a distant place, a substantial gift of bank notes, because someone had heard that "a worthy Swiss is still without employment." This my dear husband returned very politely with gratitude, explaining that we did not want

155

to impose on such kindness as long as we were not in actual need and could maintain ourselves.*

It is really remarkable how strikingly the attitudes of the American people vary, especially in rural areas, toward different types of people. Toward honest, worthy people they show unusual compassion and good will. But on the other hand, to those who they consider are falling ever deeper into the disreputable German riffraff, how cold, unfeeling, withdrawn, and, I must add, hard and insensitive they can be. If it had not been for the good letters of recommendation and introductions we brought with us, we would often have been in danger of being mistaken for the latter. And they do not even trust the best recommendations any more because, as they say, they have been misled and betrayed too greatly and too frequently.†

About American luxury, display, and the sumptuousness of clothing, I could, dear parents, write you volumes. The serving-maid of a farmer living in a desolate farmhouse is hardly to be distinguished from the daughter of a wealthy city merchant. Only in certain sects do you see a difference, but this is more a matter of design and color than quality or cost. Every wife and daughter wants clothes of the finest satin, Indian shawls, silken veils, and on top of this an English straw hat bedecked with the most expensive decorations and feathers possible. If the husband or father goes broke because of it — what's the difference!

Neither in the city or in the country do you see any woman going into the kitchen who is not wearing a hat and shawl. Even when they go to the toilet they dress as though they were going to church. I must remark here in all fairness, however, that Americans have their necessary-house about two hundred paces from their dwelling in some outbuilding so that every unpleasant odor can remain hidden. Because of this such clothing is somewhat necessary, especially in winter.

At home on weekdays the women wear white caps with little ruffles. This style is not attractive to me, and I am keeping my homeland ways, although I have to listen to a lot of reproaches because I do not care to wear any American "feshen."

* Who does not love such warmhearted givers and such honest receivers?! Such characteristics of the human heart deserve to be carefully noticed in a world where self-seeking egotism and stark selfishness not infrequently arrogantly parade their alleged virtues. [C. K.]

† A shameful truth! Such unscrupulous tampering with testimonials and recommendations must certainly damage public trust immeasurably. In the meantime a man finds it difficult to gain cognizance, and often he will be known from only one point of view. [C. K.]

To the American democratic use of "you" I could not accustom my-self at first. But now I find it pleasing.

Cleanliness here goes beyond all reason. Every week each house is washed clean and scrubbed from top to bottom, and not just with sand but with soap too. I have to participate in such activities also, otherwise I would be considered a detestable oddity. White things are not washed with lye but rather with rainwater and soap. Everything is thrown to-gether in a tub, boiled a while, then with the speed of lightning it is rinsed in cold water and brought to the clothes line. In this, as in other things they do, the Americans show an incredible dexterity and speed. For instance, a woman can sew three new vests or the finest silk dress for a woman, including trimming and ruffles, all according to the latest style, in a single day. You rarely, or actually never, see a female working in the fields. Instead women do the things which belong to household man-agement, such as knitting, sewing, spinning flax, wool, and hemp. They make soap, candles, and not rarely they dye their work clothes. They can prepare all manner of baked goods, *Lebkuchen*, pastry, and cake; in short, everything which belongs in the realm of delicate gluttony they understand well. In each house, even the humblest, a kind of pastry is prepared which they call pie. It is very easy to make and to me excep-tionally delicious. It is not expensive to make and so, dear Mother, I would like to recommend it to you. Take milk, flour, and fresh butter in the desired quantity and make a heavy dough. Roll it out to barely a quarter of an inch (or a few marks on the ruler) thick. With the dough, cover an earthenware plate which is first greased with butter. On this you lay pared slices of apples. Then with the same dough as on the bottom cover this. The plate and all is placed in a heated oven and so it is quickly done and ready.

The Americans live very well on the average. The humblest day-laborer enjoys all the most elegant and costly of foods in a profusion which I would call gluttony rather than moderation. Meat, bacon, butter, preserves, and white bread are the daily diet of the common people. None of these things can be missing at any meal, morning, noon, or night. As proof of an indescribable display allow me, my dears, to tell you the following. We were invited by a well-to-do farmer of the Mennonite community, in which my dear husband teaches music, to attend a butcher-ing party (*Wurstmahl* we call it in Switzerland). The farmer lives an hour's distance from here on a lonely farm in the woods. All the con-ceivable costly dainties that the culinary art has discovered were carried

157

to the table in the finest procelain dishes. The household consisted of an old man and his wife, an only daughter and her husband, and the master butcher. During the course of the dinner, it came out in the conversation that these people had about fifty head of cattle, an equal number of pigs, six horses, and more than a hundred and fifty geese and chickens. From this stock they had slaughtered six oxen and sixteen pigs for this winter alone, as the butcher affirmed.

Despite the fact that these Mennonites belong to a class of people who do not believe in luxury, we found, in two attractive homes, that all the rooms were furnished according to the latest style, with gorgeous beds, armchairs, chests of drawers, desks, tables, and curtains. We had to remain there overnight. The next morning, when we departed, we were loaded down with presents. I had to promise the elderly lady that I would teach her how to make cheese; this is not well known here.

The females around here are mostly all tall and well built. It's such a shame that they seem much older than they are. All of them look ten or fifteen years older. An eighteen-year-old girl resembles a woman who has had ten children. At twelve they are already fit to marry and by fourteen usually fully grown. You know what an aging appearance I had at home, and yet here they insist on taking ten years away from me.

I would consider myself fortunate enough in my new country, if it were not that I am so completely robbed of your dear companionship! I have learned, however, to adjust to circumstances which formerly would have been unbearable to me. For example, my dear husband was gone for an entire three months, during which time he crossed the country from one end to the other, through vast desolate areas and forests. The mere telling of such travels, surrounded as he was by considerable danger, would once have given me chills. He may go again tomorrow or the next day; he may go alone or take me with him. I accept this now without worrying. So you can see I have already become half American.

So far the language hasn't bothered me or held me back in the least. The principal and national language is English, yet German is spoken everywhere as well, mixed with anglicisms but nonetheless intelligible enough. The children in all areas are sent only to English schools.

Since my dear husband is still busy with his diary, I must tell you into what an unexpected occupation he entered this winter. At Christmas time when he returned home from his trip, we learned that the Mennonite community in Millerstown had a schoolteacher who could not give lessons in singing. He visited the town, which is about two hours from here,

158

and made inquiries. On the recommendation of the schoolteacher, and through his good offices, they agreed to take singing lessons from him. Of course, he wanted to do everything properly, and so he decided instead of just one-part congregational singing in the church he would teach them three- or four-part singing. What a failure that turned out to be! The good people suspected something heretical in this innovation, and because of this they wanted to withdraw from the agreement completely. My husband was annoyed at himself for not having understood the people better and for having handled them ineptly. For that reason, and not for the sake of the salary, he said, he would try to win them back. Everything possible was done and he succeeded in bringing his singing school back into being. You would die laughing if you could hear these farmers talking about their singing school. One day I went with my husband to his singing school. The community schoolhouse lies in a remote area near a forest of giant hickory trees. Opposite the forest is a grassy knoll over which our road led. Just as we were coming over the knoll, there was a swarm of people coming from all directions, on horseback and in carriages, making their way to the school. As we got nearer the school we saw horsewomen dressed in elegant gray riding coats dismount from their horses with the lightning speed of Hussars. These slender, pretty female figures were marvelously adept and poised as they led their horses to the handiest tree and looped the reins around it, and the horses were secured in no time at all. These horsewomen wore English straw hats with gorgeous swan feathers, and silk veils floated over their Indian shawls. Then another crowd of men, women, and children got out of large two-horse sleighs in great silence — not twenty words were exchanged. The whole assembly took their places and instruction began. Oh, my goodness! I squirmed in my chair. A fiendish witch seemed suddenly to have changed these stately students into blockheads. Hardly half of them could follow my husband in singing the scales. I felt impatience and shame alternately for these well-dressed Amazon queens. Finally, after expending great effort they were able to sing a whole song in a bearable manner. It cannot be said, as the old people bragged, that the song had been sung pretty well.

Now that evening had come, they vied with one another as to who would drive us in his sleigh to his home. When we arrived at one of these homes, I thought I was being led into a palace. Then food was brought in; no other dishes but porcelain and Wedgewood appeared, and in such abundance that I would almost have believed that I was in the shop of a houseware dealer, if it had not been for the food in them. The meal consisted of coffee, sugar, honey, preserves, butter, cucumbers, a variety of sausages, cold ham, jelly, all kinds of roasted things, apple turnovers, cakes, and goodness knows what else. Cider and applejack were drunk.

As soon as this gluttony was over they reached for their songbooks. For two solid hours they sang away without mercy. The schoolmaster — my husband — also had to play the clarinet, which they thought he did very well. Finally, late at night, they went to bed. How amazed I was when we first entered the bedroom! The magnificent beds covered with artistically worked spreads, the floors covered with Turkish rugs, all dazzled our eyes. Costly drapes covered the windows. We stood there transfixed. Never would we have expected such things in a Mennonite farmhouse. We will find the same thing, my dear husband said, when we accept other invitations. From all these tales, my dear parents, you will realize the degree of well-being which most people here in this country enjoy.

Furthermore, the Mennonites are the ones who want to spend the least possible amount on education. Supposedly it is even a fundamental principle of their religion to shun education. This is also the reason why they pay for instruction in music in such a miserly fashion. My husband manages to get twenty dollars (fifty florins) for three months. "I have undertaken this," he says, "not just because of the salary, but rather because it permits me to come in contact with these well-to-do people. These people could be very helpful to us in other ways because they are in close touch with all other Mennonites in the country. How advantageous their goodwill might yet be to us?!"

But space is coming to an end and I must cut this short. At any rate, my scribbling has been too long extended. If I were to tell you to my heart's content all the things I have seen and experienced, I would have to scribble up many a page more. But I still have one obligation, and I ask you, my dear Father, to please help me fulfill it. I know that you will grant my request willingly, because you will be in sympathy with it. You will well remember, as I wrote you from Texel, the many kindnesses which we received from the unforgettable firm of Mandach and Lang in Amsterdam. Even upon our arrival in New York we found new evidence of the tireless goodness and magnanimity of these people. Sometime, when you have the opportunity, please write to this firm and thank

161

them fervently in our name. Also express our gratitude to Mr. Bidermann, in Winterthur, and to Mr. Weniger and the others in St. Gallen, whose excellent recommendations led to our being received by the firm of Mandach.

Please, dear Father, do not let us wait so long for a letter. Every night I dream that we receive one from you — but when I awaken, ah! it was but an empty dream!

PART TWO

JOHANN JAKOB RÜTLINGER was born in the Toggenburg region of St. Gallen in 1790 and died in Ohio in 1856. His father, Johann Jakob Rütlinger, was a teacher and encouraged his son to follow his profession. His mother was Ursula Tütschen. Rütlinger married Anna Margaretha Baumgartner, daughter of a town councilor of Hemberg, April 8, 1823, a few weeks before the young couple left for America. See Oskar Frei, *Johann Jakob Rütlinger von Wildhaus (1790–1856), Sein Leben, Seine Dichtungen und Schriften* (St. Gallen: Historischer Verein des Kantons St. Gallen, 1915), pp. 13–14.

Day book on a journey to North America in the year 1823

by J. JAKOB RÜTLINGER

MY DEAREST ONES IN SWITZERLAND:

What new things have been happening there? How are all of you, my friends? Ah, these are questions which I would like answered all at once. But distant lands and seas separate us. The sounds of our words disappear in the valleys and heights, streams and rivers, broad and inhabited plains, high cliffs and castle ruins, the mirror of the ocean and its foamy waves, and are so long delayed that they seem like the tales of antiquity.

Formerly, when I wrote to my friends, it was from Wildhaus or Hemberg, but now it is from America that I write. How wonderfully this name steals through my mind! Once, too, I lacked suitable material to write to you about, and so I had to make up something funny and write about that. But now I have so much material before me that I would like to pour it out to you by the bushel.

My beloved wife and I arrived very happily here in America at the home of our dear friend Schweizer. May God be thanked and praised! How and when this happend, my dear friends, I will tell you briefly. It will not matter to you if, while I am telling you about this, I dream that I am in the warm little winter room, smoking my pipe, or on the greening meadows at the beginning of a friendly Swiss spring day, or at the silver spring, or at a murmuring brook in the forest of Erlen, or on the peaceful Alps in summer, on a precipice where the majestic cliffs echo every jubilant shout again and again, or up on the peaks and pastures stretching to the sky where the morning and evening sun spreads a purple carpet and illumes the still clouds in the blue heavens with a rosy hue.

Our friends accompany us

WE STILL remember with pensive joy the bright May morning in the spring of 1823 when, accompanied by a few friends, we left the friendly little village of Hemberg; just as the morning sun began to dip over Toggenburg, Hemberg disappeared behind our backs. We would never see it again. A very special mood was attached to this scene which we viewed so lovingly. The meeting with many friends in Lichtensteig and the farewell to others in Bütschwyl will remain in our memories forever. The solicitous escort of others to Zurich, their deepest sympathy with our purpose, and finally the painful parting from them and from everything dear and familiar – oh! how we felt when we heard the last farewell from them forever.

An unknown benefactor and an unexpected traveling companion

WE TOOK lodgings at the Rössli in Zurich. After we had gathered a few more letters of introduction, we were ready to travel on. When we asked for the bill, we were told, "It has already been paid." We were amazed to have such benefactors in a place which was strange to us. We could not imagine who it might be. We were truly sorry to continue without being able first to express our thanks. May God bless you, unknown benefactor, whoever you may be!

Now we were alone, without friends, without acquaintances. Yet we wanted to venture out into the great unknown where, at every step, we would encounter strange events! We did not feel quite so jolly even though a magnificent morning sparkled over the mirror of Lake Zurich and the high towers of the city shone like gold, and even though the benign spring sun spread its caressing rays over the soft vine-clad hills around Zurich and tried to radiate brightness to our souls. We stood and marveled; it was just then that we received unexpected news of a coach which was headed for Brugg. We presented ourselves to the coachman, who was willing to take us along for a small sum. We had to wait until after the noon meal. Here again we were told, "It has already been paid." The coach rolled up, we climbed in, and as we departed we waved many a farewell to that unforgettable Zurich.

Among others in the coach was a man from Glarus by the name of M. B. from S. — a very proper man, it seemed. After mutual inquiries about the purpose of our travels, it turned out that B. was traveling on business to London by way of Amsterdam. He had already done this several times. You can readily imagine how the wonderful meeting with this man pleased us, even more than it otherwise would have because, like us, he had not planned a specific itinerary, but wanted to travel by foot or by water, as opportunity and circumstance provided. Now we were very happy and of good cheer, and the blooming fields of the blessed Limat valley had a thousand charms for us. We left him in Brugg because he still had some business to finish in Schinznach. He recommended the Weisse Kreuz in Klein-Basel as a place to stay and where he could meet us again later. We went there alone. It was the first time I lugged my valise along on my back, and I decided that it would be a lot more convenient for me to make the whole trip in a coach or by ship. Still, the beautiful weather, the lovely season of the year, and the marvelous countryside decked out in all its spring finery made me forget what I carried on my shoulders.

We found the inn recommended to us to be a good and inexpensive place to lodge. B. came the day after we arrived. We felt as though we were meeting an old and faithful acquaintance, so warmly and sincerely did he greet us. It was the time of Ascension, and for the last time we attended a Swiss church service in the cathedral. That afternoon we strolled to Kleingundeldingen, where our friend Schweizer spent a year; then we strolled to the enchanting heights of St. Margarethen from which can be seen the greater part of the city of Basel with its glorious setting, a part of Wiesental which gave Hebel material for his endearing German poems.[1] We watched the birds dive into the distant blue sky. We lingered in contemplation and wished our beloved homeland many more farewells in the solemnity of this sacred day.

[1] Johann Peter Hebel was a contemporary poet whose works were prized by Goethe and Jean Paul. Hebel, known particularly for his treatment of rural life, was born in Basel in 1760 and died in 1826. Rütlinger was influenced by the farm subject matter and the use of dialect through his reading of Hebel's *Allemannische Gedichte*, published in 1803. His collected works appeared in eight volumes, 1832–1834. See *Grosse Brockhaus* (Wiesbaden: F. A. Brockhaus, 1954), Vol. V, p. 322.

We visited Pastor Burkhard who received us with much friendliness. We spent a memorable day with this charming family and received an English grammar from them as a souvenir of friendship.

Time brings wisdom

WE WOULD have liked to travel on and save our shoes, but no opportunity arose. We stood for hours on the shores of the Rhine, looking up and down the river to see if by chance the gods of good fortune would bring some kind of ship on which we could glide gently downstream. However, the river remained smooth as a mirror without any sign that a boat had once disturbed its surface.

It was the ninth of May. We strolled through the crowds on the Rhine bridge. As the evening sun shone its purple rays on the smoothly flowing Rhine and lighted the golden spires of the city like sparkling chandeliers, we noticed on the other shore two newly arrived ships whose cargo was being unloaded. We hurried to the ships and asked their plans. We were told that they were leaving early the next morning for Strasbourg. They were willing to take us along; the fare was four thaler a person. We expressed great eagerness for this. However, B.'s passport had not been signed yet. The office was already closed for the day, and it would not be open tomorrow till eight o'clock. We seemed to be in a rather desperate situation. Either we had to abandon B. or miss our chance for the boat. We did not take long and decided on the latter because such a travel companion seemed too important to us. Therefore, we slept peacefully and unworried that night because we thought that when the time comes we will know what to do.

B. got his passport from the police and then we planned how we were going to travel. Our fellow-traveler proposed that we buy a boat and navigate it ourselves. As much as I wanted to continue, I did not have any particular desire to entrust myself to a board nailed together three ways. However, the thought of my heavy valise, and the suspicion that it could be a long time before we had another chance to travel, persuaded me to consent. This was quite all right with my wife. B., like an enterprising native of Glarus, boasted that he had undertaken other such daring enterprises. If this was so, I do not know, but I did find that he could manage the boat a bit better than I did. Enough, a new boat was bought for one doubloon. You can well imagine that this was no merchant ship. We prepared for departure, loaded on our equipage, and took one more man to help us as far as Neuburg because this was a dangerous stretch for the unskilled. The boat rocked along. At the slightest movement, it lost its equilibrium and threatened to toss us out first on one side and then on the other. Now we were floating over the borders of our beloved fatherland. Feelings of deepest gratitude to it filled our bosoms for the many blessed hours we spent in its folds, and the sincerest wishes that it might always remain an independent, free, little country, and that it might aspire to show more appreciation of old customs, old loyalties, and the old integrity and simplicity than it has for more than twenty years. Silently indulging in reveries of our past, present, and future lot, we arrived in Neuburg without having noticed the surrounding country. We paid our boatman and dismissed him.

An opportunity to travel another way

WE THOUGHT that we would use our boat only when there was no other opportunity of traveling more advantageously and unconcernedly. Here we met several men who were busy equipping a raft in order to travel on it to Strasbourg. We did not fail to appeal to them to take us along. They were very willing to do so, if we would wait until morning. So we stayed overnight here with a very friendly and reasonable innkeeper. He was not, however, wholly enthusiastic about emigration. Despite this, we slept in undisturbed peace.

Morning came and then we could see clearly for the first time where we were. The moment of introspection was past, and I was again bright and happy. This town stands on a height. Below it a part of the majestic Rhine thunders over a rock weir. We could see now that anyone losing his course on the river would be the prey of death. The innkeeper told us that a few years ago a whole boatload of people perished there, because they could no longer battle the strong current. They could not be saved and plunged over the falls. They were, it is said, also emigrants.

Just as we were stepping onto the new boat, the golden sun was coming up making snowy patches on the Alsatian mountain range shine brilliantly. On the right the charming vine-clad hills of Baden still lay in shadow. The raft glided gently down between the unvarying shores of the Rhine along which the vegetation reached down to the water. From time to time, the steeples of a distant town projected above the green forest. After the raft had made a turn around a bend, magnificent Breisach, built upon two hills, rose into view in the blue distance. The day was so clear that we were able to see the tall cathedral of Strasbourg when we were still seven hours away. Like a blue cone it floated over the high forests, thrusting boldly into the air. One must marvel at the colossal work of Erwin of the Middle Ages.[2]

We stayed overnight in Kehl. It was a rather noisy evening because of all the different kinds of people in the inn — it was Sunday — so we went out into the open and feasted our eyes on the lovely sunset. In this festive setting we thought with deep emotion of home and our dear ones whom we had left behind. "The same sun sets for all of us, the same blue sky stretches above us all; one Father in Heaven protects and sustains us all, as long as it is His will, whether we are on the Rhine, the Mississippi, or the Nile," this was the hopeful expression of our deep feelings in the midst of the noisy tumult of the world.

Our own boat trip, for the first time, May 12

WE NOW equipped our frigate and sailed away on our own. My heart was beating a bit hard, but B. and my little wife just laughed at me when they noticed this. They had more courage than I did. This is the way it was. I could not change things so I had to take the oar and do the best I could, come what may. B. was the Captain and was in charge of the rudder. I took the job of sailor, and my wife, serving as kitchen boy, handed around a jug of wine or beer to the entire crew when thirst set in.

In reality, our voyage was a bit ridiculous. Until we had gotten somewhat accustomed to rowing together, sometimes one end of the boat and sometimes the other went forward; and sometimes neither. My little wife had to sit in the middle of the boat as still as a mouse, so she would not upset the boat's balance. At first we did not know the course of the water and its current very well, so we frequently hit shallows and were stuck in the middle of the Rhine, and had great difficulty in freeing ourselves again. Just at this time of year, even during the clearest weather, it was very unpleasant. This prolonged our trip a great deal. When the wind was strong, we had to land at the first good place. We often had to camp there for hours in the desolate brush; laughing and joking, we emptied the wine or beer jug and let the wind roar through the trees.

---

[2] The cathedral or Münster was built in the eleventh to fifteenth centuries. Rütlinger makes reference here to Master Erwin's design of the west façade of the cathedral (1277).

170

A kind of man-hunter

ONCE our boat was gliding quietly and smoothly in the middle of the glistening stream. The birds in the forests on both shores sang, and we sang, too. We felt wonderful, because it was a bright morning. All of a sudden the blue sky was covered with dark clouds, and just as quickly a storm roared through the forest. The Rhine changed color and tossed its waves high into the air. Only with the strenuous effort of a William Tell were we able to land, finally, on the French shore, where we pitched our tents under the trees. A notice was posted there, stating that anyone bringing anything back or forth would be severely punished. The sinister forest and the sighing of the wind in the trees made us feel uneasy and weary of mind. We were afraid that we would have to spend the whole day there. We explored the woods to find a suitable place to spend the night should the need arise. After about half an hour's walk in the woods, we came upon a little village named Neuhäusel ("New-little-house"). A better name would have been Jammerhäusel ("Woeful-little-house"). God! What poverty reigned there! Certainly we could not have found anything to eat or drink in the whole village, not to mention a place to stay for the night. The people, all without work or income, stumbled about half starved, pale, and joyless. Their clothing was miserable. So we went back, considering ourselves lucky. Just as we were half asleep under a tree along the shore of the Rhine, we heard a rustling in the bushes. Running toward us came a tall, haggard man with an exhausted, pale-yellowish face. He held a musket stock in his right hand and the barrel of the gun rested in his left arm, as though he were ready to shoot with one movement. This encounter, in a dark forest on French soil, did not make us feel very secure; we did not quite know what to make of it. Perhaps, we thought, he was a man-hunter. It was something like this, only not quite so bad, as we discovered. He was just the customs officer at this place. He greeted us in a very friendly manner and spoke to us like a sensible person. Oh, how he complained about the present situation! The common people, he said, would perish completely if things continued as they were much longer. The nobility was gaining strength again and crushing the vigor of the state. He expressed the cautious hope that Spain would win the war that had just broken out,[3] and then every-

---

[3] In April 1823 French armies under Louis Antoine de Bourbon, Duke of Angoulême, invaded Spain to restore Ferdinand VII to his throne after a liberal revolution. The French forces with some Spanish elements supporting them were successful within a few weeks of crossing the Bidassoa.

thing would take a turn for the better. But alas, the good man and many thousands more were betrayed in this hope.

Now we were able to continue our journey, but we had to land once more because of the storm. This was the first rain since we left home. The sky cleared up quickly and we untied our boat and departed. It was a delightful evening. The river lay before us as smooth as a mirror. The usual rustling of the forest changed to a peaceful stillness; only the concert of the crickets sounded louder to us. So, singing and slowly dipping our oars, we glided to Neuenburg.

Another ride on a raft

I T I S raw and rainy this morning, and we feared that we would have to spend the whole day in the inn. Then suddenly things took a very different turn. A whole group of men came in and sat themselves at a table with as many wine bottles. They let it be known that they were sailing by raft as far as Mannheim. They readily agreed to take us with them. Now unexpectedly we were making progress. We departed in cool, rainy weather. The hut built on the raft offered us a roof and the warmth of a blazing fire. Toward noon the sky cleared up, and we spent our time outside. The shores of the Rhine were gradually getting lighter and more beautiful. The current flowed in its bed, unruffled and gentle. The mountains behind us disappeared and only hills were seen against the distant blue. Towns shimmered everywhere in the plains. Philippsburg, on the other side of the river, shone in the evening sun. From now on the Rhine region is enchantingly beautiful.

While we listened to the evening bells from many villages, the raftsmen began their feast. They cooked, roasted, ate, and drank quite royally. We, too, had to take part in the banquet. We kept sailing all night. We lay down to sleep on the straw next to the fire, but the strangeness of the sleeping quarters as well as the noise and the commands of the dour old pilot would not let me sleep. I got up and walked about. By the time I had taken a hefty swig from our wine bottle the others were snoring and sleeping soundly. There was a half moon in the sky, and the stars twinkled like candles above it. The oars of the rowers splashed on the smooth, silver stream. From the groves on either shore, thousands of nightingales sang their flute-like, enchanting songs. A short pause occurred in the middle of the night, and both woods and forest rested. All nature became silent. But before dawn the woods were awake again. The thousand-voiced concert of the nightingales began again. As soon as it dawned and the sun turned the gay little clouds of morning to gold, the heavenly singers closed their throats, and the day songs of ordinary feathered folk began. These nightingales were the first and last I have ever heard in my life. It was a blissful night for me!

The raft on which we are floating is 84 paces long and 12 wide, and farther down the river we saw some that were four to six times as large. It is no small matter to steer such a raft between the pilings of a Rhine bridge. Our boat rested on the raft's flat surface like a zero on a map.

This morning we saw the most beautiful Rhine city, the lovely Mannheim, with its princely surrounding woods, its beautiful buildings laid out in square blocks, its large open marketplace, its tree-lined streets. We boarded our own frigate in Frankental again and we did not have to pay our honest raftsmen more than twelve batzen.

To Mainz: Arrival and tour

WE VISITED ancient Worms. It is an ugly city. Old fortifications lie in ruins. The dark, old Catholic church has many an art work of pre-Gothic antiquity.

Now we sit down in our boat again and splash away with a silvery, shimmering beat of the oars. The land about the Rhine is again hilly vineyard country. Little villages appear here and there. We glided down the spine of the Rhine to Nierenstein, singing on the way.

We had hardly taken our feet off our water bug when a crowd of bold fellows descended on us, offering lodgings and the care of our belongings. We spoke to them brusquely, saying that we wished to do everything ourselves. Two of the most aggressive ones figured out immediately that we were emigrants. Because of this, they followed us like well-trained wh——s. They wanted to advise us and help us in finding the best opportunity for traveling on. Among other things, they told us that a respectable family from Landau, also going to America, was to arrive here Saturday. It was now Friday. A boat had already been bought for them and a boatman hired who was engaged to take them to Amsterdam. That would not be too bad, we thought, for we had planned to sell our boat here anyhow. We did not pay much further attention to the gabbers, because we wanted to gather more information about this matter later, and to do this we waited for morning in a peaceful sleep at the Stadt Frankfurt inn.

A beautiful morning dawned over Mainz. Everything came to life. The golden Rhine swarmed with gliding boats, and on the large bridge travelers tramped back and forth. The hammers of the smiths rang out. The streets swarmed with all sorts of people; we could now look over the bustling throng and the activity of Mainz.

The city is beautifully spread out on the left shore of the Rhine. A person who has not yet traveled much sees an astonishing sight here. A whole forest of masts juts up into the air all along the shore, their flags playing in the wind. Literally hundreds of large and small boats lie at anchor. All day long cleansed and uncleansed little gentlemen and ladies slip in and out of the steaming swimming-baths. Ha! we thought as we looked at this great water palace — on the ocean there are bigger ones, and who should be afraid of riding on such a floating island!

We inquired now about the tip we heard yesterday. We actually found the boatman who had contracted with the expected family. We tried to make the same arrangement, but he asked six thaler a person, and that was a bit too much for us. We decided to wait for the people themselves, because we figured that they would have their own boat and the boatman arranged for. We would deal with them and not with him. So we let the matter rest and familiarized ourselves a bit with the city and its surroundings.

Mainz has about 10,000 to 12,000 inhabitants. It is situated in a place blessed by nature and also convenient and advantageous for trade and industry; but its inhabitants do not live happily. Wherever one goes one hears complaints about oppression and unbearable taxation. And it is true. Even a foreign traveler is not comfortable and free anywhere. Everywhere you bump into soldiers strolling about. There are now soldiers of Austria, Prussia, and Darmstadt here, living off the work of the people in the country and the earnings of the people of the city like useless servants. Like drones, they consume the honey gathered by the worker bees. But unlike the bees, the working class cannot rise up and kill the drones. In this case I praise the far better arrangement which the bees have. We were told that Mainz and part of the surrounding country had to pay monthly a sum of 84,000 florins to the princes of Hesse-Darmstadt without quarter or mercy. A pretty little sum!

Today we made a little tour across the Rhine bridge to Kassel. It is an ugly, poor, filthy dump. We strolled upon the walls of the fortification, thinking there was no harm in it. Many cannons were placed in the trenches; a guard saw us and — wham: "Beat it out of here or I'll shoot you down," he thundered up at us. We would have liked to plague the fellow a little, but this did not seem the right occasion for it. So we lowered our sails and left this hateful place, where you could not take one free step.

By now evening had come, but the expected family had not arrived.

An unexpected departure

TODAY is Whitsuntide, May 18. B. is getting a bit restless and does not want to wait any longer. Either we would continue on our own or get passage on the packet boat, he thought. But we wanted to spend Whitsuntide here, and because of this we tried to calm him down.

We went to a Catholic church and listened to their service for a while, but since we could find nothing there of the spirit of Whitsuntide we left, and sauntered along the Rhine to our lodgings to order our dinner. We noticed then, among all the boats, one that had just arrived, and we hoped it was the boat expected yesterday. Loudly and in jest, I yelled down (B. was not with us at the time) as though a new part of the world had just been discovered, and stuck my head in under the roof of the boat. I saw all manner of people moving about inside.

A man of about sixty came forward, looked me over, held out his hand. As we shook hands, he addressed me, "Well, how are you?" I did not know at the time that this is the general greeting in America. "So-so," was my reply. I asked him, "Where do you [using the formal *Sie*] come from and where are you going?" "Call me 'you' [*du*]! I will do the same with you. I'm a Separatist and that's why I want it this way. Now then, I came down the Neckar with my people from Stuttgart. We want to go to America together, if we're lucky. This is the third time I've made the trip, so I know a little about how to do it. What are you doing here, anyway? I can see you don't come from around here." "I come from Switzerland and want to go to America, too. We could go together." "That's all very well, but can you pay your passage?" I assured him I could. "Well, that's good. Otherwise I would have advised you against going. Emigrants who cannot pay their passage aren't well off these days. It isn't easy to get a captain to accept them. If he did take them, they would find, when they got there, that they didn't fare as well as they might have once. Just now they are having hard times in America, and so there's no lack of workers."

This is quite a character, I thought; and yet the man must know something and have experienced much. His original and unusual behavior seemed strange to me at first, as pleased as I was to have met this man. I had hopes of going with these people, not just to Amsterdam, but from there across the sea. We did not waste any more time and asked the boatman if he would take the three of us along. He said he didn't have anything against it, if the man I had spoken to permitted it. He was the leader of the group and had hired the boatman and the boat for the journey to Amsterdam. I hurried over to see the man (his name is Vetter and I will refer to him this way in the future).[4] I asked him to take us along. "Well," he said, "if you're satisfied with the place — we are, however, quite crowded — I have nothing against your coming. Just decide on the fare with the Skipper, then it's all right. I know how it is with emigrants; they welcome every opportunity to travel on. People should be accommodating and friendly to each other wherever they can. It is their duty. However, I have reason to be careful, because I've been betrayed and deceived by emigrants more than once. I don't think there's anything wrong with you, though; I think you're honest Swiss."

This man pleased me more and more. I saw that he had a healthy understanding of people based upon experience. Indeed, he would have to make many more such judgments. Naturally he was a bit suspicious of other people, for very understandable causes; it was partly because he was a member of a sect, and partly because he had experienced many times the fact that not everyone is what he claims to be.

Now we contracted with the boatman to take us at four and a half

[4] Vetter was a member of the Colony of the Separatists of Zoar in Ohio. In 1817 a group of 300 Separatists from Württemberg, Baden, and Bavaria assembled at Hamburg in preparation for a voyage to America. They were fleeing religious persecution; many of them, including Vetter, had just come from long imprisonment for their religious beliefs. Arriving in Philadelphia in August of 1817, the survivors of the strenuous sea voyage were welcomed by the Quakers, with whom they had many religious principles in common. Under the leadership of Joseph Michael Bäumler (later anglicized to Bimeler) a colony was founded late that year in the wooded hills of Tuscarawas County, Ohio, 84 miles south of Cleveland. The town was named Zoar after the city to which Lot fled after the cities on the plain were devastated (Genesis 19:20–23), and also because the Ohio Canal was built through their lands.

In the fragmentary documents that are still extant, reference is made to a John C. Fetter, a Caspar Fetter, and to a family Vetter. The identity of the Vetter whom Rütlinger met is not clear. See E. O. Randall, "The Separatist Society of Zoar," *Ohio Archaeological and Historical Publications*, VIII, 1899, pp. 1–105, and George B. Landis, "The Separatists of Zoar," *American Historical Association Report*, Washington, D.C., 1899, pp. 165–220.

176

thaler per person. This man also seemed to us honest. He did not have at all the character that sailors generally have. Oh, how happy we were to have found this opportunity! Why did our trip have to be so prolonged by bad winds that we reached Mainz only by Whitsuntide? Oh, this meeting was certainly not the result of blind chance! I call it the Fatherly concern of God. I would not go along with anyone making something else of it.

Now we paid our reckoning with the innkeeper's wife and we were very satisfied with her. She gave us a fair and inexpensive bill. She offered many a farewell and all good wishes for our trip. We moved into our new quarters; we met all of the people on board; then we pushed off from Mainz. It is four o'clock in the afternoon.

Bingen

THE trip from Mainz to Bingen is delightful. The vine-clad hills gradually swell into mountains. Toward evening we were completely in the mountains. It was night when we arrived in Bingen. Lights were burning everywhere, and from all the inns we could hear the sound of music and dance and the wild racket one hears in Switzerland at the annual fair. Today is Church Consecration day. We just could not connect this with Whitsunday festivities. Ah me! Religion and tradition are on the decline everywhere. The honest Swiss complains, and not without cause, about the corruption in his own country, but this corruption strikes a Swiss much more as soon as he has crossed the border.

The Separatists bought wine here, because it keeps well at sea. Not every wine, it is said, can stand a sea voyage. Our Skipper did not trust himself to navigate through the Bingenloch alone, and so he took someone from here along. I cannot see anything less than great danger here, especially when the tide is up as it is now. You can still see the ruins of the infamous Mouse Tower, but I must admit you don't hear a single one of the disgusting creatures squeaking. The boat traveled elegantly for several hours through the mountains.

If they are not too precipitous, the steep, bold cliffs are supported by stone walls. Soil is brought in and put behind the walls. Grapes are planted, and one can really say that the cliffs drip with wine.

In these mountains, rich and mighty lords must have risen. Every peak still bears the ruins of castles.

177

Koblenz

THE distant view of this city is magnificent as one comes down the Rhine. Across from the city, the gigantic fortification of Ehrenbreitstein on a bold cliff is being rebuilt. Only a Napoleon could have tried to storm it. The reconstruction is to cost millions.

We had hardly landed here when we were visited by the police and earnestly and firmly prohibited from taking anything from the boat. Soon thereafter came the inspectors to look at our crates and boxes. Vetter welcomed these guests with a drink of Bingen wine. Consequently they gave up any further inspection and took us at our word of honor.

Vetter had a few boxes of merchandise from Germany for the use of their colony in America. These had to be sealed and duty paid on them. According to their value, he had to deposit a certain percentage in cash money until the goods had crossed the border. The deposit amounted to about twenty thaler. I do not know what percentage of the value this is. The boatman would collect the money on the way back. If this arrangement had not been made, Vetter would have had to stay here until word came back that the goods had crossed the border. We were told we would have to show our passports, or else we would be sent back here at the next customs city. Vetter was astonished at this, as he was at having to pay a deposit. Three years ago, he said, it had not been like this.

This city lies in a lovely area. We rummaged through a few streets, but in a great hurry. All of them had beautiful houses. Then we came to the Mosel bridge which was swarming with people because it was Sunday. Here there is a really enchanting view of the charming environs of Koblenz: the handsome, dignified country homes on the green plains and on the rounded distant hills; above, on the heights, the gigantic fortifications; and below, the delightful river gliding along peacefully and smoothly between the forests. It flows under the high, bold arches of the bridge, and shimmering it unites fraternally with the Rhine. It is certainly a paradise. Just at the most beautiful spots the emigrant finds the greatest plots against him, which turn bitter every joyful and noble pleasure.

New quarters

ONE evening we stopped for an hour below Bonn at a little village. As usual the three of us went to an inn which, from the outside, we judged to be the best for a night's lodging. Several more people came along with us to drink a glass of beer. Among them was a druggist, a member of the Württemberger sect; by his behavior he seemed to have a bit more of a sheep's head than a druggist's head. Outside of that, he was a good fellow. When he had smilingly drained his mug, he asked for the bill. The serving maid answered, "One fat man and one fox." We all began to laugh. He asked once more and again the same answer. "What the devil, I'm not joking! What do I owe? I will not be made a fool of." But nothing different: a fat man and a fox. "That is certainly unusual money," he said, and held some change out to the girl so that she could pick these creatures out herself; he did not know them.

The most miserable language that I have ever heard is spoken here. German, Dutch, Flemish, everything so thoroughly corrupted and so thoroughly mixed that one does not understand a word. The most ridiculous sounds are heard.

Our evening meal was ready in the meantime, and it was brought to the table; we enjoyed it thoroughly. Even though they could not understand us and we could not understand them, they had so much natural hospitality that they found the right means of satisfying our wants.

Everything was fine. Then we let it be known that we would like to sleep and took our travel bundles, idly hanging them on our shoulders with hat and cane in hand. We were ready to go up numerous steps to the bedroom since the house was high. But dear God! Things were quite otherwise. This effort was beautifully spared us. They brought several bundles of straw, threw them on the floor, said good night unintelligibly, and closed the door. Here we had our new quarters.

I would like to return again to the druggist I mentioned. When you hear about certain individual characteristics of a person, you can often get insight into his whole character in this way. To present this remarkable fellow more fully, I need to tell nothing more than how he handles his money. He opened his money box, and it revealed unusual contents. Then he took out a bag and opened that. Inside the bag there was a considerable packet wrapped in paper and securely tied with wire. He untied the knot and you could see that there were many little paper packages. In each one there was a coin. The value of the coin was written on each little package. He never carried more than a few kreuzer in his pocket. Each time he had to pay for something, he had to unravel the knots. I asked him why he had the money wrapped up in this fashion. He answered me that he could not bear to hear the clinking and rattling of money. It was lucky for this man that he did not have much money, otherwise he would have spent his whole life packing and unpacking it.

All sorts of things, as they come

IT WAS barely dawn when an alarm came from the boat, signaling departure. We left our beds as reluctantly as though we had been sleeping on featherbeds.

The day rose bright and golden in the east. The lovely sound of a spring concert came from the treetops. The boat splashed agreeably onward. Now for the first time we saw windmills on the shores of the Rhine, their gigantic wings swinging. It is an unusual sight for us.

By seven o'clock we had already arrived in Cologne. We had our breakfast there. While my wife passed the time at a piano, B. and I strolled through the gray and ancient city. You no longer see the 365 churches here.[5] Oh, how the old things disappear.

It seems to me that the character of the people in Cologne is a praiseworthy exception to all other Rhenish cities.

Today we traveled as far as Düsseldorf. This is a beautiful spot. All hills and mountains have disappeared, and the lowlands stretch out before us.

At every town, we were stopped by the disagreeable customs men. The offices never opened in the morning before nine o'clock and were closed again by six o'clock in the evening. If you do not get there at the proper time, you have to wait until the gentlemen are in the mood to do business. They do not inconvenience themselves very readily for travelers. One after the other, in quick succession, we passed the toll cities of Koblenz, Cologne, Düsseldorf, Orsoy, Wesel, Emmerich, and Lobith.

Once in a while, we had Dutch cooking served to us. Potatoes boiled in water, complete with their clothing; roast meat; then melted fat, vinegar, and salt mixed together and lettuce were brought to the table. Each person then prepares the salad and potatoes as he wishes. For the evening meal, salted butter, fat cheese, pumpernickel, and unsalted white bread were served. You take a slice of white bread, spread butter on it, then a slice of cheese is placed upon it and covered with a slice of pumpernickel, and eaten this way. It is really very tasty.

[5] See p. 58n.

180

How to advance quickly

HOW to do this cannot really be learned from us, either from our experience as we rode our water horse alone, or from our experience traveling with the Württembergers.

We had hardly come to Emmerich one evening, the last Prussian city and toll station, when the family from Landau arrived that I had heard of in Mainz. They had not left until the Tuesday after Whitsunday, in the afternoon. This fact did not seem too unusual to me; I could believe that they had arrived at each customs place at a more fortunate hour than we, and so had lost less time. The morning we came to our boat they were already gone. When we got to Lobith (the worst place for emigrants, usually necessitating a stay of several days), there were no Landauers there any more. We were told that they had passed by there long ago and could already have reached Arnhem. It was this that really surprised me. Even Vetter could not solve this puzzle for me. Finally, I figured out that their passport was good only as far as Amsterdam and their effects were listed as merchandise and naturally had to be taxed as such. A boatman, familiar with everything, could do a great deal if one slipped him a good tip. This way of travel is certainly the fastest, but it seems to me to be somewhat risky, and, in any case, costly.

If I were ever to emigrate again, I would take nothing along, not as I did this time. I would have my passport made out for Amsterdam or any other coastal city. Once there, I could go on wherever I wished. When you make a contract with a ship's captain, he asks for no other passport than the payment.

At home, we deliberated when I was given a passport written in German as to whether it should not have been written in French. This did not cause any difficulties on the trip. It would not even have been necessary to have the passport signed by the Prussian and Dutch consuls in Switzerland.

Anxious anticipation of things to come

IN LIFE we often exaggerate what is to come. Either the evil which is to befall us is projected into a too horrible picture, or the pleasant things which we anticipate take on the features of exaggerated attractiveness. Both are only foolish illusions. The reality is neither terrible nor beautiful in the way we imagined it to be.

That is the way it was with Lobith. Such a disgusting picture of this place was drawn for us that it was difficult for us to rise above it and to approach it without being anxious and concerned. We could hardly think that out of hundreds we would be the only ones who got out of here with skins intact.

We had heard so often how people were held here sometimes for from fourteen days to three weeks, and how they had to use up the greater part of their money. We had heard also that no emigrants were permitted to leave this place without depositing three hundred florins in cash until they could produce an affidavit from an authorized person in Arnhem, Utrecht, or Amsterdam vouching for them until their departure for America. This gave me cause to reflect. I had planned to write to Amsterdam from Mainz for such a voucher, which I hoped to get so that the delay in Lobith could be shortened a little.

But now that I was acquainted with Vetter, I thought I would pay exact attention to every step he made and then do what he did. But even this was not necessary, because he offered me his help and counsel. He said this we would, indeed, do. Back in Wesel he had gathered all our passports together and had quickly sent a qualified acquaintance who dealt with such matters to Arnhem with them to bring back a voucher by the time we reached Lobith. Everything was in order, and thereby a considerable load was lifted from my mind. I knew that Vetter did everything very carefully, and so I thought it would not turn out so badly. I was not short of money, God be thanked, should the deposit I described before be demanded of me.

May 24, on a Saturday afternoon, we came to this dreaded place in Lobith. At eight o'clock the passport man came also with the vouchers. Since it was already fairly late, we were afraid our things would not be cleared now, and that we would have to stay here over Sunday. On this day, no such transactions would be made. However, the toll officials were very considerate of us. The inspection and sealing was carried out with dispatch. None of the boxes was searched. Because Vetter was here for the third time and was known as a straightforward, honest Separatist, his declaration was accepted in good faith. For the same reason they accepted the voucher without a deposit. The honest way is still the best and surest of all.

The next morning they made another claim; they showed us an invoice for our passports, and asked that five florins and twelve stüber be paid for each person. I alone had the honor of paying eight florins; why,

I did not know. Perhaps because there were two of us, but still there was not more than one passport, and that certainly was not any heavier than others. I just thought of it this minute! Perhaps it was harder to read than the others. Enough of this; I was very happy about the whole thing. The situation could have been much worse.

Lobith lies in a really lovely area. But most people, having such a difficult time here, rarely notice this. The thought of all the plaguing, hustling, and bustling spoils even the most beautiful things surrounding us. The town, with many very attractive houses and pretty little gardens, lies somewhat elevated in this otherwise flat region. There is a really beautiful view of the lower plains on the other side of the Rhine, where you can see the towers of city and village rising.

My wife and I wished we could cook our own meals, too, like the others on the boat. Our fellow travelers very considerately provided us with all the cooking utensils we needed to cook our own food. We accepted these with sincere appreciation and set ourselves up. It is truly expensive to board in inns for such a long time, even if you try to live simply.

Not far below Lobith the Rhine branches into two channels; one goes to Dordrecht and the other to Rotterdam. Here there is a firmly emplaced boat on which cannons are mounted. At this point one must show proof that all transactions required have been fulfilled in Lobith. Anyone trying to get by this point without giving this proof is fired upon and must pay a fine besides. If he has the proof required, and it is accepted as valid, a horn is blown until the boat has been lost to view downstream.

The flying bridge

IT WAS already late in the afternoon. The sun peeked drearily through the rain clouds and was about to set when we arrived in Arnhem. The city is quite beautiful; the bells from the towers ring joyfully. We had to pay another insignificant sum on our passports here, and then we went on our way. Our patience was about at an end. Every moment we wished we were in Amsterdam. We rowed on without stopping half the night, even though it was pitch dark and rainy besides. Midnight brought a glimpse of the stars through parted clouds. Suddenly the boatman called "Halt!" We were approaching a flying bridge. The boat had to be taken back a little way, so that we could tie it securely to the shore.

We had certainly passed many bridges like this before, and this was nothing new to us. But if we had traveled on, and grazed the roof of the boat against the connecting segment of this bridge, that would have been something new to us.

A flying bridge is really a vessel which, wholly without hand labor, travels back and forth across the river quite by itself. In the middle of the river, a boat is secured by a chain which is attached to the bedrock of the river bottom. Another chain connects the downstream end of this boat to another boat about twenty or thirty feet away, and that boat is connected to another, and so on. In this way six or eight of these boats one after another stretch downstream in a row. At the end of the line of boats and perpendicular to it is the bridge, suspended between two large boats. Ordinarily the bridge is tied to one or the other bank of the Rhine. When the bridge has a cargo of people or merchandise that must be carried across, it is untied from the shore, pushed out, and away it goes, without anything further being done. They swing it back and forth from bank to bank like a pendulum as long as it is needed.

The trip on the canal

FAREWELL, Father Rhine! You have rocked us on your back so often, shown us many things worth seeing. You have never failed us. You helped us night and day, carrying us so well and carefully from our homeland through strange lands to this spot! Thank you, companion of our fatherland, for your friendship and for all the services you have rendered us. We will never see you again. May you always flow so clean and clear and benignly through your lands! May your clear waters never be clouded by the blood of men in battle! May the tears of sorrow and poverty never drop into your silvery waters! May no unfortunate soul seek his grave in your course! So we called back, as we came to a canal, leaving behind this oldest of friends who had accompanied us longest. The gates of a lock opened, a horse was hitched on, away flew our boat, and we saw the Rhine no more.

What a pity that we cannot wander through this area from here to Utrecht at leisure! It is so enchantingly beautiful.

Like the most charming, perfect picture of a living fantasy, the most beautiful country estates were presented to our fleeting view. The houses, tastefully painted and enhanced by Grecian porticos, lay half-hidden in picturesque, shady groves of trees. The beautiful gardens with their attractive garden houses lay next to them. All this gave evidence of the former wealth and prosperity of the Dutch, as reflected in the best taste by this country splendor. Such a festive, comfortable, quiet, and peaceful atmosphere characterized this heavenly place.

One drawbridge after another opened for the quickly passing boats and packets, and just as often hands were extended demanding money for transit. Utrecht is a magnificent city. Here it took a long time until all the locks and drawbridges had been crossed; always money had to be handed out. All of these charges had to be borne by the poor, honest boatman. He had to pay for all incidental fees in tolls and bridge charges as well as lock payments. The passengers traveled free. In truth, the good man had little profit when you consider that he could not take the boat back with him. He had to sell it at any price in Amsterdam.

A little fraud

IN UTRECHT a contract was made with another lightboatman to take us to Amsterdam for six florins. The lightboatmen pull every vessel on the canal from one station to another with horses hitched to the boats. When we were halfway to Amsterdam we made a stop. The lightboatman wanted his six florins. "You'll have them as soon as we get to Amsterdam," our boatman said. "Not so," said the other. "The contract is in effect only to here." Together they went to a commissioner. He told them that people from Utrecht did not have the right to go farther than this place, and by law they could not accept more than two florins. Our boatman was being cheated of four florins. Since the contract was in writing and the lightboatman was only a servant of the man with whom he had made the contract, our boatman should pay him six florins (the agreement actually was written in Dutch and did not extend farther than this place). The official would give the boatman a paper which the lightboatman had to sign, and he assured our boatman that the four florins would be paid back to him on his return trip or a severe penalty would be assigned. I wonder how it turned out. I am afraid that the good man received nothing back. A stranger is a stranger. Out in the wide world one is exposed to cheating and villainy everywhere. A man pays quite dearly for experience and foresight, and when he has purchased a goodly portion of it and wishes to use it to advantage, ha! he finds himself at the end of life's journey when he cannot make much of it. And what does he get out of it?

185

Arrival in Amsterdam and what happened there

ANOTHER horse rushed away with us. Happily we headed for the world-famous city. In the distance we could already see its towers projecting into the sky. We approached with yearning anticipation.

May 27 was the day of our arrival in Amsterdam, and it marked the end of our European journey. We landed on the Amstel in front of the Visopper port where we awaited a new part of our trip. It was two o'clock in the afternoon. We disembarked and went in gay and leisurely mood through the gates of the city, which excited all our wonderment and amazement. It is large, astonishingly large, crossed everywhere by canals.[6] One can traverse the whole city in all directions by land or water. Along the canals, almost all the streets are shaded and made beautiful by trees. I think this is an advantage this city has over many others. The most beautiful streets have magnificent and formally arranged buildings. On both sides of the streets which run into the main street, the houses on both sides rise, step by step, to the middle, and this middle building is incredibly high. Everything is built of brick. Every hour the bells from the main towers ring. Each plays its own melody. All the sounds blend harmoniously, but each is distinguishable. This music was very appealing and attractive to us.

To see a city of 230,000 inhabitants is really no small matter for a Swiss who never came out from behind the mountain peaks before. It would be even more interesting if one of these mountain colossuses would rise to the sky next to such a city, from whose heights one could look down at one sweep upon the mass of buildings on the shores of the sea.

You bump into Jews at every step. They say there are no fewer than 30,000 in the city.[7] Oi weh! oi weh! How they bargain and haggle here!

[6] See p. 68n.

[7] The Jewish population in Amsterdam in the early nineteenth century was heterogeneous in cultural traditions and identification, language, occupation, as well as in social and economic circumstances. The Jews were still subject to restrictions which had burdened them with inequalities. There were, to be sure, as Rütlinger unsubtly points out, Jewish itinerants and charlatans as there were Dutch counterparts — quite possibly in similar proportions. It must be noted in this regard that neither Schweizer nor Rütlinger has been as critical of any other national group as they have of the Dutch.

The Jewish community in Amsterdam was at this time sharply divided between the newer Ashkenazic and older Sephardic inhabitants. It was the latter groups from which most American Jewish colonials derived.

The Marranos, the Portuguese and Spanish Jews, were expelled from the peninsula in the late fifteenth century. Many of them fled to what is now Belgium and,

186

If you just consider the Israelite bootblacks, you are certain that they alone make up this number. It is downright annoying, and funny, too, how these fellows plague you. There is always a swarm of these craftsmen who scream into your ear incessantly, "Boots polished, shoes polished!" Wherever you stand, half a dozen of them quickly set their little boxes down in front of you. They tear at your legs because each one wants to be first, and often one of them tests the durability of his brush on another's head. It is indeed true that you are often in danger of having not only your shoes torn from your feet but even your legs torn from your body.

B. is our guide; otherwise we would get so lost we would never find our way out of here again. He accompanied us to the wharf. Here the Amstel opens into the Zuider Zee. Far around on all sides, everything is crowded with large and small boats, a countless mass of them! We only saw a few large three-masted ships. These rarely come to Amsterdam. They anchor at Helder or on Texel. There merchandise is loaded on smaller boats and brought to the city, or merchandise is transported from here on smaller boats to the big ships.

Evening was approaching so we returned to our boat. We could not sell this until we had made arrangements for a big ship. The Separatists offered us an opportunity to stay entirely with them. Something like this is a great advantage to emigrants, especially if they have to wait a long time in Amsterdam for ship accommodations.

in the late sixteenth century, to Holland, particularly Amsterdam. People in various conditions of life arrived, physicians, merchants, diplomats, lawyers, professors, and others of more ordinary accomplishments. These Sephardic Jews remained strongly identified with the Iberian culture to which they had contributed so much over many centuries. Between the ninth and the fifteenth centuries, Spanish history was Christian-Islamic-Judaic. It was, moreover, as Castro emphasizes, during these centuries that the definite structure of Hispanic life emerged. The Jews expelled from Spain in 1492 rightly regarded themselves as being as thoroughly Spanish as the Christians. They long remained only sojourners in the other parts of Europe to which they fled.

These Sephardic Jews in western Europe, particularly in cities like Amsterdam, were given opportunities to prosper by the developing commerce of the succeeding centuries. They made signal contributions, on their part, to the emergence of European capitalism.

The Jews in Amsterdam developed a considerable literature. Baruch de Spinoza was one of the most distinguished of the Sephardic Jews born in Amsterdam. See Max L. Margolis and Alexander Marx, *A History of the Jewish People* (Philadelphia: Jewish Publication Society of America, 1927), pp. 488–498, 552, 562–563, 611–616; also Americo Castro, *The Structure of Spanish History* (Princeton, N.J.: Princeton University Press, 1954); and Henry V. Besso, *Dramatic Literature of the Sephardic Jews of Amsterdam in the XVIIth and XVIIIth Centuries* (New York: Hispanic Institute, 1947), pp. 1–84.

When we got to the boat, the street nearby was filled with a swarm of people. Dutch shipbrokers were gathered there, because it was already known that we were emigrants. Smoothly and with flattery they offered this or that fine accommodation to America. Long and fat lists were produced of people they had already made arrangements for — whether to America or eternity, I do not know. Others told us that they had almost a full load of passengers, but there was just enough space left to take as many as we were. They were expecting those who had already signed up to arrive any day, coming from Hesse, Prussia, Hanover and so forth. Vetter just laughed at their chatter and handsomely let them spout on. He said that such people were not to be trusted. They were common, arrant cheats. But certainly these rogues could put on such a show that it is no wonder that often people who are inexperienced were shamefully cheated and deceived by them. Whole swarms of ragged Jewish vagabonds crept around here like the plague of the Pharaohs and wanted to trade, or even steal. You had to be wary of these, too.

Vetter said that if in a few days no opportunity arose to continue, he was going to Antwerp to seek passage for his people there. We had decided to go along with him in anything he might undertake.

A beautiful day dawned. Gloriously the sun shone down on the sparkling towers of Amsterdam. The many windmills about the city turned their pinions busily in the golden rays of the sun. This day greeted us in such a friendly way, as though it wished, you might say, to instill a pleasant hope in our souls that we would soon find suitable accommodations for a happy sea voyage.

Today I sought out Mr. von M. and found him and his family to be worthy people with the noble character of honest Swiss. This good, friendly man was greatly interested in us. He immediately inquired about ship accommodations for us, and his tireless efforts were not without results. He sought out Captain Kurz, a well-known, honest American seafarer. He was to take on his cargo in about fourteen days, and he was willing to take us along. Mr. M. said that even if we had to wait three or four weeks, we should wait for this chance. He would also find us inexpensive lodging until that time. I was deeply grateful to him for his more than friendly efforts on our behalf. I told him about our traveling society and how well and cheaply we were able to live with them; I also told him that we would not think of going overseas with anyone but them, because we already knew them well. In Vetter we had an experienced and honest leader. Mr. von M. was so concerned about our welfare that he wanted to see this man personally and speak with him, to be sure that we were not dealing with a cheat. Just as we did, he found Vetter to be an honest man. There was no danger with this man, he said. We visited these good people daily, as long as we were there. There is something inexpressibly wonderful about meeting such people in a completely strange country.

I asked also about the little box which I had sent ahead from home and addressed to this man. But he did not know anything about it yet. What were we to do? We could not and would not wait for it if a chance arose to sail earlier. In that event, I would leave it to Mr. von M. to send it after me.

Now I told Vetter about Captain Kurz. He answered, "I know about that already. I know him personally as an honest man; but we will be delayed too long if we want to go on his ship. It usually takes longer for departure than the captains promise. This one will certainly not leave for another month."

We thought that because we were staying outside of the city, we would not have to deposit our passports. But a police official came to our boat and earnestly informed us that if we wanted to avoid unpleasantness, we should bring our passports to the office immediately. We did this. These gentlemen too wanted a few more guldens from us.

Vetter returned from the city with the news that he had found another ship accommodation. One of the best business houses of Amsterdam, named Karthaus, had received a shipment of merchandise through an American, Captain Browe. His ship was returning to Baltimore completely empty within the next few days. It was the same boat Vetter had crossed on three years ago. The ship is called the *Massasoit*; it is a large three-master. The Captain would permit us to feed ourselves. We would have to provide ourselves with enough food for no less than one hundred days. He asked one hundred florins per person for our fare and promised sufficient fuel and water. This was very pleasant news for us.

I have forgotten to report that we met the family from Landau at the same spot where we landed. Vetter, the Landauer, and I went to the exchange together. This is a place where merchants, ship captains, and whoever will, gather daily. We arranged our contract there and were able to lower the fare to ninety-five florins. We had to pay the full sum here at Karthaus, however. Vetter said there was no danger in this, because he had known this business house for a long time. Furthermore, our passports would not be returned to us until we could show the receipt for our passage payment. This meant that we had to deal carefully. But there was nothing to worry about, even if the rope were put around our necks. We had the means in hand to see that it did not get knotted.

Our fare was paid, and we received our contract papers. Now for the shopping. First we bought a bed and the necessary clothing. Then we bought food supplies: zwieback, meat, butter, white flour, rice, barley, peas, cheese, dried prunes, coffee, sugar, tea, figs, lemons, various spices, and brandy and wine. The latter we got from the Separatists. It is a good idea to do as they do and bring these along from the Rhineland. You do not get a good medium wine here. The French, Spanish, and Island wines are too expensive. You have to think everything over carefully to be sure that nothing is forgotten. Once on the ocean you cannot go off to cities and towns to shop for necessities.

How many times we had to scour the city from one end to the other until we had everything gathered together at the proper place. During this time we often got lost on streets in which there were nothing but disorderly houses. Everywhere the wh———s stood at the door, gaily dressed, and called out to us, "Come on in, farmer!" Or sometimes they even pulled us by the sleeve. When you come upon parts of the city like this, you begin to think that there is not one decent house to be found. I got very angry at being accosted like this, and would have liked to lash out left and right like a Hussar with his sword. Young, inexperienced people have reason to be careful in such places. It is no wonder that some return home from foreign lands ruined in body and soul.

The trip to Helder

ON THE fourth of June we took leave of our dear M. family after they had given us some books, gelatin tablets, and a bottle of a costly beverage as a souvenir. It certainly hurt us to leave these good people. We did not see our B. again. I do not really know what to make of his stay in Amsterdam. Every time I visited him in his lodgings, it seemed to me he looked as though he had just returned from a long journey which had tired and strained him very much. I hope that he did not penetrate too deeply into the dark alleys and become lost. I would be exceedingly sorry. In him we had an excellent traveling companion to whom we could entrust everything. He took care of all that needed to be done since he had accurate knowledge about what had to be provided for. Thus we did not have to worry about anything.

191

Our things were loaded on a lighter, and at seven o'clock in the evening we left Amsterdam. We glanced back often at this beautiful city and watched the last rays of the sun fade upon the peaks of the towers and at last disappear from our view. It was a beautiful moonlit night. The wind chased away the fleeing clouds from over our heads and rocked the boat vigorously. We looked in astonishment at the first surge of the sea and at the waves which broke against the ship in the silver light of the moon. Our attention, however, was directed to something else. Seasickness was already beginning, especially among the women. They could not bear this kind of sedan chair very well. They began to vomit, making so much noise that you could no longer hear the sound of the waves. They looked very comical, because it was all new to them. I hied myself to the deck and was spared.

The following afternoon we arrived at our large ship in Helder. It lay near shore. What a palace! Our eyes widened in amazement, and we looked forward eagerly to moving into such an edifice. Many boats lay at anchor and awaited a good wind for departure or waited for the cargo which was to be loaded into them. Now our things were put on board, and we ourselves boarded the ship. The sailors were working on the sails and rigging and the ship's carpenter was setting up our sleeping quarters. The bunks were in pairs, one on top of the other, near the Captain's cabin, in each of which three or four people could lie comfortably. Several of the sailors can speak German, and this pleased us very much. The Captain also speaks German as well as he does English. The cook is a black man, which is usually the case on ships. Now our own cooking began. We divided ourselves up into groups, so that it would be less inconvenient to cook. A single man, a Württemberger, joined our group. He was a cooper by trade. From him we bought another sack of potatoes. These are delicious things on a boat.

We are now waiting calmly for our departure. The time does not seem long to us at all. We stroll frequently on this island at the edge of the ocean. Even though not a bush or tree grows here, and only sparse grass sticks out of the sand, this area has a certain attraction for me. The many ships, always coming and going, enliven the place. The shores are rather rocky. The grass which projects so sharply from the sand reminds me of high alpine lands. Often, in the warm sun, I imagined I was resting in the green mountains. And I looked out upon the churning sea and I felt happy inside.

Our Captain has just returned from Amsterdam. He informs us that

192

he plans to leave with the first good wind. I have a letter from Mr. von M., telling me that he has received a notice about our crate. We would be very happy if we could still get it on board, because it contains our books.

Passengers are still coming on board our ship: a little man and a young lady with a boy, a bird dealer with about one hundred live songbirds of all varieties, and a Dutch woman. Now our entire passenger list has reached twenty-five.

Trip through the channel

AFTER the water had been taken on and everything was ready on the ship, the favorable wind promptly arrived. A dark, stormy night produced it.

The anchors were raised and our ship began the great sea voyage on the morning of June 10. Here, unfortunately, one must wait for a favorable wind before passing through the channel. Some passengers have had to wait for four to six weeks before a favorable wind came. Moreover, we were still a bit worried that we might be thoroughly buffeted about in the channel. Things were going well now, in any case.

Toward afternoon, the wind got stronger and by seven o'clock in the evening we had lost sight of all land, and only sky and water surrounded us. Since this is a light ship, there was considerable motion all night, and a general revolution of seasickness occurred. My wife is one of the first to be troubled by it. Hardly anyone wanted to get out of bed this morning. I had to make my own black coffee and drink it alone as well. My little wife lay in bed almost the entire day. She did not vomit, but she felt like it, and she got very dizzy when she tried to get up. I persuaded her to go out on deck to enjoy the fresh air there, and this helped her a great deal. The enjoyment of fresh air on deck is the best remedy for seasickness. One should drag people up on deck, if they do not have strength to go up themselves.

I got up very early on the morning of the twelfth. How wonderfully changed was the scene. To the left the high coast of France was visible; to the right that of England. That's how close we were to these two important countries, which have made such a great impression upon the world. But just as in the course of fate, France sank before England. By nine o'clock we had lost all trace of the French coast; England, on the contrary, appeared closer and closer. The snow-white chalk cliffs sparkled dazzlingly before us. We could clearly distinguish houses, meadows, and fields on the soft, rising hills above the white shore. The waters were teeming with large and small craft. A Dutch war frigate, about forty cannon strong, sailed proudly and splendidly past us. They say it is bound for Gibraltar. The delightful weather made everything gay and bright today. With a fresh northeaster we moved rapidly away from the friendly shores. Sometimes we saw hills, blooming gold with turnip fields, extending down to the ocean. Sometimes we saw high, perpendicular cliffs, sometimes high lighthouse towers or dwellings scattered about in the green meadows. These were the lovely prospects which appeared to us. It is too bad that one could not see a bush or a tree or a forest. All of a sudden we were in a dead calm. It was strange, because the boats we could see near us had continued good wind, but we did not get it again for almost an hour.

After two days we had lost all sight of land. There was not a trace of Europe to be seen. It was a good thing that regret for the step we had taken did not awaken in our hearts, or we would have been in a sorry state. The ocean voyage would have become hell to us. But no, we were of good courage and determination; we were ready to meet whatever came along.

The curtain has fallen behind us; it shuts out so many tender images which we saw on the stage of Europe. All that is beloved and pleasant we carry over in our hearts to another world; the things which once caused us unpleasantness we are happy to leave behind and try to banish from our minds. The theater of our surroundings is a sceneless void; it has been transformed into a bare stage. Every object has withdrawn behind the hazy circle of the horizon. We cast our eyes forward and wait patiently until a new curtain goes up in the west. This will reveal to us other objects, which, with exact observation, we can compare with those that once surrounded us in the east; we can absorb everything beautiful and good into our beings. So the charm of reality and the joy of memory will blend together, and nothing more will remain for us in life but to keep these well-ordered and pure.

Now the compasses are being hung up; the quadrants make their appearance; the keeping of the log begins. The plumbline will be thrown out in a few more days. We must still be along the English coast.

In the far distance we see a ship. Our Captain observes it through his telescope and reports it is an English frigate. Quickly he has the American flag hoisted. This surprises me because of the distance. The other ship, however, does not return this friendly sea greeting with its flag.

194

The sea has changed color all of a sudden. Earlier it was light green; now, however, it is completely blue-black. It seems that we have come into the open sea. Bottom can no longer be found.

Description of our ship

OUR ship is really large, but it is rather old and uncoppered. It can hold 380 tons of cargo. Now it is quite empty and has nothing but ballast. Three large masts rise skyward, the foremast, mainmast, and mizzenmast. Projecting in front is the bowsprit. On all these masts twenty to twenty-four sails fly when the wind is favorable. On both sides of the ship rigging is attached, running up to the tops of the masts and holding them fast. Ropes extend from one crow's nest to another and beyond. The mainmast has three sections, on which four sails of various sizes billow out. These hang on large, sturdy spars which can, by means of ropes, be turned, raised, and lowered. On these bars, and on hundreds of taut ropes, the sailors climb about, even in stormy weather and darkest night, like spiders in their webs. The foremast has two sections and three sails. The mizzenmast has three sails and another one nearby. In front, on the bowsprit, three more sails flutter. If the wind is very favorable auxiliary sails are put up everywhere. It is a glorious spectacle to see such a ship in full sail move forward proudly.

There is a floor over the entire boat, with a railing so you won't tumble over by accident. In back, below deck, the Captain's cabin is located. It has windows and is beautifully furnished. There are small side rooms for eminent passengers. In front is the sailors' cabin and between these two is the area for passengers or merchandise. The lower hold is a damp, dark hole in which the water barrels and other wares are kept. In the middle of the deck is the kitchen, which is bound to the deck by ropes and chains. In front of this is the big lifeboat, and to the rear of the ship a small lifeboat is tied on. We would set out in these if the large ship were crushed against a cliff or stranded in shallows. I am willing to forgo such a pleasure outing, however.

In the rear part of the deck there is a neat little cabin, comfortably equipped for sitting, designed for the use of those who need to relieve themselves. It offers each person relief as well from pressing and burdensome concerns. In front of this is the wheel of the great rudder. Before the pilot's eye is a case in which the compasses are hung, illuminated by a lamp at night. In front on the deck is the anchor pulley.

On a small crossbeam there is a bell about the size of a chapel bell, which is rung at certain times of day. One stair leads from the deck to the Captain's quarters. Another leads down to the middle room. On both sides of the case which contains the compasses and under which is the staircase to the cabin, there are comfortable benches to sit upon, and under them are neatly fashioned chicken coops. Next to the mainmast there are two water pumps which go down to the lower hold. These give the sailors a great deal of work when the ship is leaking and taking on a goodly amount of water. On the bow of the ship, under the bowsprit, the god of the sea is carved in wood, life-sized, with hair and clothing streaming backward. Even though our ship is large, it is easily moved by the wind because it does not lie deep in the water. They usually do not take on more ballast than is necessary.

The ship's crew

IN ADDITION to the Captain, the ship had a first and second mate, a cabin boy, a cook, and eight sailors. There was also a cat, but I am not certain whether it was a member of the crew or not.

We had been given many unpleasant descriptions of ships' crews in the past. Consequently we did not have a very good opinion of them when we boarded the ship. But we were soon convinced that even among these rough, raw fellows there were some laudable exceptions.

The Captain was a modest, friendly man, not at all proud as most of them are. He spoke with everyone on board, showed consideration wherever he could. He gave us the freedom of the whole ship, as well as of the kitchen. We could use as much water as we wanted, and we could cook whenever we liked. He was an experienced and diligent seaman, but besides that he had little knowledge. Only when the trip was taking too long in his opinion and the wind was unfavorable did he show his rough seaman's character. He cursed and complained on such occasions quite woefully.

The mates, the cook, and the sailors were altogether very pleasing, fine people as long as they were on board ship. I must say that I did not hear them utter one coarse word. Among themselves they were always peaceful. Toward the women they were so modest and well behaved that they were far from ever allowing themselves any discourtesy. We became very fond of all of them, and we treated them like old acquaintances. When they had to do hard and dangerous work, we felt sorry for them. They

196

did everything so willingly, without complaint. During the day they were all together. They took turns at the wheel every hour.

They always had something to do. In addition to moving the sails, either they were unbraiding old ropes and making and twisting new ones out of them, or they had to tar the ropes and rigging. There was always something to improve or mend. In calm weather or in good wind their work was fairly light; but in rainy weather and storm I would not care to be a sailor. They took their bearings every two hours. Only a few times did we have such a good wind that the ship made eight or nine miles in an hour. At eight o'clock in the evening half the sailors went to bed. At twelve o'clock at night a bell was rung and the second half went to sleep and the others came on deck. At four o'clock they changed again; at eight o'clock in the morning they all came on deck again. During rough, raw weather they all had to remain awake the entire night. The Captain and the mates always took turns as well. One of them always had to take command. It is no joke to go out in a storm on a dark night and climb to the high masts and there crawl on your belly to the far end of a yardarm in order to pull in and gather up the sails. Every noon the Captain, and often the mates too, came on deck with quadrants, observed the geographic latitude of our ship, and determined the moment of noon, when the bell was rung again. Every morning and evening the water had to be pumped out of the hold again. Toward the end of our trip the deck was scrubbed every morning and cleaned with sand. The whole ship had to be newly painted, and the big ropes and rigging freshly tarred. The food of the sailors consisted of salt meat, bacon, peas, zwieback, tea, and coffee; they received no whiskey. The Captain treated them rather meagerly, but he lived very simply himself. A sailor gets around twelve to fifteen dollars a month. Ours, however, had to provide their own tea and coffee, which they drank morning and evening. On Sundays they usually mended their clothes or wove themselves straw hats. They were very good at this.

The passengers

I WILL be through with the passengers quickly. All ate and drank and felt fine. They cooked and roasted three, four, or five times a day. Some of them got as fat as monks on board ship. The women, after they had seen everything thoroughly and time began to drag, started to sew and knit when they were not cooking and eating, or sleeping, or being

197

seasick. You can well imagine how much time was left over to work in. The men were always making clever plans for the future. Often they looked back and observed themselves in some past foolishness, whereupon, with a smug little laugh, they rejoiced in discovering how much wiser they had become. Sometimes they all got together, stuffed their pipes or had a little snuff, and then one or another pulled out a tale from the chamber of his experience, in order to instruct or shock with it. Among the single men and women love affairs developed. That is the way it goes when they live well and do not have anything else to worry about. They dwelt in the Elysian fields, though there was neither a gurgling spring running through the woods, nor a meadow in bloom, nor yet shady trees hung with golden fruit anywhere to be seen. The children played together and were happy. In them one could clearly see manifested the poor rearing of their parents, which was unfortunately all too characteristic. But now to the important matter.

First, something about the Separatists according to what Vetter has himself related to me. As is well known, these people would have nothing to do with military service. The former King of Württemberg was a zealous persecutor of this sect, and wanted to force them to serve in his army. They defended themselves vigorously against this, however. He had several hundred brought to the prison at Asperg where they held out valiantly for many years. Vetter was among them. As soon as they were out of prison, three hundred of them decided to go to America together, where they hoped to be able to live undisturbed according to their basic principles. In the year 1817 a few men were sent ahead to Amsterdam and Antwerp to arrange for passage. This they accomplished that spring.

They migrated to the state of Ohio in the interior of the country and there they bought a few thousand acres on which to settle. They held everything in common. Everything was done under the leadership and guidance of a few directors. At first they had to fight many difficulties with great work and effort. Now, however, they are well established. A little city was built which is called Zoar, and there they already have sawmills, flour mills, and some manufacturing establishments. Every year they go down to New Orleans in their own boat, which they load with 1200 to 1500 barrels of flour and other products as well. Even if they only got five dollars a barrel, and that much they would certainly get, this would add up to a pretty sum. If other products which they cultivate are included — cattle and sheep raising they pursue vigorously — you can easily see how this colony is making progress. They want to introduce vineyards as well.

Vetter is infinitely delighted to have found this free colony in America where everyone has prospered. He has already been sent to Württemberg twice to gather money for their people and to take other people of their religious community back with him, if they wish to go. This time, too, he has several accompanying him.

Among them is a shoemaker, a widower with two grown daughters. This man has pursued the philosophers' stone faithfully for many years; he has not quite seized it yet, although he has sacrificed a nice little fortune for it. There is also a woman who had divorced her husband because she went over to this sect. The sect considers marriage wrong.[8] The shoemaker occupied himself with this slut as faithfully as with the philosophers' stone; he would have sacrificed it for her if he had had money. He had planned to join Vetter's colony, but now he has ruined everything. Almost the same thing happened to his two daughters, one because she got along so well with her father and her almost-stepmother, and the other one because she was involved in a love affair with a young carpenter. The young man's father had turned him over to Vetter almost by force to be raised and disciplined in the colony. He seemed to be a bit of a gay and careless fellow. These young people were able to keep their romance a secret for a few weeks. Then Vetter found out about it, and from then on, they did not dare speak a word to each other in the open. Now life on board ship became hell for this scorned pair.

A hefty young girl from Swabia, for whom a miserly Separatist woman was paying passage, gradually became the mistress of our Captain, who has a wife and child. The sailors often jeered at this affair because they were more delicate than he. He prattled that he wanted to marry her and claimed that his wife did not object. When we got to Baltimore, he paid her fare on a steamboat bound for Philadelphia to stay with a brother.

[8] The confession of faith which the Separatist group had formulated while still in Germany provided for marriages contracted by mutual consent before witnesses. Civil authorities were then informed of the marriage. The group rejected entirely the intrusion of priests or preachers (Article VIII). Sexual abstinence was viewed as more commendable than marital relations. Sexual relationships except when necessary to perpetuate the population were held to be sinful and against divine instruction (Article IX). Marriage became increasingly allowed with time. Efforts were consistently made to keep family interests subordinate to community interests. Later the development of family solidarity gave rise to cliques and divisions among members. In the early years of the colony, children were separated from their families, but in later years children were raised in their own families. See Landis, *op. cit.*, pp. 188–200.

The stingy woman could not figure out how she was going to get her passage money back. The girl often laughed and said that when she got to America the passage money would already be paid. Vetter remarked, "That's the way it often goes with people for whom you pay passage. You can't be careful enough. In the home country the circumstances of their lives force them to be honest; the boring and idle life on board ship, as well as the prospect of coming to a free country, develops a completely different character in them. Once they are in America, they think, the gate and door will be opened to every wrong-thinking person to do wicked things without being punished. If one or a hundred go to the devil, what will the man do who trusted them?"

The man from Landau, by the name of Lauer, whose family was used to the best, had five poorly brought-up children. At home, it appears, he had lived very well and pleasurably, spending a great deal of money. He was well able to pay his passage, but he did not have a cent left over. What were these people going to do? It was a good thing he was a cooper and beer-brewer. It is also well for him that he has a son-in-law in America with whom he can stay for a while. However, this man is still in a difficult situation, because he imagines everything in America to be so good and wonderful. If any man feels betrayed in his hopes it is this man.

About two girls I do not know what to say except that they were vain creatures, as they all are; other than that they were honest things.

The little man from Zweibrücken and his even littler wife were accompanied by their ten-year-old son. Her little mouth and little tongue moved incessantly by means of a thousand swift muscles. These otherwise good people — how were they going to get along in America? One time on the ship we got to talking about our passports. The little man showed his too, and what was it? Nothing but a letter of recommendation from one of his town officials; and yet they came through all the rascality all the way down the Rhine. From Bingen they had to pay a boatman ninety florins to get to Amsterdam. It seems that these fellows know how to manage things if they get paid enough. I still wonder now how these very simple people, even at great sacrifice of money, did manage somehow to get through. In Amsterdam they instructed their innkeeper to buy certain specific supplies for their sea voyage. The innkeeper had everything brought to the ship and gave them the bill. It was very high. They paid for everything in their honest way, without thinking that anything might be wrong with it. Only after they were on their way did they see

200

that they had been cheated. Much was not there for which they had paid; and what was there was of the worst quality. The zwieback was so black and moldy that pigs would hardly have eaten it. What could they do? They simply had to put up with it. It was fortunate that these people had a large supply of dried meat and bacon which they had brought from home; otherwise they would have been in an exceedingly difficult situation. When these people arrive in America, they will have about fifty thaler left, but no profession, nothing but their helplessness. Soon that little sum of money will be used up, and then what kind of fate is left for them? They will have to do farm work, and this is so difficult that new immigrants cannot stand it for long. Still God helped them wonderfully this far, and I hope He will stand by them in the future.

The Dutch woman has to work to pay off her passage. She found a good job in Baltimore, immediately upon arrival, in the home of the merchant who owns this ship. She speaks English well, and she is a very proper and well-mannered person. Our Captain tried in vain to start an illicit affair with her, since she lived in the same quarters with him. Single women can find employment the most readily here. We had hardly arrived when inquiries were made about them.

The birdman, who was from Saxony, was a stubborn, uncomplimentary little man. He always behaved as though he knew all sorts of secret arts, and he complained miserably about America, because he had been there once before. It seemed that his cherished hopes, instead of placing a golden crown on his head, had only put a lousy hat on it instead. As I said before, he had about one hundred songbirds with him, many of them trained singers. These creatures brought us much pleasure. They were always so cheerful, it made us think we were in the woods. Unfortunately about twenty of the best singers died. This was a considerable loss for the man. He assured us that he would not have sold a one of them under thirty thaler.

The stingy Separatist woman I mention only because she sold us a little barrel of wine; the reason she did, according to her, was that she did not dare drink it because it made her feel too good. The devil was far too crafty; he was always sneaking around, trying to lead people astray. And how easily this could happen if she drank the wine — then he could mislead her into thinking indiscreet thoughts.

My little wife and I, indeed, also belonged to the passengers; we were on the same journey to America as all the others. We got more or less acquainted with everyone, and in turn we were known more or less by all of them. Each one of them, if he wished, like me, to take pen in hand to describe us and pass judgment on us, would certainly make his own comments about us, just as I did about them. I think this picture, in its way, could be hung among them without standing out particularly. I do not trust myself to portray ourselves. The same thing could happen to me that the Separatist woman spoke of in connection with drinking wine. The devil could easily find an opportunity in this to mislead me into much too great self-indulgence and self-praise. Therefore I would rather withhold my pen from such a possibility.

Sea creatures

A KIND of sea-swallow constantly flies about the ship in a small flock, eagerly snapping up any morsels thrown into the water. Ordinarily they do not make a sound until twilight; then for a while they make a screeching sound. These birds accompanied us until we were almost on land; then they left us and another kind of sea bird, much larger, appeared.

Often I stood for hours on deck at the railing, staring into the ocean to see if I could discover some kind of sea monster about to declare war against our ship. But for many days I could discover nothing, not even one little fish. Once when I was watching the ocean in this way, I noticed in the distance, toward the southeast, a rapid change in the water. The movement came closer and I saw thousands of fish leaping to form arches high above the water. They were heading rapidly for our ship. Everybody ran to see this miracle. They lingered about the ship, rocked all around it as though they wanted to admire it. Across their backs they were reddish-yellow and their bellies were white. They must have been about four feet long and weighed about a hundred pounds. Their heads were exactly like those of pigs. Such fellows we saw almost daily for a long time. The sailors frequently threw little harpoons at them, but they could never catch one.

Once, far in the distance, a whale swam by. He shot water like a fire hose, high into the air. Unfortunately he did not come close enough for us to see him well.

Another time I saw a fish slowly swim up to our ship. This fish was fairly thin and must have been about six feet long. A horn which projected three feet in front of its head made me think that it might be a sawfish. Its color was dark brown.

202

Once we were becalmed. The ocean lay before us like a smooth mirror. Then from all sides many large fish swam toward the ship and played a saucy game around us. First they raised their heads out of the water. There was a round hole on their heads. As they dived they sprayed a stream of water into the air as though from a hose; then they gradually turned around and showed themselves full length, so you could see their entire backs down to their tails quite clearly. They played around in this manner for a long time. They must certainly have been twelve to fifteen feet long and as thick as a big ox. We interpreted their play as meaning a storm was coming, but we were spared this. This peaceful scene changed quickly, though, and again we had considerable wind.

We often saw solitary fish, rather large ones, with wide jaws. These were said to be sharks, predatory fish. If a human body, dead or alive, were in the water, instinct would lead them to it from afar to give their welcome friend a kiss, and then, out of sheer love, devour him completely.

One afternoon when the sea was mirror-smooth and the sun shone warmly, the shining water offered a friendly invitation to swim. If I had been able to swim I too would have gone into this oversized bathtub and enjoyed myself also. The Captain threw off his outer clothing and plunged into the calm water. He swam around like a fish, diving up and down. Zoom, one of those sharks came along, his fins moving fast. The Captain barely had time to grab the rope he had climbed down on and to swing himself above the surface of the water when the fish was already snapping at his feet. Now I can see that being a nonswimmer can also save your life. If I had been able to swim I would certainly have gone into the water; just as certainly such a fish would have gulped me down into his stomach. He would hardly have spewed me up on land like another Jonah.

While we were crossing the Newfoundland Banks, the Captain and the sailors often tried to catch fish from the bottom of the sea when the wind was still. The ocean was not any more than about twenty to twenty-five fathoms deep. They shared their booty with us. It was an excellent kind of fish, weighing from four to ten pounds, and as tasty as trout. Once they pulled out a remarkable fellow, with the shape of a butterfly: a thin, small tail shaped like a sword and covered with spines and two somewhat smaller webbed feet. Its broad wings had symmetrically arranged spots of yellow-brown and black. It was completely without fins. All of this gave him a truly wonderful look. He could have weighed as much as twenty to thirty pounds. I saw a fish exactly like it later in the museum in Philadelphia. On the Newfoundland Banks we often saw flying fish, too.

The Portuguese Man-of-War

WE OFTEN saw something that looked like a greenish-red half-sphere of glass swim past the ship. The Captain said that this creature was called the Portuguese Man-of-War. These were marvelous for making the skin fine and soft if you rubbed your hands with them. The women wished nothing more than to get such a thing, as acquiring delicate hands so easily and inexpensively had a much too great appeal to them. We know only too well how much this vain sex likes to pay ceremonial calls with lovely little hands. The thing was agreed upon. A sailor brought one up in a water bucket. It was like a bubble in the form of a half-moon. The curved bow lay distended on the water. It was iridescent and its colors changed from red to green to blue and white, transparent as glass. Below it, extending into the water like strings of pearls, was a tuft of fibers, which like the roots of a plant, gave the bubble balance. As soon as the plant or animal comes out of the water it expands many feet in size and then quickly contracts again, as soon as it is back in its own element. Many hands reached for it; a girl and an inquisitive boy had the honor of receiving the prize of being the first to touch it. But woe! Horrible screams rang out. They shook their hands wildly and did not know what to do. It was funny and at the same time really pitiful. The boy certainly endured hellish pain for several hours. His hands swelled and were covered with blisters as though they had been rubbed with nettles. The girl suffered less because she had only touched it with the inside of her hand.

Of wind and weather and a disappointed hope

WE ALWAYS had fairly good wind until sundown. The wind came mostly from the north and northeast, therefore we were sailing in a southerly direction. The sky had not been clouded by a single day of rain, and no great storms had shaken us. After the sun went down the west winds started; southwest, northwest, and direct west winds were always a hindrance to our progress to the very end of the ocean voyage. Every time our ship was shaken heavily by the wind, nausea and vomiting began among some of the passengers. I never had seasickness or any trace of it, and I was not envious of those who did.

One night toward the end of June, when the first mate took the night watch, he lay down on deck and fell asleep, just at a time when the high sails should have been taken in because a black cloud and a strong wind were roaring toward us. The Captain woke up and noticed that things were not quite right on the ship. He went up on deck and found the watchman asleep. The thunder was terrible, but it did not come from the clouds, which passed peacefully overhead.

About this time I had a hunch that we must be near the Azores. I had always observed the course of the ship closely, and I noticed by my pocket watch, which I had kept running since we left Holland, that we must be approximately on the meridian of the Azores.

The following day, the 28th of June, the Captain said that we would see something of the Azores Islands that day. We were very happy about this. But as it turned out it was not true. We waited for several days for the pleasure, but unfortunately in the end we never did experience it. I would have been so happy to see even one of these beautiful islands. It must be an enchanting sight, jutting out of the water in the middle of the ocean. The Captain said that we had sailed through the middle of the island group. We could be certain that we were near land because we saw all sorts of marvelous corals, various shellfish, and huge turtles.

One night I dreamed I was back home and on a botanical trip into the Alps with my friend Forrer.[9] When I awakened I thought about it and realized that it was exactly the time at which every summer we roamed through the high mountain land together, shouting for joy. These images possessed my mind all day.

The meeting of ships at sea

THIS was a pleasure we often had. Few days passed in which we did not see a ship either at a distance or near by. It is really a delightful experience when on the wide uniform expanse of the ocean ships from

[9] The botanist-teacher Johannes Forrer (1800–1844) was, like his friend Rütlinger, born in Wildhaus. Both were trained as teachers in the normal school established by Reverend Steinmüller. Both also wrote poetry in the Toggenburger dialect. Forrer wrote for the *Alpenbote* published in Ebnat, St. Gallen. The general esteem for Forrer as a person and as a teacher was expressed by Reverend Kranich of Hemberg (Schweizer's editor) in his eulogy on the occasion of Forrer's death. See Armin Müller, *Schulgeschichte des Städtchens Lichtensteig* (Lichtensteig, St. Gallen: O. Malder & Co., 1963), pp. 60–63.

all sides loom out of the vastness and pass one another like travelers on land.

When ships pass very close to one another, the Captains speak to each other through megaphones. They ask each other, "From where?" "To where?" "How long at sea?" In what longitude did they think they were? Then they wish each other good luck on their trip. Often it happens that when a Captain sees a ship at some distance and it is not going in a direction which would make them meet, and yet he would like very much to speak to the Captain of that ship, he gives a signal by a certain position of one of the sails. As soon as the other Captain realizes this, he joins the other in trying to bring their ships together. No honest Skipper tries to avoid such a request.

Several of us were still on deck at twilight on one occasion when the fog lay thick on the ocean. Suddenly the prow of a ship sailing toward us thrust through the darkness and mist. The sailors shouted. Only by means of a quick turn of the wheel was a collision of the ships avoided. Many ships have apparently met with accidents just in this way.

On the 25th of July we saw a brig far ahead of us. As we approached it we noticed that its sails were so set as to avoid moving. They lowered a boat and came toward us. It soon drew near us and the three men who were on the boat requested permission to come on board. Ropes were thrown down to them for this purpose. One of the men, the Captain of the brig, went into the cabin with our Captain. We found out that they came from Ireland, and had already been at sea for fifty-one days, on their way to New York. They were suffering from the lack of certain supplies, and that was why they were here. Our Captain gave them a sack of zwieback, vinegar, brandy, and other things. We passengers also prepared a sack full of zwieback for them since we were well supplied with this. It must be a sad predicament when food supplies give out on the ocean, the wind is constantly unfavorable, and fortune does not bring another ship to help.

Little storms, sea and sky phenomena, fog, and boredom

ONE afternoon a cloud as black as night came along from the southwest. The Captain was asleep and the first mate, who was a lazy and inattentive fellow, had the watch. The cloud approached and everyone saw that it was driven by a strong wind. The mate did not have the sails pulled in. I had hung my pants in front on the sprit to dry and since raindrops were already falling I wanted to get them. While I was getting them down, a powerful gust of wind struck the ship, and with a burst of thunder the huge bar in front broke in two at my feet like a weak pipe. It was dashed into the sea right past me. I let my pants hang where they were and got away from there. If they had been hung a bit higher, I would have learned to swim to my death in the waves.

One morning very early, when everyone was still sleeping and snoring in the room, suddenly a terrible noise and trampling of the sailors on deck began. From the shouting and commands from the Captain one would have thought our ship had been split on a rock. Everyone woke up and all eyes were wide open. Anyone who had fallen asleep on his back now found himself turned over on his stomach, and vice versa. The ship was receiving knocks more severe than ever before so that everything which was not tied fast went back and forth in the room. We arose and sought to find peace and quiet among the normally motionless sacks, which now suddenly became alive. We who were always alive had enough trouble just to keep standing up. This we were able to do only when we could grasp a post and hold fast to it. The greatest spectacle, however, was provided by our sack of peas. It was not securely tied and so it opened up. The wonderful little things made the most comical, joyful leaps all around the room. This comedy too had its clown. After a while I was able to capture it and tie it up, otherwise we would have lost this product completely. This little storm was soon over.

One evening, long after sundown, when daylight was still barely glimmering in the west, a shining brightness was visible on the northern horizon as though the sun had just gone down there. I asked the Captain what kind of a phenomenon this might be. He said that it was the so-called aurora borealis.

It is unbelievable what a magnificent spectacle sunrise and sunset are at sea — when the sun gradually sets towards the horizon and its glowing sphere seems to grow larger and larger. Its rays seem to withdraw into their own golden stream and their sparkle creates an ocean of fire; its surface glows with magnificence and beauty from within. The rays are mirrored on the foaming waves which shimmer like rubies. Then this purple world dips down into the sea and the glittering streak on the ocean grows smaller and smaller until the last purple spark merges into the sun on the distant horizon and disappears. Oh, what a glorious spectacle!

207

We often passed through ocean currents. During the quietest weather the water was more turbulent and moved the ship more strongly than during very unfavorable winds. The ocean roared and raged powerfully. The water in such currents is generally lukewarm and next to these currents it is very cold. The Captain tried to avoid the currents wherever possible because the voyage was always prolonged by them since the current always pressed strongly eastward.

While we were going over the Banks, time passed very slowly for me. It is always foggy and damp there. On such days everyone stuck to his room and each one, through some occupation or other, sought to win the battle against boredom. One person made buckets, the other barrels, but there was no wine in them. Another person carved ladles because he could not do anything else; another mended shoes without leather; and so on. I stayed in bed, thinking: I can hear best up here, and I am in no one's way. Here I studied the faces and moods below, gathered and cooked them together. The resulting extract taken as medicine would, I was convinced, have resulted in nausea and strenuous vomiting.

The Captain said that it was dangerous to sail over the Newfoundland Banks at this time of the year because of the icebergs which drift about there. Because of them most seafarers took a southern route. Sailing through the Banks was all the more dangerous because it was always enshrouded in fog, and the icebergs could not be seen from a distance and hence avoided. The previous year a beautiful new ship on its first trip from Liverpool had been completely wrecked here. The people on board had been able to save themselves by taking to the lifeboats, but they were beaten about in the sea for seven days before they found land and safety.

As soon as we had the accursed Banks behind us, bright, beautiful weather began again and we noticed that land winds began to reach us. Now we often saw green grass, complete with roots, swimming in the water; a lovely, hopeful sight. Several times we came to very unusual places. In the distance we could see a white, shimmering streak on the sea, like a road, extending as far as the eye could see from one end of the horizon to the other. When you get close to it, it looks as though you were passing a smooth, motionless silver river. On each side foamy moving shores are formed and between them the water lies completely still. The waves lap like the waves on a rocky shore. Grass and moss lie thick on these still surfaces.

Land! Land!

THE 3rd of August I arose early in the morning, but since it looked dreary and rainy I went back to bed. After we had eaten a late breakfast and the rain ceased, we drifted up on deck. A very pleasant breeze began to blow, while the clouds parted and the sky cleared. Vetter and I stood at the railing and chatted. All of a sudden one man called, directing his glance northward, "Look, Swiss, over there, I think I see land." I was amazed, looked more carefully and saw clearly that it was so. Oh, how happy we were! "Land! Land!" I cried. The news traveled from mouth to mouth and all gathered together to see the longed-for land. The sailors verified our opinion and joyful brightness streamed from every eye. Only the Captain seemed to express no pleasure about it. He looked sullen and only occasionally cast secret, dark glances toward land. We could sense that this land was not in the right place, or rather his ship was not in the right place.

It turned out that this land was Long Island. The sailors said that we could be in New York in two days if that were our destination. It was a blessed sight to me; even the coast of New Zealand would have been welcome. What a singular feeling you have when you see land again suddenly after a long sea voyage! As the sky grew lighter, the wooded dark green heights loomed larger and larger. Gradually the giant trees reaching skyward could be distinguished, and then individual buildings set in the forest could be seen. It was on a Sunday that we first saw American land. What a festive day that was! What powerful emotions surged through my soul! Would we find the things we were seeking in this land? Will we meet our friends there and find them well and prosperous or are they by chance unhappy? What will we do? How will we live? What will be our first endeavor in this new land? How soon will our goal be attained and we can set foot on dry land? We gave many thanks to Heaven that God had led us this far so well.

With evening the ship was turned toward the southeast; nothing else could be done because the miserable southwest wind continued to hold us to the north. So we went backwards and soon lost sight of the lovely land. The following day we again saw land toward the northwest; it was the same land as yesterday. Today it does not look as friendly to me because we are still in the same spot and there is no prospect at hand of getting nearer our destination. With favorable wind we could get to Baltimore in three or four days now. Because it was very sultry and warm, we had some bad weather this evening with lightning and thunder; this is the first we have had at sea. Thank heavens it passed without a storm. Land is gone again. It looks as though our Captain is still afraid of storms; he is having the empty water barrels filled with sea water. It is the most dangerous around the coast when a gale strikes. Our careless first mate, while doing this job, poured salt water into an opened barrel of fresh water containing the last of our good water. Now we have to use water which has probably made several sea voyages already. As soon as a barrel is opened, an unbearable stench spreads over the entire ship. I cannot possibly drink the coffee or herb tea made with it any more. We could still use it for sassafras tea or for soup pungent with vinegar. We had an overabundance of vinegar, which is an excellent thing to have on the ocean.

During this time a land bird made its first appearance. It flew around the ship several times as though to welcome us, then it settled on a mast to rest. A person gets a bit impatient gradually when he is so close to the goal and yet cannot reach it.

Today, August 7, the Captain said he had no prospect of getting to Baltimore for another fourteen days. He began to get very angry with the good Lord and complained woefully about the bad wind, which was keeping us from our destination. He also said that we had to restrict ourselves in the use of wood and water, but he made no move to do this and just let things go on as usual.

This afternoon we saw land again to the northwest. These were the heights of New Jersey. The land disappeared again toward evening. The following day we saw the same highland again.

During these last days the man from Landau expressed his dissatisfaction with the Captain. It was his fault that we were taking so long to get to land, and he complained and swore horribly. He proposed that we force the Captain to set us ashore, be it where it may. We just laughed at him for this stupid idea. His bad mood was caused by nothing more than his having run out of snuff. The Captain noticed his senseless behavior. He read him chapter and verse so soundly that he was happy to remain silent in the future.

So we tacked back and forth, back and forth (and I think we were pretty far out to sea) until August 16 when in the afternoon we saw many pilot boats in the west. Finally we got one of them for our ship, and soon thereafter, as our ship followed along after it, we again saw land in the west.

210

Chesapeake Bay and arrival in Baltimore

THERE was great joy again among all the people on board, among the sailors as well as the passengers. Some complained to the last about the Captain, because he had started being very miserly with the food.

The Captain and the sailors repeatedly told us how dangerous it was to sail up the Bay during stormy weather, how a ship perished here, and another was stranded there, or was tossed on shore, and so on. I was really somewhat afraid of entering the channel even though it opened beautifully before us. We haven't had a single dangerous storm throughout the long voyage, everything has gone so well and according to our wishes, I thought, and now in this Bay we are going to get a rib-cracking farewell. Just as we were coming into this promising channel the wind stopped. The clouds came together, and we were menaced by a thunderstorm, but we were all spared. There was always a mighty protective arm about us, turning away all danger. With a fresh north wind we sailed into the channel only with difficulty. The lighthouse tower of Cape Norfolk shone its friendly light in the dark, stormy night. It was the only star we saw shining in this darkness.[10]

The following morning we left our beds and marveled greatly at our new surroundings. On both sides we saw land, and amidst the giant forest we occasionally glimpsed the attractive house of a planter. We had to run into an inlet because of the north wind. Here there was a mighty fort and thousands of firepits which threatened death and destruction to anyone planning to endanger America's peace and freedom. Not far from this our ship lay anchored.

We had to remain here quietly all day, but the time did not seem long to us. A cool wind was blowing and our spirits were as bright as the heavens above us. We feasted our eyes on the green forest and on the pleasant American homes which, like Gesner's idyllic shepherds' huts,[11]

[10] Baltimore was an important port in the early nineteenth century and had been since colonial times. The port was despite this account reputed to be favorably located, being protected from storms, tidal disturbances, and adverse currents. Baltimore provided ready access to a rich hinterland. At this time cargoes of flour and tobacco left Baltimore for Bremen and other Hanseatic ports. At the time Rütlinger came, the movement of immigration tended to follow the prevailing trade routes between Europe and the United States.
[11] Conrad (von) Gesner (1516–1565) was a great Swiss writer, naturalist, physician, and professor of natural science in Zurich. Among his monumental works was his *Historia Animalium* published in four volumes, 1551–1558. This book served as a point of departure for the development of modern zoology. He was

peeked out from tree and bush. We wished for nothing more now than to get on land and stroll for a few hours in those shady oak groves. Today we saw the first steamboats with their great smokestacks roar proudly and triumphantly past us.

A bright moonlit night smiled at us on deck. Toward midnight the wind improved. The anchor was lifted and the ship sailed easily away again.

On the 71st day of our ocean voyage a delightful American morning greeted us. The bay had become much narrower and under the azure dome of the sky the view toward Baltimore opened enchantingly before our enraptured gaze. Oh, what a romantic entry between these peaceful shores! No matter how difficult it may become for new arrivals until they find a livelihood, you can see at first glance at the countryside and the scattered houses that tranquility, peace, and freedom live under the shade of these trees. The area around Baltimore and the city itself lie somewhat elevated and look so picturesque and charming that one could not imagine anything more beautiful. Sturdy fortifications lie in front of the city and protect, when necessary, the fortune and freedom of America.

In the afternoon around three o'clock we reached the quarantine station about two miles from the city. Here we dropped anchor. We hoped that when the medical inspection was over the ship would head promptly for shore. The doctor came today, a young and very friendly man. He found the state of health of all the people on board ship to be to his complete satisfaction. Our beds and everything else in the room pleased him very much because everything was so neat and clean. Now we could land whenever we wished. How happy we were about that too. Next to us lay a ship from the East Indies which had been lying in quarantine for four weeks already because of illness. No one was allowed off the ship until all were healthy.

The Captain informed us that the ship would not land until all the ballast had been unloaded; this could take from ten to twelve days. We were instructed to have our things taken off as soon as possible. We would have to do this at our own expense; according to law he had nothing further to do about it. First, however, we would have to have an inventory prepared by a notary, listing our belongings so that they could

known by his contemporaries chiefly as a botanist. Gesner was also widely known for his love of mountains and his excursions into alpine areas for the love of their beauty, for the value of exercise, as well as for scientific collection. See Valentin Gitermann, *Geschichte der Schweiz* (Thayngen, Schaffhausen: Augustin Verlag, 1941) and "Konrad von Gesner," *Encyclopaedia Britannica*, Vol. 10, p. 323.

be checked and signed at the customs house. An official would then come on board ship to check for any discrepancies.

The sailors went to the city this evening and brought presents back to us: fruit, milk, and whiskey. Of the latter they themselves consumed a good part because they were so happy and as neatly and cleanly dressed as fine gentlemen. During the remaining days we stayed in Baltimore, we met them often. They were completely different than on board ship. Their faces were distorted; they were constantly drunk; they asked us to go to taverns with them where they offered us beverages of all kinds. We accepted this invitation only once. We saw then that they would squander their hard-earned money soon enough in bawdy-houses with shameful wenches. In spite of all this drunkenness, they always behaved with modesty and good manners toward our womenfolk. A few had already signed up on a ship going to the East Indies. I would truly have liked to make this trip with them. To the cook and another married sailor who did not accompany the other sailors at all now, we gave our supply of zwieback. There was still more than a hundredweight of it. The cook was a very decent fellow. He had allowed my wife special privileges in the kitchen because she occasionally gave him a little schnapps. He had a wife and child.

The following morning, the 21st of August, a memorable day for us began. A couple of sailors took a few of us passengers to the nearest shore. It was the first place where we stepped on American soil and it was hallowed to us. If I had been alone, I would have fallen down and kissed the good earth. Every little flower was sacred to me and every green plant a thousand times welcome. Every tree was an altar under which I felt like kneeling and giving an offering of thanks to the all-bountiful Father in Heaven for the fortunate voyage and for His blessed care.

Vetter and I then went into the city in order to have our inventory prepared. Each one cost a dollar. A Quaker named Päpplein, a wealthy merchant and a friend of Vetter's, gave us the best instructions on how to handle the situation. However, we knew no English, neither speaking nor understanding it.

By the 23rd we had everything in order. An official came on board the ship in response to a flag that was flown. All the things were loaded one by one on a ballast boat under his supervision. He was not at all conscientious. Not even all the boxes had to be opened. This time smuggling would have been easy if only we had some merchandise. All effects which were listed as being for personal use were not subject to duty. At least that is the way it was in our case. The Captain brought our things to the wharf free of charge. After we had all our plunder on land we looked for a place to store it. About a quarter of an hour's distance from the wharf we found a German coffeehouse. The innkeeper offered us a wide, spacious room where we could stay until we had an opportunity to journey on. He promised us complete freedom to cook in the kitchen. Vetter had his own place for his people. The remaining sixteen of us moved into this suitable house. The innkeeper and his wife, people in their sixties, received us with as much hospitality as if we were their beloved friends.

First welcoming ceremonies in America

UPON closer acquaintance with our innkeeper I discovered that he was the father of Dr. Gall, who has recently published an extensive description of America.[12]

Truly these people did not paint a very pretty picture of the country which we were just entering. "It is a cursed land," they said, "inhabited only by rogues and rascals. There is absolutely no order. Justice is nowhere protected. The law benefits every thief. It is now four years since we came to this country. We brought twenty young people along and paid for their passage.

"It was in the fall that we arrived, so we kept these people all winter and fed them. During this time we bought 415 acres of land for 1100 dollars. With this land we wanted to provide work and income for these people. As soon as spring came, they all got the devil out of there; not one remained. What could we do? America is large and there are no laws that take care of such rascals and punish them. If we could sell our land, which we would gladly do now for 400 dollars, we would return to Europe in a minute."

Later I was given the most reliable assurance that his son, Doctor Gall, never left Harrisburg, where the assembly or government of Pennsyl-

[12] L. Gall, *Meine Auswanderung nach den Vereinigten-Staaten in Nord-Amerika, im Frühjahr 1819* . . . (Trier: F. A. Gall, 1822). Heinrich Ludwig Lampert Gall (1791–1863) came to America in 1819 with a group of German immigrants intent on founding a nonreligious community. The immigrants formed an organization in 1820 in Harrisburg, Pennsylvania, but the communitarian enterprise failed. In the winter of 1820, Gall returned to Germany where he worked for a more revolutionary kind of socialism. See Arthur E. Bestor, Jr., *Backwoods Utopias: The Sectarian and Owenite Phases of Communitarian Socialism in America, 1663–1829* (Philadelphia: University of Pennsylvania Press, 1950), p. 100n.

vania has its seat. There he wrote his glittering work, using English sources and the information given him by members of the government.

We remained here over Sunday and searched everywhere to see if there was not a teamster who was driving to Lancaster. We could find none.

Today many Germans who lived in Baltimore visited us. Some gave us courage and made us feel very optimistic; others came armed and fought every good opinion which we cherished about this country. One blessed and the other damned. All of them, however, asked, "Do you know a trade?" This left me a bit perplexed. It was soon evident that I would not be able to beat a source of income out of the cliffs with my schoolmaster's stick in this country as Moses got water with his staff. Now I would gladly have exchanged my discipline rod for shears or a shoemaker's strap, or even a soldering stick, or anything else, if I could have done it readily. "Where are you going then?" they asked further. To Lancaster in Pennsylvania. "Ha, there you would do well! That is the best and richest place. New immigrants get along well there." Each person also added, "These are hard times; there is no money anywhere. Eight to ten years ago it was different, you could make money then." And also, "Beware of swindlers; there are many of them among the Germans as well as the Americans and English. The Germans have lost the great trust people had in them before the past few years, because of their recent behavior." Germans told us all these things, and we thought that perhaps these were not the worst of them.

First travel in the New World

BECAUSE we could find no opportunity to have our belongings shipped, Lauer of Landau decided to stay here until he could find one. We should just go on without worry, if we wished; our few things could be transported with his. He wanted to go to Reading; the road there led through Lancaster. No sooner said than done. Three of his children and our cooper came along too. We had a distance of 74 miles before us. We checked out with our innkeeper and were well satisfied with him. Since we still had peas, rice, tea, coffee, and other things left over from the ship, he bought these from us. Thus we got some money out of the provisions. Then I packed the essentials into my valise. Early on the morning of the 25th we started out, taking something to eat on the way.

Occasionally we got milk from farmers. That night we cooked some soup in a farmhouse and then slept on the straw in the barn.

In the morning we flew out of the feathers early. In Strassburg, a little city, we had breakfast at an inn. We did not know the American custom yet and ordered coffee. The people understood German. Our fellow travelers were too frugal to turn in and eat with us. They went on and knocked at a farmer's door. This is the customary way for immigrants when they come from their ship into the countryside. We were curious, however, and wanted to know what the customs were in American inns. After about fifteen minutes food was served. We prepared our mouths for plain coffee, but how pleasantly we were surprised. In addition to the bubbling brew, boiled and roasted meat, butter, honey, and bread and other baked goods suddenly appeared on the table. We ate with relish and only had to pay half a dollar, which would amount to about 37½ kreuzer per person. From here on the others took the opportunity of riding in a coach because they were very tired. We branched off from the main road alone and took a country road which we were told was a little shorter. The land on which there are scattered plantations and still a great deal of forest is generally called the bush here.

This noon we came to a magnificent farmhouse. We knocked and asked if they would give us a little milk for money and kind words. "Ei! I should think so, come into the living room," said the woman. Then milk, bread, butter, and honey were set out and she said, "Pull up close and help yourselves." We knew well that no ceremony was necessary here and we ate heartily. Much was asked about Germany and much was told. At the end we asked how much we owed and reached for our pocket. "You can certainly use your money. You are welcome," was the answer.

In another place we sat down under the shade of a tree because it was very warm. Not very far away there was a house, but we had thought no one would notice us. Now a woman comes running toward us and hands us a big apple pie on a plate, saying, "You must be hungry!" We thanked her, and like the other woman she said, "You are welcome." If that is the way it is in this country, we thought, things are not going to turn out badly after all. When we had gone on again, an old man met us who addressed us in German. He asked us this and that and then at the end said, "I am happy every time I see a German here," and added, as he held out a bottle of brandy, "Take a drink, but drink well."

This evening we stayed overnight at an inn which had a German innkeeper. We decided to treat ourselves and drink American wine. We did not know the right word for the measure so we told him to give us as much as it was customary to drink here. Now, we thought, he would do the thing well and double or even triple the usual portion as a German innkeeper would do in Europe. He served a small glass about the size of two kreuzer's worth of brandy at home. We had to laugh and told the innkeeper how we drank wine at home in Switzerland. "Here," he told us, "this drink is very expensive and strong; it comes from southern France, Spain, Portugal, Madeira, and so forth." This wine is very strong, like liqueur. I would much rather drink a good Schaffhauser. This little glass cost us elevenpence, about eighteen kreuzer. Except for this, we were fairly served.

The reunion with our friends in Lancaster and what else happened there

AUGUST 27 marked the day of our arrival in Lancaster. We hoped to get there today fairly early. We were happy at the thought of surprising our friends so completely. We could easily have let them know from Baltimore, but we purposely refrained from doing so.

It is a very hot, sultry day. My valise weighed heavily and we often took refuge under shade trees. Now we are approaching Columbia, where the Susquehanna glides along, still and silvery, stretching out like a sea. A masterfully designed bridge, a full half hour's walking time in length, spans the river. Here every person has to pay six cents (nine kreuzer) toll.

Now the towers of Lancaster appear and our hearts begin to pound. Near the city we encountered a German street laborer who knows our Schweizer well and showed us exactly where he lives, so that we were able to walk directly to the house without having to ask further. We found his wife and child fine and healthy; they already knew about our coming. Our traveling companions had come here before us. Not only that, his wife had just received a letter from Amsterdam which came by way of New York, also announcing our coming. We did not meet dear Schweizer; he happened to have gone to Philadelphia. He returned the evening of the following day. He also knew about us already. So our plans for surprising our friends were in vain. Of our happy reunion, our joy and emotion, of the questions and replies — back and forth — of these I will write not one word. It's something that must be experienced personally before one can understand it fully. It is enough to say that even in faraway America we found each other again, happy, healthy, and well. To our Father in Heaven, who bestows upon His people so many joys even in this world, we offer our deepest thanks.

Now we are with our friends; we rested a few days, chatted a few days, and were filled with deep joy for a few days, and only now do we begin to take stock of the situation. What can we do, what sort of business? In a word, how are we going to get along in an honest way? These were the questions which first roused us out of the giddiness of our joy. They could not be answered satisfactorily. Hope is life's comfort. We found this place quite different from the way it had been described to us in Baltimore. Our friends had just made the decision to move away from here. They had a position in Middletown, Maryland, ninety miles from here. There Schweizer could work in a drugstore. Here, he said, there was nothing more to do. They had been here three years and had gone backward more than they had advanced. It was getting worse day by day. Everyone streamed here because this place and all of Pennsylvania had been so praised. They knew many good people here and had sincere friends, whom they were reluctant to leave, but what good was it? They had to leave if they wanted to continue honorably in the future. We protested mightily and yet we found that this was really true. If there was nothing for them, what could there be for us? We therefore decided to go with them. The city and its surroundings would have pleased us very much. We had already made the acquaintance of people of good character and considerable education. What can be done, however, when a suitable livelihood cannot be found? One cannot remain even though the country and the situation are pleasing and the people express the wish to have us stay. In our homeland we had worries of all kinds. Troubles accompanied us on our trip. Now we are here and troubles will not be missing here either. If God just grants us health, we will not be in need.

While we were here, I went to Baltimore once more because my things were too long delayed in arriving, and I had them sent here. In the last week before we left here, I received news from Philadelphia that our trunk had arrived there. I went there myself to make arrangements to get it. I made this trip quite willingly; only one thing was missing in this pleasure, and that was that Schweizer could not come along. He had already left for his new residence to check this and that and make arrangements.

Philadelphia is indeed a beautiful, large city. All the streets, small and big, cross one another precisely at right angles. If you stand at one end of the city on a street, your eye can see in either direction until the houses are lost in the distance. If this city were embellished by several really high towers, it would compete with the most beautiful cities of the world for the prize. There is no lack of beautiful buildings and magnificent squares. The waterworks itself is an authentic example of Roman architecture. About an hour's distance from the city, the water is pumped out of the river by means of gigantic machinery and pumped up to a rocky hill where it is stored in a broad reservoir. From there it is conducted under the ground along all the streets. On both sides of the streets outlets are placed at regular intervals. It is only a few steps to such an outlet from every house. A turn of the faucet and as much water flows forth as you want. If the machinery is run for one or two hours, the entire city has enough water for the day.

I also went to the museum.[13] A magnificent building. It seems to me to contain a rich display of remarkable things in art and natural science, especially in the latter. The skeleton of a mammoth attracted my complete admiration, so that I forgot almost everything else. The size of this creature, as well as the fact that it no longer lives any place on the surface of the earth, held me in amazement. It must have been the largest land animal by far. And — it was — and now is no more. Is this the only kind of animal that has disappeared from the world? When? How? Were all the animals now known already here at the time of creation? Oh, Creation, how mysterious thy essence! Creator, how marvelous and unfathomable are Thy works! We worship, praise, and reverence Thee!

It is indeed pleasant to get around in the world a little! You often see things you would never see around the hearth at home. I think it is well worth while to stroll around a bit in the Lord's great household to see how things are going among his scattered children. Do they quarrel and show envy over a handful of earth everywhere? Because of this do they forget themselves — what they are and what they should become? Do they not realize that on this earthly shell, over which they plague and torture one another, the grave for their death slumber awaits them? Is there still a small place somewhere, perhaps, where people get along well together — people who keep their destiny in mind, and peacefully

[13] The museum was established by Charles Willson Peale shortly after the American Revolution. In 1781 Peale, who had studied portrait painting under Benjamin West, established a portrait gallery of Revolutionary War heroes. This soon grew into a museum, which was housed in Independence Hall. The collections were highly varied, including stuffed animals and the skeleton of a mastodon as well as the portraits. The museum became famous throughout the country and served as a model for other communities.

220

and harmoniously enjoy what their Father has given them? To find this, perhaps, a trip to the moon or even to Sirius might be necessary.

In Philadelphia I met a couple of good German men. I had now settled the matter of my trunk at the customs house, at a cost of eight dollars. If I had had it with me, this expense would have been saved. The way it was, the trunk was considered merchandise. I returned then to Lancaster in a leisurely and contented spirit.

The move to Middletown and our activities there

IN THE first days of October we said farewell to Lancaster and began a new journey. We arrived here, where we still remain, in four days. We rented a little house with a living room, a narrow kitchen, and a dark storeroom under the roof. It has a small garden which we can cultivate in the spring. There was no cooking-stove, no stove in the living room, and no cellar, and for this stately house we had to pay forty dollars a year. Yes, I said forty dollars. We still had to rent a stove and buy wood. There are no other stoves here but cast-iron ones. One of these cost us three dollars for the winter. Oak wood costs two dollars a cord and hickory two and three quarters to three dollars a cord because this is excellent wood for heating. We generally bought this kind and used six cords a year. We had to bake our bread at the neighbor's when we wanted some. When we heard about all this, our eyes opened wide. We knew we would have to pay for all these things; we knew we had to live, but a job and an income we still did not have. We realized that these expenditures, even the minor ones, could upset the balance. Still we did not permit ourselves to be discouraged and tried to sit fast on the saddle of fate, so that we would not be thrown easily out of the stirrups into the pit of hopeless despair. We reflected that all beginnings are difficult and let it go at that.

Now we began to develop our skills. Schweizer, who understood book-binding quite well, made me somewhat familiar with it, too. Since there was no other bookbinder in this area, we had considerable work for several months with old books. For a small hand Bible, bound in full leather, we received one dollar. For a Testament we received one half to three quarters of a dollar, and so on, proportionately, with other books. My wife sewed bonnets and knitted stockings. In addition to that, we made hatboxes out of cardboard, and other little things. We were well paid for all of them. If we had had enough work, year in and year out, in this sort of thing, I could not imagine a nicer living. I would not trade this easy business for the best country school in Switzerland, in that case. All the things we made had then to be sold from house to house. My wife mostly occupied herself with this task. She was very successful. She brought home in exchange many a round dollar, pieces of meat and bacon, pots of lard, and whatever else we needed in the household. She always praised the hospitality of the farmers. Perhaps many people in Europe would shrug their shoulders at this lowly-appearing trade. Oh, vain folly! Here the very richest person is not ashamed to earn his money with the lowliest honest labor. He who can make a pot himself and mend his own pants and shoes counts for more than a foppish little gentleman, even one with money, who tries to keep his hands soft in his pockets. This is one advantage in this country which greatly shames the cultivated part of the old world. All honest work is worthy of recognition; only his own ineptitude holds a person back.

Among other things, we started a singing school, too.[14] We held it all winter long every Sunday for several hours. We had about twenty-five students; each student had to pay us a dollar for a quarter of a year. What am I saying? Each *was* to pay us, because even now we have not received payment from all of them, and it will be difficult to get. We did not keep it up for more than a quarter of a year when we saw how things were. If I wanted to describe this singing school, I would have to give a word-for-word repetition of the one that is described in Schweizer's *Journal*. Therefore, I am saying nothing but that there is something pitiful about conducting a singing school in America.

In the meantime spring came. The old books were almost all bound, and most of the women had been provided with bonnets, stockings, and hatboxes. Now we had to think of something else to do. All through the summer you could indeed get work and good pay with the farmers. This, however, means ruining all your strength and health, as well as digging yourself an early grave if you are not accustomed to such hard work.

---

[14] Rütlinger played the organ, flute, violin, and clarinet. Wildhaus, where he was born, had particularly strong musical traditions. Pastor Franz of Wildhaus reported in 1819 that probably not a home is without a musical instrument. On summer evenings and on Sundays the whole family played music together. There were fifty zithers and ten to fifteen organs in addition to other instruments. People with little formal musical training sang and played instruments very capably. Pastor Franz is quoted in Albert Edelmann, "Vom frühern Musikleben im obern Toggenburg," *Toggenburgerblätter für Heimatkunde*, Vol. 23, Part II:2–3 (1962), p. 2. Rütlinger is cited as having been active in such musical activities as a young man.

Straw hats are in great demand here in the summer. The foremost people generally wear finely woven imported hats which are very expensive. Among the farmers you often see homemade ones, very crude and ugly. And so we thought, if only we had learned how to make straw hats like the ones worn all over Switzerland. There is a popular proverb here: Help yourself. There was nothing else to be done but apply this proverb to ourselves if we wanted such hats. I tried something which at home would have seemed impossible. I bought straw, and started to work. The experiment was successful. A straw hat was produced, truly not the finest and most even, but through this means we saw the puzzle solved, and we learned that they could be made in this fashion. Now I began to work away, and the rest learned to do it later, too. At first it took me three days to make one. Later I made seven or eight pieces in one week during the long summer days. The hats were shown, and they pleased people. Soon we got several orders from the most prominent people in the little city. They paid us a dollar and a quarter for each. We worked away all summer and sold them, on the average, for half or three quarters of a dollar for a medium quality farmer's hat. This brought in many a dollar. If things continue like this, I will certainly try to make dresses, pants, and shoes, and learn to use a plane and a smith's hammer. In this way a man learns to know the skills the benevolent Creator gave him.

At the end of the year we began to look for other housing. I rented a little house about an hour's distance from town in what is here called the bush. This house has more room and is more convenient than the other. My wife and I moved out there by ourselves; we have to pay a dollar a month. We also get wood more cheaply from our farmer. Our friends are moving into another house in town which is also a bit cheaper. Because of the drugstore they can not very well move farther out. However, we visit each other often, exchanging visits between town and country. We are content and live very happily.

Already I have another job. In the area in which we are living the farmers are all Germans. There were several who wanted to maintain a German school. I applied and now I am, in fact, already the teacher of eight or ten children. How long this will last I do not know. If things go on like this, I will finally advance to pot-mender, chimney sweep, and rag-collector. I receive two dollars for a quarter of a year for each child. If I had fifty students, I would soon earn enough to buy a plantation of two hundred acres of land.

I will tell more about running a school later on.

Now, dear friends, I have told you briefly but truthfully and in detail how things have gone with us to the present moment. You can see that we are healthy and of good courage, and that thus far we have been very fortunate. Do not worry about us; there's no need of that. America is big, and in a large part of it roads have already been built on which you can travel freely and unhindered, where and how you like. When you travel far, you see and experience a great deal. How much then there is to tell about. I think the next news that I send to you will be gathered around the Wabash, the Ohio, or the Mississippi, where herds of buffalo graze along the shores and Indians with bows and arrows hunt in the forest.

My song is not yet at an end. Be forewarned. I will now tell you all sorts of other things about America. Everything is new here and we see and hear much that seems truly marvelous.

About housekeeping

THERE is quite a difference between housekeeping here and at home. My wife always talked about this each time she returned from her selling trips. "In every house I come into," she said, "the husband and wife form two separate household regimens. Neither one is concerned about the other's. Each manages his or her affairs as he or she can and wishes. Sometimes you would think that they didn't know each other. The wife has jurisdiction over the cows and poultry. The husband's jurisdiction extends over pigs, horses, plow, and field. He sees to the cultivation of the land, pays what it costs, and takes in the money from its harvest. He gives none of this money to his wife. He also has to provide part of the food for the table — that which involves meat and flour products. The wife is as little concerned over the good or bad farming of her husband as I care about the harem of the sultan of Turkey.

"The wife milks and takes care of the cows. The butter she makes, with the exception of what is used in her own household, she sells as she does also the eggs and calves. From such sales she must provide coffee and sugar. What is left is indisputably her own. From this she can provide herself with luxuries, and this often costs not a little."

Also, she often remarked, "The richest farm women don't have any money. I had to give credit to this one or that one until she can sell some more butter and eggs. They don't even have credit with their husbands. Many have tried to borrow from them, but received nothing. The husband says either, 'I have no money,' or 'First you must return what I loaned you yesterday or a year ago before I give you any more.' I can deal freely and openly with every woman. Even if the husband sees it, I don't have to be afraid that he will ruin my sale. If a wife would like to buy something and she asks her husband, 'Shall I?' 'Well, you may if you have the money,' he says, and laughs. But the farmers often claim they haven't a cent in the house. I brought a hat to sell N. at the big plantation with the beautiful brick house. He told me that he couldn't pay me for it until I came next time."

As far as the women are concerned, they certainly never keep any money in reserve. They give every penny to the fashion merchant as soon as they get it. This is not the case with the men. Even a farmer with a medium-sized holding has 100 to 300 dollars lying around the house all the time. His house is a savings bank, and if he does not have any other money in his current money pouch, he would rather borrow on credit than pay out of his savings box.

The women are generally skilled in managing their household. Each makes her clothing and finery herself. Roasting, cooking, all sorts of baking in addition to making bread, they understand from the ground up. They are masters at spinning flax, hemp, or wool. Many of them can weave as well. Linen and half-woolen material for work clothes they always weave themselves. Beds and household furnishing are very elegant and beautiful but scant. They are very clean and exact in everything with the exception of their private functions. These occur in the open. In the country one rarely sees a little house erected for this purpose. Even in the cities one does not see them everywhere. The back of the house or a shady little shed or behind a hedge — these places must serve for the relief of the body.*

How work is done

ALL work is done very quickly and efficiently. A farmer who has 150 to 200 acres of land works it alone. Some may have one or two sons and a slave. During the hay and fruit harvest, however, they hire day labor, as much as they can get, so that everything is quickly completed. When you come to a harvest field you see twenty to forty people. They

* This seems to contradict Johannes Schweizer's *Journal*, p. 127 — perhaps the general comment made there applies particularly to certain areas. In other areas, according to friend Rütlinger, it must look different. [Publisher's note, 1826.]

225

are mowing, cutting, tying, shocking, everything all at once, as though it were a matter of life and death. The farmer does not check to see how things are done as long as a lot of activity is going on. The whiskey bottle goes around every minute and everybody works industriously at that, too. Much is done — that is true — but all without consideration of the loss of fruit. It is a grubby mess whereby a shocking amount of fruit is spoiled. That is the way it is with all farm work. They cultivate an appalling amount of land with few people, but everything is very superficially and sketchily done. They have really never understood that through careful, better regulated operation a lot of produce could be raised on less land. There has been little evidence of a desire to apply this yet, because America is still too little populated.

The corn harvest is carried on just as speedily. A few people go out into the field, pick the ears, and throw them on little piles. They are then loaded on wagons, driven home, and all thrown on one pile. The farmer then calls 40 to 60 people together of an evening, and in a few hours they husk 60 to 100 bushels of corn. This does not cost anything but whiskey and a good supper.

A woman on the average spins 2600 linen threads calculated according to the spool measure which we use in Switzerland. They estimate that a man going into the woods can split 250 battens of cordwood. First, of course, he must fell the tree and then chop it into logs with the axe. We must marvel at these two accomplishments no matter how we look at them. Here there can be no superficiality; it must be executed with particular dexterity and skill.

When a farmer wants to build a beautiful house, he sets up a shack with a straw roof on a suitable spot. He opens a loam pit and forms and bakes and fires the bricks for his house himself. It is astonishing how in an incredibly short time a beautiful brick house stands there, with roof, rooms, doors, windows, kitchen, and chimney. But when you observe everything about it, it is only made for appearance and not for durability. That is the way everything made by American hands looks to me. By this maxim they have developed unusual dexterity. If you consider, as well, that their implements and tools are efficiently and functionally planned, then the American worker is not nearly so amazing as we think and even less worthy of imitation. It seems to me that the American is not capable of solid, sustained, enduring work; he is adept, however, at grasping every useful means at hand to help himself. It is also true that

226

with this turn of mind comes an inventiveness which is expressed in many daring, ingenious works.

This careless speed in work leaves many craftsmen, professional people, and day-laborers without work for weeks at a time. Yet wages remain high. You have to pay two or three dollars to a shoemaker for a pair of shoes, and three or four dollars to the tailor for making a coat, even if neither has had any work for weeks and none in prospect. No one will work for a reasonable wage in order that he might always have something to do. He wants big wages and little work and wants to spend the remaining time doing nothing rather than working for a lesser wage. This is characteristic of the day-laborer. In these days when money is scarce the farmer hires him only when he has to — because of the high wages. Even now a day-laborer during the haying and fruit harvest gets three quarters to one dollar a day and food and drink. This periodic labor has the disadvantage which the proverb confirms: *Müssiggang ist aller Laster Anfang*, Idleness is the beginning of all evil. Most of them, when they are not employed, spend their time in taverns. A great many dissolute fellows are hatched out in this way.

What the situation of the people is in this country

PEOPLE who have no land of their own or no home of their own and who must depend on something other than themselves are in as difficult a position as someone who can't skate and is chased out on the slippery ice. They have no firm base, no secure foundation. If they are very careful and capable of much work, they can make a living, but it must be sought ceaselessly and anxiously. Everything you begin is so uncertain and is subject to capricious change as nowhere else. A man in a particular business can be making a good living on one day and the next his business may stand idle. He has to think of something else to do. It is not rare that a man has to struggle through dozens of occupations until he can become a farmer. However, once he has reached this goal, he is in the safest and happiest position in this country, as long as he is just a bit careful and keeps his head on his shoulders. Then he can enjoy the fruits of his own labor. He can acquire and maintain livestock of all kinds so that year in and year out he has an untroubled living. If he wishes to be rather modest and simple, he makes his own clothing, which does not cost him very much. If he has little money, he also has little expense. His taxes and expenses are not worth mentioning.

Our farmer has about 150 acres most of which is cleared and put to use. We got to talking about taxes. Yes, he said, he had to pay considerable taxes. "How much, then?" I asked. "Why, they come to eight dollars a year, and that's a lot." I answered him, "In Europe you would have to pay at least 200 dollars a year with your land and money." This seemed unbelievable to him.

Yes, indeed, here the farmer is his own master, and no one can order him around. And when it comes to giving orders, he is the one who gives them.

It is not easy to become a farmer, however. Many a man in striving for this goal has spent his entire lifetime in grim labor, and before he reached this objective, he had to step out of life's drama. Furthermore, many a man has lost his big farm and ended up a bum.

Cleared land in accessible places is already very expensive. If a farmer buys bushland he has great difficulty establishing himself in the midst of the forest.

An acre of cleared land currently still costs 30, 50, up to 100 dollars depending upon quality and location. It used to be even more expensive. During the time of the European war land prices increased incredibly. Farmers enjoyed a golden age. If a man had his 200 to 300 acres of land, a third of it planted in wheat which yielded from 25 to 30 bushels an acre, and if 5 bushels of wheat made a barrel of flour weighing 200 pounds and he received 12 to 16 dollars a barrel, this made money! Besides, you must consider how much corn and rye he plants and how many pigs he keeps. Many people bought land on speculation, not as much as they could cultivate, but rather as much as they could get at 100 to 125 dollars an acre, and stupidly thought it would continue to rise in the same way. In this way untimely speculations were hatched out just as there are at home in manufacturing businesses. Then peace came and the price of land suddenly fell unbelievably. There they were, the rogues. It was not any barrenness of the land that was responsible for this. This land rewards its cultivator richly. Certainly it is unbelievable, if you haven't seen it for yourself, with what strength the invisible power of nature reigns on earth and what a variety of growth it brings forth for the benefit of man.

At present all the farmers are complaining about bad times, because they no longer get more than four to five dollars for a barrel of flour.

228

Because of this, many wish another bloody war on the heads of the Europeans. They think that the fishing would be good again in murky waters.

Luxury

A SOFTENING of moral fiber and a multitude of desires for all sorts of luxury are found in these once happy farm valleys, even in the most remote hut of unhewn logs that stands alone in the forest. Who would believe it? This is especially true of the women. Are you, sisters of the same sex back home, laughing a little and blushing because you feel this refers to you, too? The matron and the maid, the country girl and the city girl, are not distinguishable one from the other. Every cent they get into their possession they carry to the store. And most of them have large sums after their names in the merchants' account books.

You come through a lonely woods. In the middle of a clearing you come upon a rather unusually high log cabin. In it you hear a few weak human voices in what sounds like a miserable song and you stop. Suddenly the doors open, and in a moment you feel that you have been transported into the crowds of a city. You are surrounded by females who resemble a princely entourage. The magnificent shawls and green gossamer veils on the finest straw hats flutter in the wind, and silk parasols with fringes float over these gay dolls with bold, saucy faces. Men with fashionable tailcoats of the finest English cloth and hats made of beaver fur step onto the scene. You are astounded and puzzled; then you find after a closer look that this is a church, where ordinary farm people living in the bush had gathered to give praise to God. A moment more and all the sprites fly away on magnificent horses in all directions, raising clouds of dust that make the forest dim.

If you should meet an old man and get into conversation with him he will soon say, "It's really terrible the way people carry on nowadays. There was no such luxury and frivolity before. Once the women went out in the field and worked; not one of them shrank from work, and they were healthy and strong. Now they loll in the houses and study the fashions and can no longer withstand anything. They sicken and fade and get old before their time. Once if a woman had one pair of shoes in her life, she was satisfied; they were her wedding shoes. When she went to church she carried them carefully in her apron and put them on in front of the church door. After church she wrapped them up again carefully and went home the way she came. She made her clothes herself from home-

229

made material. Neighbors were friendly and helpful to each other; they helped each other in their work; but now it's no longer like that. People must get back to the old, simple ways. It can't go on like this any more."

Trade, prices of merchandise and food, and other things

BUSINESS is a very risky thing. A man who has no money cannot very well start anything, and a man who starts with a lot often loses a lot. The most incredible speculation often goes on in this field. In the port cities, if a man has a large quantity of merchandise, or has just received a large amount, he often auctions it publicly if he thinks that with this money he may make even more through speculation. Because of this practice there is frequent bankruptcy. Merchants and traders in the inland cities often have regular connections with people in the port cities. The latter are always prepared to buy merchandise at public auction at a very low price. Then they send this to their associates in the interior. In this way the balance in trade is ruined. The English are completely flooding America with their wares. It is surprising, too, how cheap cotton articles are here. Even though they have to pay a fairly high import duty, what of it? The English are as cunning as foxes; they smuggle in an incredible amount. Otherwise they could not possibly survive. This too is the reason the domestic manufacturers and factory people cannot rightly get on their feet. They all, or rather many of them, think that they cannot make the merchandise as cheaply. This is America, which dares to undertake the impossible. It is a pity that this spirit of enterprise is not also directed to the establishment of domestic manufacture. Only then could this country become a self-sufficient, happy country. America could produce enough materials, raw stuffs of all kinds. There are already a fair number of hands here to make things out of these raw materials. There are already a good many poor people who have nothing to do. There would also be no lack of intelligent people to install the best, most functional machinery. As people see the present situation more clearly, and realize that every year much more money leaves the country than comes in, domestic manufacture will eventually be achieved. Recently the import duty on various foreign goods has been raised. In time it will certainly happen that all products that America is capable of producing will be completely excluded. Once this point has been reached, there will be no lack of ingenious machinery, thus making almost all human hands useful. Even now, you can occasionally find admirable products of human skill. These inventions will not spread poverty and misery among the common people in America, as they have in the old world, as long as there is still so much unsettled land. Preparations are already being made here and there for the advancement of expanding trade and commerce. Roads are being built and advantageous canals opened.

A little more than twenty years ago, a man bought a couple of thousand acres in the area around Lake Erie at half a cent an acre. In time Lake Erie, which is connected with other large lakes, was connected to New York by means of a canal. The land I have mentioned lay just along this canal. The owner laid out some of it in lots for a city; a lot is one third of an acre. At present these lots cost 6000 dollars. One acre of land then would have risen from half a cent to 18,000 dollars. This seems unbelievable but it is nevertheless true.

It was decided by the Congress to connect the large lakes by means of a canal to the Wabash. This is a very important enterprise and of the greatest advantage to the western states. These can then use the market of New York as well as that of New Orleans. These two cities will someday fight for the honor of being the greatest trade center of the world.

If you live along the Wabash, you can make a pleasure trip every winter down to New Orleans for the Mardi Gras. In the spring, after the sowing, you can go to New York. Once there I wouldn't give a cent for the annual fairs or church consecrations that I used to visit in the old world.

At present white cotton material costs from twelve to twenty-five cents a yard, and printed dress material from twenty-five to thirty cents a yard. Linens have a rather high price. Domestic cotton costs about ten to fifteen cents a pound. Wool cloth costs one to ten dollars a yard. A pound of wool costs thirty to forty cents. It is somewhat finer than that of our sheep in Switzerland, however. Tanned leather is very expensive; rawhide, however, is quite cheap. Iron, copper, and brass articles are expensive. An axe costs two or three dollars. A hundredweight of fine white flour costs two and a half dollars. Medium fine flour, which is like our choice flour, is a dollar and a half per hundredweight. Rye flour, which is whiter than over there, is a dollar a hundredweight. Corn is also very cheap. Butter is eight to ten cents a pound. Lard, which is used everywhere here for cooking, is ten cents a pound. Pork is six to eight cents a pound, beef and mutton three to six cents a pound. A dozen eggs is six to twelve cents. A pound of coffee is twenty to twenty-five cents, and sugar eight to fifteen cents.

One dollar has 100 cents. One cent according to our money is one and a half kreuzer. A yard is three feet long. One pound is 32 *loth*.

These standard weights, measures, and moneys are the same throughout the United States. This is not a bad idea, either.

The greatest evil in this country is indeed the slave trade

HERE in this area it is true that slaves are not treated as harshly as in many other places. Still they are creatures that are looked down upon, and numerous examples show how low they are in the eyes of the whites. To the merit of the Germans, it must be said that fewer slaves are found among them and that these are treated much better than those of the English. At least around here they are generally well fed and well dressed, and not more work is demanded of them than they can bear. The black woman is often dressed in the very same way as the white. It is quite remarkable to see a figure in a snow-white dress wearing a stylish straw hat from under which peeks a shiny black face.

What a contemptible degradation this is. Nowhere in any house does a black person eat at a table with the family. His share is given him in a far corner of the kitchen. Also, not one of them can take one step into the living room. They must stay in the kitchen, with the exception of the women, who in most places carry the food on and off the table.

It is shocking, indeed, how these poor people are treated in the southern states. There a farmer often has from one to three hundred slaves. They are driven to work with whips. Each day a certain portion of unroasted corn and a few salted fish are given them. They can eat the corn raw or roast it by the fire. They have to get along with that and work all day like animals. A stiff punishment is inflicted on anyone who gives a black an opportunity to learn to read and write.[15] They are cut off from any

[15] Laws prohibiting the teaching of slaves to read and write were passed by southern legislatures on several occasions when slave insurrections and rumors of plots had heightened public alarm. Such laws were passed particularly around 1830. The southern white stereotype of the Negro as docile and unintelligent was severely shaken by the uprising of slaves in Santo Domingo in 1791–1795 and by the massacres of the whites. The plot of the free Negro Denmark Vesey and the Nat Turner Insurrection in Virginia increased the concern in the 1820's and early 1830's. Nat Turner had through his reading of the Bible received ideas that impelled him to

opportunity to learn anything or even to get together socially. Many times plots have been divulged that the blacks wished to destroy the whites, but they have never succeeded. The number of Negroes is much larger than that of the whites.

Since we have been here, slaves have been driven through this little city several times, bound and chained and with whips at their backs. Since it is so hot in these southern lands and because these wretched creatures are, moreover, so harshly treated, they die like flies. Then other young and strong ones are bought from other areas and delivered down there. This is just the way the Swiss do with cattle when they export their surplus.

There was a farmer in this area at one time, he is still living, who had a black family with children. The father was sent to market one day by his master. While he was away, slave dealers came to the farmer, and the farmer sold them the wife and children of the absent father. When the poor thing came home, his loved ones, to whom he was tenderly attached, were gone — sold. The Negro, full of despair and anxiety, took the first opportunity to escape at night and made his way without rest straight through the uncultivated woods, far from the road, to Pittsburgh, about 270 miles away. The very moment he got there, he saw his wife and children boarding a boat to go down the Ohio. Breathless, he tried to plunge in after them. Just as he was about to jump, like a flash his pursuers, who had been sent after him, seized him and took him back again.

One evening a dealer in souls came to a plantation in the southern area with a transport of slaves fresh from Africa and wanted to stay there overnight. Many Negroes worked on this plantation and they belonged to its owner. While the slave driver and the farmer discussed the terms of the overnight stop, the new and old slaves stared at each other and drew closer together. Suddenly there was a loud outcry. A woman among the newly arrived slaves and a man from the plantation fell on each other's necks and hugged each other. They were husband and wife who eighteen years ago had been unfortunately separated. Now they met again in this manner. This heartrending meeting moved the slave trader at least to the extent that he offered his slave to the farmer at a lower price

revolt. The laws passed against Negro literacy inhibited the Negro's education but were never so effectively enforced as to prevent a Negro from learning to read and write if he was set upon doing so. One southern editor, arguing the obsolescence of the laws, wrote in 1862 that he had never known a case of punishment for its violation. See Clement Eaton, *A History of the Old South* (New York: The Macmillan Company, 1949), pp. 260–273.

or offered to buy his at a higher price than he would otherwise have done, so that these two people could be together. But the satanical farmer would do neither of these things and took devilish pleasure in separating these poor wretches again.

Ah, one could tell many such heartbreaking tales. The slave trade is an inerasable stain of shame for the United States of North America. A few states, God be praised, have done away with the practice.

The people of Colombia in South America have given a laudable example. Hardly had they made themselves free and thrown off the harsh Spanish yoke when they also expressed the desire to have no more slaves. They were to enjoy freedom like other people. A law prohibited all slave trade and gave the Negroes the same rights of citizenship as any other inhabitant. In addition, another law forbade the import of all foreign merchandise which it was possible to do without. This province wishes to establish a truly independent self-sufficiency. This puts North America, which has boasted of its freedom and independence for forty years, to shame on two counts.

The president of the free island of Haiti offers all freed slaves in North America freedom and land on his island, as well as free transportation to the island. Several shiploads have already sailed there. Haiti and Colombia are perhaps the morning stars which precede the day of freedom from all slavery in all of America. God willing, may the dawn come soon!

There are several sects that must be praised because they are fervent haters of slavery: Moravians, Quakers, and others.

Condition of the church

THE government does not give preference to any particular religious denomination, but respects them all, as long as none of them disturbs the others' worship of God.

Among the Germans, the Lutherans are the most numerous. They have six synods, more than two hundred preachers, and in excess of one thousand congregations. Then come the Reformed, with about eighty preachers, one synod, and about five hundred communities. In Ohio there are many who call themselves United Brethren. Then there are Mennonites, Moravians, Anabaptists, and so on.

Among the English, the Presbyterians, Baptists, and Methodists are

234

the most numerous. There are also many Episcopalians and Congregationalists. In several seaport cities there are also many Quakers. Catholics are numerous in several cities. They have the outstanding churches in New Orleans and Baltimore. The monasteries are insignificant. Altogether there are over fifty sects. All of them, indeed, have the same God. He is worshipped and called Father differently, but these are only external differences.

The preachers in almost all denominations are chosen by the congregations and supported by voluntary subscription. As a result of this all shepherds are dependent upon their sheep. They do not have an assured position. If a preacher does not preach in a way that pleases the farmers, they say, "Well, we want to have another one." It is true that the Germans are mostly very miserable preachers with a very narrow education. The English are supposed to be much more capable.

A minister often has to serve several congregations. The Lutheran minister who lives in this town and is our good friend has in addition to the city congregation five other congregations in the country which he must serve. In these he preaches every two weeks and in the most remote places every four weeks. His income can rise to six or seven hundred dollars. In some places a minister gets over a thousand dollars. There is also a Reformed Church here. Their minister lives eight miles from here, and comes only every four weeks to hold services. I have not seen any religious instruction provided for children. They say it is given in some places.

In the churches there is certainly too much freedom, that is, during the services. Each comes and goes as he wishes. Still, this is sometimes a great blessing, if you cannot stand it for the whole time.

Last Whitsuntide we attended the confirmation exercises at the Reformed Church. After they had completed their examination they had to go to the altar to take their vows and to be confirmed. Several communicants had to be baptized before they could be confirmed. This really seemed a bit strange to us.

Small children are rarely baptized in church. The farmer frequently waits until he has two, three, or even four children before he calls the preacher to the house to have them baptized.

The synods also elect and pay their own itinerant preachers who are sent to the western regions in which there are still few inhabitants and no churches. There they preach the word of God to the scattered settlers.

235

Schools

THE country schools are generally still in a very bad condition. There is not one school board anywhere and no principal. The whole matter is up to the farmers. Ten or twelve and sometimes more get together and build a little schoolhouse in the middle of their district. If a man comes along who wants to be a teacher, whoever he may be, he goes around to the farmers and signs up the children each farmer is willing to send. If he gets a number sufficient to maintain himself, he starts the school. If not, he goes on to another place. For each child he is generally paid one third to two thirds of a dollar a month. They learn only to read; little writing is taught, rarely arithmetic, and never singing. So the children are registered for school; now comes the question whether they will attend or not. They have their way at home and at school. If the schoolteacher wants to maintain order, and he seems too strict to the children, they just do not attend any more. Their parents do not force them to attend, either. Discipline and seriousness are not at home here, anywhere. Through my own experience, however, I find that the blame lies mostly with the teacher himself when the students contradict him and say right to his face, "Well! If you do this I'm not coming back again." The teachers are mostly rough fellows with little understanding. They know as little about sensible treatment of children as a heathen wandering about in darkest ignorance knows about the Light of the Gospels. It is true that there is great freedom for the child, and the stubborn little mule won't be guided by command or beating, but the teacher's intelligent, impartial concern, and a certain awakening of pride in the child make him a bit more tractable. Gradually through a sensible treatment he would become more willing and capable of love and obedience.

Here and there the Lancaster method has found acceptance.

Since the English language is the dominant one, all the schools in this language are the best supported. Even though the German church service is maintained in many places, still on the whole the young people are raised in the English language. Now and then you will find children of German parents who will no longer speak one word in their mother-tongue. The splendid German language, which has so many great advantages over the English language, will in time perish.

In the northern states school instruction is said to be better than in all the others. This is because the state governments have taken charge of education and have also seen to it that poor as well as rich can enjoy education. In the middle and southern states the children of the poor, and often of the rich as well, learn little more than reading. These are the slave states. This is not true of the other states and the new states. In the new states of Ohio, Indiana, Illinois, and so on, a square mile of public land in each township is kept to be used for schools. In every state some land in a number of townships, up to ten square miles, is also designated for high schools.

At present there are nine universities, thirty-eight colleges, and seven theological seminaries in the United States, at least in name. I cannot and will not pass any further judgment on them.

Perhaps one of my friends here or there is shaking his head and is a bit taken aback by the description of church and school instruction. But friend! I beg you to withhold your harsh judgment until you have looked about a bit and studied the situation. Take our farmers, our country people, even our city and town people at home, think how they are. Would they without the compulsion of law, without any external impetus whatsoever, get together voluntarily in groups of fifty to a hundred families to build a church or in groups of ten to twenty families to build a schoolhouse? Would they support and pay a preacher and a school-teacher? Would they do that generally, I ask you? *

It may be true, furthermore, that there is much that is disorganized, undisciplined — much that is immoral — to be found here. There may indeed be a great deal of crudeness, lack of polish, lawlessness, and freedom poorly used. Despite all of this, it must be said to the honor of America: Religion is held in much higher esteem here than in the old world. The farmer and everyone else hold more firmly to the reverence of God and the Bible than is true over there. A minister, even though he may be dependent upon the farmers, if he is sensible, if he has love and dedication to his calling, and if he preaches the word of God clearly and without confusion, is not the pawn of the people. He achieves for himself trust, respect, and love.

Nowhere among the people do you hear anything said in ridicule or with double meaning about any religious truth. In no company is material chosen from the Bible subjected to ridicule as entertainment and passed around for each to attempt a derisive joke. The worst sinner still has

* This might not happen generally, but in most places it would if it were necessary. The effort of the people on behalf of school and church in Canton St. Gallen, for example, gives proof of this. [Publisher's note, 1826.]

some respect for religion. No newspaper editor is ashamed to accept genuine religious essays for his paper and to write about religion himself with warmth and respect. A few of the seaport cities may already constitute something of an exception to this, because they may already have absorbed somewhat more of Europe's fashionable enlightenment.

The camp meeting

WE WERE told that ten miles from here a German camp meeting would be held by the United Brethren and the Methodists.[16] We were told about many miracles and wonders that were supposed to take place at these meetings. As a result of this, we became curious and wanted to see this thing too.

We went, and we found a great crowd of people in a remote forest, under high, shady oaks. All around, tents had been set up (a gathering such as this usually lasted eight days) in which were beds, boxes, trunks, tables, and chairs. Behind each tent a fireplace smoked for cooking and roasting. Rows of boards on blocks were set up for seats. An alley divided the men from the women. Below this a pulpit was erected upon which at least a dozen preachers parade. In front of this and adjacent to it a square enclosure is set aside as a holy place for new converts. Daily as long as the thing lasts, from early morning until deep into the night, there is preaching, praying, and singing. When one preacher is through another one steps up. Today we had the honor of hearing three of these men of God. How those fellows hack away! How they blast open and shut the gates of hell! How they summon forth the flames of eternal

[16] The holding of religious camp meetings in groves and forests apparently began shortly before 1800. The practice spread rapidly so that by 1820 there were perhaps a thousand such encampments held each year. The *Grosse Versammlungen* held in the ample barns of the Pennsylvania Germans and Swiss in the late eighteenth century were ancestors of the camp meeting.

The leading minister on this occasion may well have been Jacob Gruber, who was an active revivalist among German-speaking people in Maryland in Rütlinger's time.

Like many American churchmen and lay people of that period, foreign visitors (like Frances Trollope) and immigrant observers often wrote very critically of the exaggerated emotionalism of camp meetings. One writer suggested that more souls were made than saved. More significant is the fact that the camp meetings had a strong influence upon the religious and moral life of people, particularly on the frontier, which was poorly served by established churches. Camp meetings served people often completely deprived of religious services for years, who were therefore willing to gather from great distances and to spend three or four days. See Charles A. Johnson, *The Frontier Camp Meeting: Religion's Harvest Time* (Dallas: Southern Methodist University Press, 1955), pp. 29, 85, 147, 149, 181.

damnation from the smoky abyss is something frightful! They jump into the air so that the rafters crack under their leaps. They beat their hands together over their heads, shout and scream with all the strength of their body, and work up their enthusiasm until they can no longer draw breath from their lungs. They usually do not give up until their most ardent brothers and sisters are sighing loudly, moaning and groaning, throwing themselves on the ground, and rolling in the mud.

The last one who appeared while we were there made noise in English. I will see this one as long as I live. A tall, old, ice-gray man. Oh! How he carried on! How he whipped the tails of his old English straight-cut coat about his legs! Unfortunately I could not understand him, but his gymnastics and noise must have had a very unusual power. Many people surged into the sacred place, making a great noise and writhing on the ground like senseless animals. A screeching song was begun by the ministers; in between, you could hear shouts: "Come in, whoever feels awakened. Now is the time to be saved by grace." Several ministers went down, prayed over the new converts, laid hands on them, and blessed them, while the shouting and singing rang forth from all sides. My wife said, "Let's get away from here. I've seen and heard enough." And so we did.

Witnesses told us that at night, when fires and lights were kept going in the sinister darkness, it reached the point where people were carried from the place unconscious. Some people had already died on the spot. I will not say another word about this except that this description is really the truth.

We attended a meeting of Moravians in Lancaster during their love feast.[17] The service began with solemn organ tones and soft song. Then the minister gave a simple sermon in gentle tones and with a smiling face in a manner that touched the spirit most delicately and tenderly. Then a steward and stewardess appeared and handed each person an excellent cup of coffee, hot off the fire, and a fine bun. This we enjoyed in great comfort, sitting in our chairs while the minister continued his sweet discourse. This service is the opposite of the service described above. The former seeks to shake the soul through thundering and with

---

[17] The Moravians used the term "love feast" to describe informal gatherings at which light refreshments were served. These partly devotional and partly social gatherings were held frequently throughout the year. The simple meal of which all partake in common symbolized the fact that there is no respect of persons before the Lord. See P. E. Gibbons, *Pennsylvania Dutch*, 3rd ed. rev. (Philadelphia: J. B. Lippincott & Co., 1882), p. 177, and Fredric Klees, *The Pennsylvania Dutch* (New York: The Macmillan Company, 1950), p. 101.

frightful threats. The latter touches the spirit softly through gentle example and friendly, warm agreeability. To both of these all spiritual powers and strength of soul seem to be nothing but emotion.

I would have liked to visit a Quaker meeting as well. They have no definite minister. They sit in church and contemplate in solemn silence, their eyes glued to the ground, until one of them feels moved to speak. This person then stands up and says, "I feel awakened." And then he begins to pour out what is surging through his heart. They say that often very amusing things come out.

I am far from criticizing this or that religious sect with disparaging remarks or ridicule. To the contrary, for those with which I am more familiar I have respect. They honor God ardently, they are generally useful, and they are tolerant of other ways of thinking.

Something about courts and government

IN THE year 1776, when North America was still an English colony, it declared its independence. After a war of seven years it was victorious with the aid of France and its freedom was recognized. The United States of America were then formed, a federal Constitution was drawn up, and the plan for a national government was designed.

The president is the highest officer of the United States. He is indirectly elected every four years. The people elect one man out of every 36,000 who is to vote for president and vice-president. The Senate consists of two representatives from each state without regard to population. They are elected alternately by the state government for six-year terms. Members of the House of Representatives are elected every two years; one representative is chosen for each 36,000 people. This body and the Senate form the Congress or national legislature. Any member may propose a law, but the proposed law, after careful study, must receive a majority vote in the House of Representatives and in the Senate and also the approval of the president before it becomes law. The president receives an annual salary of 25,000 dollars and the vice-president 5000 dollars. Every member of the Congress receives eight dollars a day while it is in session.

Washington, beloved by all and still honored, was the first president of the United States. He was a great, noble, and excellent man. The world may never again produce such a man.

The president appoints his cabinet with the consent of two thirds of

241

the Senate. There is a secretary of state, a secretary for the treasury, one for war, and one for the navy. These together constitute his cabinet. The seat of government is in the city of Washington.

Each state also has its own legislature and a governor who is elected by the people. The legislature is organized like that of the national government with a Senate and a House of Representatives which make the laws for the state.

In the election of a governor, as in all elections, the people take extraordinary interest. Many weeks before, you hear shouts along the streets and in the taverns: Hurrah for D.! Hurrah for G.! Children who can barely talk chime in. In the newspapers opposing opinions begin to appear, trying to extol or decry the matters that are coming up at the election. Huge bets are made, won, and lost. Once the election is over, everything becomes quiet and everyone seems to be satisfied until the time of the next election.

Every state is divided into counties, and each of these has a judiciary called a court. This examines and judges all criminal cases and all quarrels among the citizens. The chief judge in most states is appointed by the governor. Two or three citizens are made available to him to help and advise him in civic matters. When court is held, 48 men are chosen from the county. These are veniremen for this specific court and are made known to the public. When court begins, their names are placed in a little box. When the court clerk has read the case to be heard by the judge (the cases are taken in order), the judge asks the defendant if he is ready for his case to be heard. If there are no mitigating circumstances to merit postponement, the clerk draws twelve names out of the box, and these are the arbitrators or the jury. They are sworn in. Then the case is heard, the witnesses testify, the lawyers are allowed to speak or to lie. After this the judge gives a short summary statement of the law pertaining to the case, and then the jury withdraws to its own room. They must stay there until they have reached a unanimous verdict. Then they come back and announce their verdict to the court.

Nothing counts in this country but the letter of the law. The judge can do nothing but abide by it. The decision depends on the skill of the lawyers. They are said to be mostly very capable and fluent men who know how to cleverly circumvent and confuse the letter of the law in each case, to twist and to procrastinate according to their advantage. What motivates them, whether conscientiousness, money, or pride, I do not want to try to decide. I only know this, that whenever anyone asks

242

a lawyer for advice, even if the lawyer has only a few words to offer, the man must pay a few dollars for it.

The court is held with open doors

HERE is an example of how the letter of the law may be circumvented: A young fellow came to a lawyer and said he loved a girl and that he wanted to steal her because he could not get her any other way. He therefore wanted his advice as to how he should go about this in order to avoid being subject to punishment. They lawyer said, "Good, but you can't just go and steal the girl straight away. You will be caught by the letter of the law. But, do you know what, have the girl ride ahead of you on a horse in the direction you want to go. In this way your sweetheart has abducted you, and the law can't do anything to you at all. A girl who abducts a boy doesn't have to fear the law; only the other way around." No sooner said than done. The young man paid well for the advice, thanked him, and went on his way. The lawyer's only daughter was very beautiful, and I do not know what kind of special gentleman he was saving her for. On the morning of the following day she was gone. That was indeed a good trick!

Every county is again divided into townships. In each of them one or more justices of the peace are appointed, by whom all petty quarrels are tried and decided. In some states these are appointed by the governor, and in others they are elected by the citizens of the township for a specific term. In addition there are also several constables; they are somewhat like a sergeant or a gendarme at home.

In most of the states the laws favor poor debtors. No one can be put in jail for debt unless fraud in the transaction can be demonstrated by the property owners or creditors.

If someone is put in jail for debt, and he swears that he has nothing to pay with, or as they say here, "that he isn't worth anything," then he is free of his debts. Then as long as he is stuck in jail his creditor must support him. In this way many a man has turned over his money and property, whether much or little, to his wife, and then sworn himself out of jail. The common expression here, "He isn't worth anything," applies very well to such a person.

A murderer, unless it can be proved many times over by witnesses that he killed another with premeditation and in cold blood, does not have to pay with his life.

In assault cases, there is a fairly stiff punishment for the aggressor who strikes first.

Here as everywhere, it is a blessing not to become involved in a lawsuit. It is really better to suffer injustice than to seek justice in the courts.

All official duties must be carried on under oath. If someone has scruples about taking an oath on the Bible, he is asked: "Will you speak the truth before God and man?" If he answers yes, this is accepted. The reason for this is that certain sects, Quakers, Separatists, and so on, will not swear an oath. They confine themselves to yea, yea, nay, nay — anything else is bad.

The military

ALL men from 18 to 45 years of age belong to the militia and must practice the use of arms on certain days. They may, however, buy themselves free of military obligations for a certain sum. Several sects do this because they consider war unjust. The military training is very simple and rather limited. Each person wears his own civilian clothing, whatever he has. What they say about the Appenzeller exercises is true here too: *Vor altä Zitä händ si ä Hauä än Ax furnä Füsi, und än Stekä fürnen Degä gha, und si händ no viel thuä asä* (In the old days they used a hoe or an axe as a gun and a stick for a sword, and still they got a lot done). If a man does not have a musket he takes a stick or whatever he can find, appears, and practices with that. The volunteer corps and the military in the larger cities are well equipped and also better trained. But in the ordinary land militia, as I said, one man carries his gun on his right shoulder and the other on his left. Yet they won their freedom, and they are very proud of this. It is certainly true that when land, blood, freedom, and life are involved, it will not help much to have uniforms all made from the same material and of the same cut, with buttons of the same size and shape, or muskets of the same kind with shining metal. What counts is courage, loyalty, brotherly love, honesty, a common devotion to country, home, property, and justice.

America maintains a standing army of only a few thousand men. These are not a curse for the country but a true blessing. Through them useful roads are built, advantageous canals are opened, and fortifications for the protection of the country's liberty are erected. The forest yields before them, and the wilderness is transformed into fertile fields through which plow and harrow pass.

244

The post, roads, and the conditions of travel

THE United States has about 5000 postal stations or post offices. Every little insignificant village has one. These offices are all branches of the general post office in the seat of government. All of them belong to one circuit which contains over 80,000 miles of post roads. The postal system is still in a very defective state, since no repayment is made by the post office for lost or stolen articles. No doubt an eye is kept on the honesty of the men who run the postal service, but it is still risky to turn over money or other valuables to the post.

From what I have already said, it can be concluded that the United States is fairly well cut through with roads. Still, these passages have many inconveniences for travelers, especially in the less inhabited areas. In many places there is a lack of suitable building materials to maintain and build roads. Because of this a foot traveler in rainy weather sometimes is almost choked in the mud and muck. Often he comes to a swollen brook where there is neither bridge nor plank to help him over. There he stands, not knowing what to do, until perhaps a wagon driver or a man on horseback helps him out of his predicament. Not much attention is paid to doing away with these inconveniences, because the American traveler never sets foot upon the roads. He travels by horseback or rolls over the roads in a wagon. Anyone can find an opportunity to ride in a convenient stagecoach, but that is very expensive.

Bridge and road tolls are perhaps nowhere more expensive than here. Most of the roads, and the bridges over big streams, were privately built. These, besides being useful, are a source of great gain for those who have invested capital in them. All that is needed is permission of the government, and that is rarely denied. Because of this the toll stations on the roads are legion. Anyone can avoid paying toll if he knows of a road that goes around the toll station, or if he pleases to make a road himself, without penalty.

If a traveler wants to eat and drink in a tavern, this costs considerable money. For every ordinary meal a quarter of a dollar is charged, and for a bed one eighth of a dollar. If he comes to the tavern between meals, he can rarely get any other refreshment than that miserable whiskey which the Americans gulp down standing up, without even a little piece of bread. To a new immigrant it seems completely strange that he cannot have his little bottle of wine, his small loaf of bread, and whatever soup or bit of meat he wants whenever he wants to. However, when a family leaves

245

home and moves many hundred miles away, it is less inconvenient and less costly than it would be at home. If they have their own horse and wagon, they pack up the most necessary things, take their food along, do their own cooking in inns or at farmers' houses, and sleep on their own beds. If they do not own their own vehicle there are opportunities enough to have their things hauled by teamsters. The charge for this is not more than two or three dollars for a hundred pounds on a two- or three-hundred-mile trip. If boat transportation can be used, it costs even less.

Excellent gun factories

JUST recently my friend and I returned from a very ingenious factory which is located about eighteen miles from here.[18] It deserves all admiration. I think that visiting this artistic production alone would merit a trip to America. The whole thing is too complicated and big for me to venture to describe. The entire works is water-operated. There are regularly from 300 to 500 workers, and none of them has to work very hard. From fifteen to twenty thousand guns are made here annually. All are made so precisely that bayonets, locks, and screws are interchangeable. Even for the gunstocks, a piece of wood is set into a machine, and it comes out shaped to the correct design, so that only a little handwork is required to finish and smooth it. At present there are 75,000 of the most beautiful guns stored in the arsenal.

There are said to be three such gun factories in the United States, but this is the best of them.

The little city itself, which is called Harpers Ferry, is situated in a wild, romantic setting in a narrow valley shut off by cliffs and mountains. Through it the Potomac flows, pure and silver, over rocks and boulders.

What is even more praiseworthy about this place is the fact that any

[18] During the presidency of George Washington, the Congress authorized the establishment of a gun factory and federal armory at Harpers Ferry. The factory began production in 1801, and by 1810 was producing 10,000 guns a year. In 1819, John Hall of Maine, a gunsmith and inventor, was given a government contract to manufacture a thousand rifles of his own design — a breech-loading flintlock rifle. So exact was the manufacture of parts that all could be used interchangeably. Hall's guns proved excellent and thousands more were ordered. Several buildings were assigned to Hall for his use. This was the first completely successful example of the system of mass-producing manufactured goods. See Francis A. Lord, *Civil War Collector's Encyclopedia: Arms, Uniforms, and Equipment of the Union and Confederacy* (Harrisburg: Stackpole Co., 1963), pp. 242–243. See also United States Department of Interior, National Park Service, "Harpers Ferry National Monument, West Virginia," n.d.

stranger, without regard to person, can enter the factory freely and un-hindered. He can look and stare at everything and everything is shown to him. He does not first have to ring a couple of dozen doorbells until he has found a money-hungry guard or watchman who will agree to let him in only when he sees that his efforts and politeness will bring him a considerable tip. At this place you come in and observe a group of modest working people. You do not recognize the great man who runs and orders this important business. Nor do you recognize the genius who drew the plans for this astounding factory, nor the architect who executed it. It is only the mark of genius on their faces that identifies them. Each one has his hat on the right spot — his head, that is — firmly and fast. It is not often removed in deference. They say to you, "How do you do?" (pronounced "howdy do?"); this is the usual greeting when people meet. Here you do not see a special office in every corner with about a half dozen little clerks with slicked-down hair sitting at desks, keeping their eyes glued to their papers not because they have a great deal to do, but from sheer perverseness and rigidity, as if it would be just too vulgar to turn around to see who was there. Oh, no! You do not find miserable creatures like that here.

Our hands got confused after the long tour of admiration and wonder, and found some money in our pockets and offered it as a tip to the man who had made a special trip to show us the arsenal. He refused it so modestly and earnestly that we would have been ashamed to press it further.

Not long ago I read in the paper that a wool-spinning machine had been invented that can spin a pound of wool for a cent.

Indians

THIS summer for the first time we saw the original inhabitants of America. Chiefs and their followers, representing two tribes, traveled through this little city.[19] They had been at war with one another, and

[19] This is the delegation of Chief Keokuk and other chiefs of the Sacs and Foxes (but not Black Hawk), traveling to Washington in the summer of 1824 under escort of the Indian agent William Clark. Because of their particular eminence, Keokuk was allowed to take one of his wives and the Fox chief Tiamah, his wife and daughter.

The advance of white settlements not only had impaired the relations between the Sacs and Foxes and the Americans but also had stimulated conflict over tribal lands between the two tribes and the Sioux. In September 1823, the Sac and Fox

now in order to arrange peace they were going to the president of the United States in Washington. They must have traveled a few thousand miles for this mediation.

There were some really interesting faces among them. They are very different from the Negroes. They have a copper-brown color, small, sly, suspicious black eyes, a very strong chest, and thin, slender arms and legs. They are covered from their feet to their hips with soft deerskin clothing. On the upper body a wool cloth is draped. This is taken off when they retire. Some of them had part of their faces painted red and a tuft of hair on top of the head tied together with gay feathers in it. Others had a narrow, cropped strip of hair going from the forehead to the nape of the neck. The rest of the scalp was smooth and brown. The hair roots seemed to have been killed. On the upper edge of the ear, in large pierced holes, they wore ornaments of iron rings and chains; several thick brass rings were worn on the upper arm. One carried a deadly weapon very carefully on his arm. It had a spike set in a wooden shaft and was designed for striking, not for pushing. Marks were scratched into it, showing how many enemies the Indian had already brought down with it. He seemed to be very proud of this. A whole cluster of gay silk ribbons fluttered from it.

Duty and laws are supposed to be sacred to Indians. No one need fear them who has treated them honestly. If they are offended and cheated, however, then their revenge is said to be terrible.

Purchase of land, and what a person must be aware of if he wishes to settle

SINCE the government of the United States was formed, it has purchased additional territories of great size. Louisiana, a large strip of land to the west of the United States and extending to the Pacific Ocean,

chiefs asked permission to send a delegation to Washington to present their claims. Secretary of War John C. Calhoun, who had refused a similar petition two years before, now reluctantly gave consent. Keokuk persuasively presented claims to lands west of the Mississippi in Missouri, but in the end signed away claims in return for minor financial grants and annuities.

Members of the tribal delegation were taken by Clark on a tour of Baltimore, Philadelphia, New York, and other eastern cities. The tour pleased Keokuk and convinced him more than ever of the unwisdom of fighting the United States. Later Black Hawk led his band of Sacs and Foxes in a vain struggle against Americans in the Black Hawk War. See William Hagan, *The Sac and Fox Indians* (Norman: University of Oklahoma Press, 1958), pp. 93–97.

was bought in 1803 from the French for 15,000,000 dollars. A few years ago both Floridas to the south of the United States were purchased from the Spaniards.

At first these wild lands were given free to settlers. Experience taught, however, that this was not a good way. There were disputes about boundary lines among the farmers. Two, three, and sometimes more people fought over the same piece of land. As a consequence of this, there are many lawsuits to this day in Pennsylvania, Ohio, and particularly in Kentucky, and it is very difficult to decide who was the first to mark out the claim. After this the government surveyed all the lands and laid them out in squares of 160 acres and had them numbered. The land was then sold for two dollars an acre. A quarter of the price had to be paid immediately, the other three parts in triennial payments. Then many people bought more land than they could possibly pay for, so they lost their land. This, too, caused much dissatisfaction among such purchasers. Then they made a law that all land must be paid for in cash at a dollar and a quarter an acre.

Whoever wants to buy land goes into the forest, hunts himself up a piece of land (you cannot buy less than 160 acres from the government), notes the number, township, county, etc., which are marked on the trees. Then he goes to the courthouse, presents the land description, and pays for the land. Then he receives a guaranteed bill of purchase from the land office of the government. With this he can occupy the land undisturbed or sell it at will. The right is undisputed.

In purchasing land, a man must pay special attention to location and fertility. He should never settle more than ten to twelve miles from a navigable river, and avoid swamps or too rocky land. Swamps and places too near rivers are unhealthy, and in rocky areas there is a great amount of difficulty and labor.

Many immigrants fail because they are not aware of these things. They settle either too close to rivers or in damp hollows, and then suffer terribly from fever, so that the most beautiful situation would repel them. Or they go too far inland where they lack the opportunity of bringing their products to market. The distance is too great, the roads bad or completely lacking. Besides, it is very difficult to bring things in from the outside. There they sit, and the richest harvest brings them no joy.

Another reason so many immigrants have had a hard time earning a satisfactory livelihood is that they have settled individually, not knowing the land or its inhabitants, among all kinds of people. There they find strange customs and a strange language; they are often taken advantage of and cheated. Because of these difficulties they lose all courage and fortitude; they fall into poverty and are held in contempt.

Settling on wild land is often not as difficult as one would imagine. If the family is fortunate enough to come to a good spot, the neighbors gather to help. They bring their piece of bread along and build a house in one day. This costs the settler nothing but a couple of gallons of whiskey. The logs, untrimmed and with the bark still on, are placed one on top of the other. Stone and mud are placed in the cracks and the roof is made of coarse shingles. If the settler wants to prepare a place for a garden, the small bushes are simply cleared away and burned. Then a fence is built around this place. The ground is broken as well as possible if there is no plow; seed is planted between the big trees. In the spring, before the sap rises, the bark is chopped through so that the trees will die. In this way the land is cultivated for two or three years among the dead trees. Then the land is left idle for one or two years while other pieces of land are prepared in the same way. The branches fall from the trees; in three or four years the trunks themselves begin to fall. In the late summer, fire is set to them so that they will be burned up by planting time. Then the field is seeded again. Wheat and corn are said to do very well among the dead trees.

How to settle to best advantage

WITHOUT any doubt the best and most sensible new way to cultivate these lands would be to have a number of families who know each other settle together. With the help of God they would be sure of their good fortune. They would have a big advantage in building their houses and could help each other in clearing the land. Not all of them would have to buy all the necessary tools at once. Selling and buying of products could be done more easily. Sawmills, flour mills, tanneries, and factories could be established more quickly and more easily. It would be far easier to provide for churches and schools. Widows and orphans could receive advice and help from their fellow countrymen. If the colony were of Germans from one country, manners, customs, and language could be preserved.

There are numerous colonies in America and I do not know of any which in a few years did not achieve success. But I know of hundreds and

251

hundreds of individual settlers who are unhappy; they must spend their lives in hardship and need.

There is not a year when whole boatloads of Germans and Swiss do not come over. As soon as they reach dry land, they disperse; one goes one way and the other goes another way, and rarely does any one know what he really wants and where he wants to go. If a person could see them again a few years later, one would be a day-laborer, another a tramp who had been cheated out of his possessions, another would find himself helpless and hopeless in the forest on a piece of bushland that he would like to pay for but can't. By the fiftieth case you might find someone who is in a passable position.

Why does it have to be this way? Why hasn't experience and example made people smarter in this respect by now?

How splendidly the cultivation of grapes would succeed, especially in the western states. The price of wine here is very high. On one gallon, a little more than one of our measures, there is generally a dollar import tax. In spite of this over 3,000,000 gallons are imported a year. In the state of Indiana, near Vevey, there is a colony of French-speaking Swiss who cultivate grapes for wine. The colony is doing very well. I am assured that in fifteen years there was not one bad year. The wine is sold fresh at a dollar a gallon. About 5,000,000 grapes were harvested in one year. This Swiss colony is said to be very prosperous already, but in their first year they had to struggle along by making straw hats just to get enough to eat.

Why wouldn't sheep raising be a profitable enterprise? Even now a sheep produces the value of its purchase price in wool each year, and how cheap the land for pasture is! It must also be considered how many millions are spent yearly for the importation of woolen cloth. Could this not be made in the country as well? That it can be done Rapp has proved in his colony on the Wabash. He established woolen mills and his cloth is sought after; a yard costs from eight to ten dollars.

Something could also be done about cotton. Many millions of pounds are grown in the southern and southwestern states. In the state of Carolina alone, in one year, over eight million dollars' worth of cotton was harvested; the price is eight to fifteen cents a pound. Rice, indigo, and tobacco are also grown. In Indiana successful experiments in the cultivation of all these products have been made.

In this state and in the state of Ohio they still raise a lot of cattle and pigs. Last fall and winter 33,000 pigs were driven through Middletown

252

to Baltimore alone, and many oxen as well. Many farmers keep from one hundred to five hundred pigs. In the summer and winter they feed themselves in the forests and in the fall they are driven into the corn fields. After that they are sent off to market. The breeding of horned cattle is still completely neglected. A great deal could be accomplished by it.

He who has ears to hear, let him hear!

Luck is round as a ball

LUCK appears in the new world with the same round shape as in the old. Many a man sees it rolling around in front of him. He watches it for a while, and before he has planned with which expedients it can most certainly be caught, it eludes him. Or he goes empty-handed in his attempt to catch the round thing and stick it in his pocket. But he reaches for it in vain! It always eludes him. Many a man is plagued this way his whole life long by lack of success.

Another is clever; he sees it too and thinks: I will just wait for you until you cross my threshold by yourself, then I'll close the door behind you and you are mine. It happens just that way, but not for long. He is so trusting of it, as though no special attention was any longer necessary. Luck flies out the open window and never returns. Another carries it in his pants pocket and does not know it. It follows at a third man's feet without his coaxing it; sometimes he even strikes out at it with his shoe when it gets too close to his heels. It just moves out of harm's way a bit but remains faithful.

N. came fifteen years ago, which was still in the Golden Age in this country. He was a distinguished man and an excellent musician. He knew nothing of a trade. He thought that through musical tinkling he would soon have luck in his power. He did not succeed so readily, however. He wandered from one to the other of the large seaport cities. Nowhere, not even for nothing, could he give music instruction. The man was not very happy because he had already spent a few years this way and saw all his economic resources going. Still he did not let all his courage flee. He took up very menial work. He went to an inland city where he earned his bread by working as a chimney sweep. Everyone appreciated him because he was industrious and performed this black work very well. In this manner he earned a handsome living and also became acquainted with the families. In the course of time he discovered that in many homes they wanted a music teacher. He never said that he was one, however, although he planned not to let this opportunity escape him. Suddenly one day, a music teacher appeared with white, delicate skin, beautiful clothes, and powdered hair. He went in the evening from house to house, wherever he was wanted, and gave instruction in piano and other instruments. Thus he earned four or five dollars every evening. People were astounded by this excellent teacher; he seemed all the more unusual because they did not know where he came from or where he was actually staying. By day this gentleman was nowhere to be seen. Every evening he appeared as though he had dropped out of the clouds. He was the chimney sweep, who did not want to give up this occupation even now. With great care he tried to remain hidden. With great effort every evening he made a music master out of the chimney sweep. He had learned enough from experience to know how uncertain every occupation is; that is why he wanted to keep his chimney-sweeping in reserve, so that he would not lose his customers if the music instruction should suddenly come to an end.

S., an excellent, broadly educated man, a poet, painter, and illustrator, immigrated here a few years ago. He was well informed in numerous branches of higher learning and was even listed as a scholar in the encyclopedia. People recognized the value of his knowledge, yet he did not find a place anywhere or a suitable position in which he could be effective in his fields. He moved in vain from one city to another and from the north to the south. He found neither support nor help. He was not even given the opportunity of earning his living in a lower school. This summer the good man died in the southern states, helpless and unhappy, in great need and poverty.

D. and F. came across the ocean together. D. could not pay his passage and first had to work this off before he could taste American freedom. The latter, however, still had about two hundred dollars when he left the boat. D. wished for nothing more than to be in the same situation as his traveling companion. Still, this could not be and they parted. A baker took D., and he worked there for three years to pay for his passage. He got along well and in time learned his master's trade. He stayed on two more years after he had served his time. He earned so much money that he later had a bakery of his own. Now he is a rich man. F., on the other hand, went into the country and bought about fifty acres of land on which he spent his two hundred dollars. Then the ownership of this land was challenged and he lost everything because he lacked a valid bill of sale. Now he is a poor day-laborer and his wife and children must starve.

Tailor Nix was a good worker and a fine, polished little man with a very fast tongue. He shipped across the Atlantic Ocean a few years ago and came to the land of free thought and free trade. He envisioned himself practicing his tailor's art in America too, and also airing his dull-scissors philosophy in the bright daylight of reason. He hoped to smooth it with the costly, new-style flatiron of American liberty. This anyone would loan him until he had acquired one of his own.

My tailor, surfeited with life on the boat as was everyone else, hopped joyfully on dry land and looked back philosophically on the trip he had just endured. It was due to his own cleverness that he had crossed the sea so successfully. "I knew that's how it would be," he told himself. "I knew that it would not turn out badly. Didn't I choose the right time of the year for my journey and a good ship with a good Captain sailing to the best American harbor?" Thus he made one decision after another until it couldn't turn out any other way than it did, and he came to admire himself as a very clever little fellow in whom foresight and understanding of cause and effect were all combined under the name of common sense.

With this self-satisfied feeling of comfort, Nix filled his pipe with the silver mounting, lit up, and began to smoke. He took his cane in his right hand, and, holding the bowl of the pipe with his left, he strolled through the streets of the city. He bent his back every few moments out of courtesy and his cane would be tucked under his left arm. His ruffled-up hair was almost purged from his head by his frequent tipping of his hat as he greeted the people who passed him. It is true that this fancy behavior attracted attention. Everyone stood still and stared at the German, but without returning his polite bows. A whole gang of boys gathered about him, shouting, "Look! the Dutchman, look! look!" The screams rang piercingly through his ears. He regained his composure, however, and thought: At home in Germany, such behavior toward a stranger would be considered highly crude and stupid; but here there is freedom, and its products are the results of naturalness and free thought, and not slavish compulsion. He let his hat remain on his head, but he could not stop smoking. Certainly not everyone looks at things this way when he first comes from Europe. He soon figured out that there was nothing for him in this city. He would not, as many did, try to become a big city man by force, risking the money he still had for something uncertain. He went to the country, to a small town in which there was only a single tailor

255

who had not learned his trade at the crossroads. He rented a little house and soon had enough work and income. And so he concluded, "That's just what I thought; things won't go as badly for me as they have for others. Some people manage their affairs so stupidly. One must be a bit clever and exercise good judgment."

In this town everything was English, and since Nix knew French he learned the language of this country very quickly as well. Really his talents came to his aid. Then he subscribed to one of the best English-language newspapers. In the very first issue that he read, he found an article which discussed a religious truth with honesty, forthrightness, and simplicity. This appalled him, and his pale cheeks burned red. He felt shame for the editor for having accepted such old-fashioned stuff for his newspaper. He soon composed himself and decided that in this country there is freedom of expression, and this must be the work of a stupid farmer. He will find his opponents soon enough. He watched all the newspapers week after week to see if a refutation would not appear, but none did. It seemed to him that he could easily have marched into battle with his scissors-philosophy and fought against these views and carried off the victory. The enlightened and educated classes, he was sure, consider this thing too simple to be concerned with. So Nix stood again in complete greatness.

The man worked very industriously; his customers increased and everything went well for him. He got acquainted with many people, and wherever he went into a home he found kindness and order. In every home he noticed a Bible and several prayer books lying along with other books on a shiny mahogany commode. None of them, from the smallest to the largest, was covered with dust or cobwebs. They looked as though they were used every day. Nix was greatly surprised, but, he reasoned, there is freedom here; these good people are mostly just farmers who do not know of superior tastes since they live in their traditional simplicity. In their farm life they have no contact with the educated world. Again he stood there in his great self-affection and felt compassion for the ignorant. He wished for nothing more than that these people could use his German library. It was not large, but it was devoted to the best philosophers of the modern period. He heard that in every little city certain societies had been formed which considered questions and propositions that came up about various topics. That is where the enlightened people must be, he thought, here there must be a better atmosphere. There was such a society in this town, too. He soon joined it and it pleased him very much

256

that as a stranger he would be so graciously received. Every subject, to his wonderment, was intelligently developed and, indeed, he felt that in this ability he was not as advanced. However, the people concerned themselves only with topics of general interest: nature study, mechanics, agriculture, geography, political economy, and in general the experiences and work of everyday life. Not one subject concerning religious philosophy came up for discussion. In this respect, he thought, they must be as stupid as the fat Swiss cows. He felt that in time he could arrange to have a subject brought up which in Europe every sensible man who considers himself intelligent has often answered for himself to his own satisfaction — but yet has left many people dissatisfied and misled so many that they abandoned what God's Word and the Bible made so clear, enveloping many in doubt so that they could find no peace within themselves. He went home very pleased and scanned all his books on philosophy once more to be sure to be well armed when he appeared the next time.

He was given the honor of speaking on the subject first since everyone had noticed how interested he was in it. Everything was heard very dispassionately as though his thesis was not particularly shocking to anyone. Occasionally he noticed an expression of compassion on some faces, but there was never a chuckle of approval as he had anticipated. There was a solemn pause when he was finished. He thought he had done the thing so well that no one could possibly say one little word against it. He was wrong, however. The seemingly most simple person sitting in that circle took up the question and spoke with the greatest consideration and respect of the religious truth in question, and so thoroughly and incontrovertibly did each make his plain and sensible objection to Nix that the fire went out of his eyes and he did not dare say another word.

From then on he did not attend the society any more and stuck with his philosophy. Occasionally he tried to pass it on to the farmers, but here also he found no sympathetic ear. Each of them had a better philosophy of life than he did, and each was intelligent and remained with his Bible and prayer book. Then he thought again, this is the land of freedom and the people here are either much more stupid or much more intelligent than in the old world. He accepted the first conjecture. To accept the second would have cost him too much personally, even though now and then he was torn by involuntary doubt.

His philosophical attitude was known to all. Everyone let him know that they still regarded him as Tailor Nix and that no one pointed a finger at him or changed his manner toward him. They changed only in this respect, they no longer gave him any clothes to make — even the people who were a bit vain and concerned with outward appearances and who had been well pleased with his cut and fine sewing. This is what happened; he lost his customers and could not win them back. There stood Nix again; he could not have been anything but stupid not to realize why this had happened. All he said was, "I never would have thought it would be like this." His scissors-philosophy was not broad enough to help him over this moment. He had to leave town and try his luck somewhere else. That he became a little more careful and learned to be silent when he didn't know what was what, I do know. But whether he began to reflect more wisely and nobly about himself and his beliefs, about God and immortality, and about the relations of concepts that, like the terms of a sequence in mathematics, begin with the simplest and most obvious notions in the visible, material world, and then order themselves ever more meaningfully and marvelously, and so continue outward without limit to all eternity — that I don't know.

Sickness and its foes

I AM neither naturalist nor doctor, physicist nor chemist. I do not know, therefore, whether it is the climate of this country or the way of life of the people which is the most responsible for the sickness which exists here. I do observe that a whole host of fevers, from the cold to the hottest, both quick-killing and wasting fevers, as well as rheumatic ailments, make people toss about on their sickbeds. Everyone says that it is very unhealthy in damp and swampy places and too near brooks and rivers. It is true that in such areas you meet sick people most often. But no one escapes these evils entirely, even if he lives on dry, airy heights.

The summers here are generally very warm. People work unreasonably hard in the greatest heat. Strong whiskey is always ready to refresh and cool, as they believe, the parched lung. A cool night often follows a hot day. Not enough attention is paid to this rapid change of temperature. Three times a day they take strongly salted pork, without soup, along with rich pastry. All this taken together would be enough, one would think, to cause persistent disease. A doctor once said that when the fruit harvest was over the doctor's harvest began. It is true that just at this time the fevers spread everywhere.

The malignity of illness may have causes which one should, perhaps, look for among the doctors and among the sick themselves.

The doctor is generally an unashamedly expensive disease-mender. He thinks nothing of charging fifty dollars for two visits three miles away and a dozen pills. Because of this people do not seek the doctor's help except in the greatest emergency, or when their own home remedies no longer help. Every farmer and every wife is half a doctor here. Many people know a surprising number of home remedies. Some of these may even go back to the original inhabitants. It is well known how the savages of bush and island are familiar with the powers of nature. The fault which often lies in the sick person is this: He is so spoiled and so dainty that when he does need a doctor, instead of following his instructions to the letter, he takes the bitter brew once or twice and throws the rest away. And off he goes on his merry way, completely unable to control his impulses. A fine European doctor, accustomed to treating every illness in a deliberate, cautious way and prescribing one pot of herb tea after another, would not find his fortune here.

It is said of an English doctor here that in his prescriptions he charged five dollars for every dot over an *i* and that he did not forget a single one. The American doctors practice in the same dollar-hungry way.

A tale of three Bernese

IN JUNE of this summer one of the newspapers stated that twelve honest Swiss had arrived in Charleston. They planned to go by way of Baltimore to the western states to settle there. Their interest was mainly directed toward establishing vineyards. They ought to be received with good advice and friendship as well as good wishes for the success of their enterprise. We were eager to know from what canton these people might be.

Not long after this newspaper article appeared, three people from Bern came through the town. Because they inquired about German-speaking people they found us. We welcomed them with sincere Swiss handshakes. Now we discovered that they were from the party of twelve we had read about, and recognized in them the prosperous Bernese type. There was a grandfather in his sixties, a forty-year-old man, and a young unmarried man who was a wagoner by trade. The men were of rather good cheer, and it seemed that thus far everything had pleased them. The two older ones had families at home, but since conditions were so bad there that

259

a farmer could not survive, they had decided to come to America. If they like it here they will buy land and then send for their wives and families. Many other rich farmers would then also come along. We were very happy about this because we thought the path might be opened in this way for a Swiss colony. The minister of our town, who has traveled in the western states and has a brother in one of the best spots in Indiana, joined my friend Schweizer, who has made all kinds of inquiries about those parts, in providing them sincerely and truthfully with all possible information about the advantages and disadvantages of the area and giving them the best advice as to how to conduct themselves in various situations.

These three well-stuffed Bernese stayed with us for three days, and we showed them every consideration. When they left they promised to get in touch with us on the way back, come what may. We did not expect them to return for two months. We thought we would give them letters then and get some back through them in the spring. We did not doubt in the least that the marvelous landscape of the west would please them greatly. About five weeks went by and then we happened to hear by chance that there were two Bernese in Baltimore who had passed through in the spring. They were returning to Europe by ship within the next few days. The manner in which they were described indicated that these were the same ones who had stayed with us. Could it be possible that they were there already and had sneaked by us like scamps? That could not be. Schweizer immediately wrote to an acquaintance in Baltimore where this Bernese delegation was supposed to have stayed. The answer came that it was the same party. The fools had made the pilgrimage to Rome, but they had not seen the Pope. They had related that they had proceeded no farther than Pittsburgh, and that since they had not liked it they returned directly. Consequently they saw nothing but the poor mountain land of the Allegheny range. The dunces thought that all of America was like this and that people had just been trying to hoodwink them, or tie a bear on their backs, as the phrase is. We discovered that they had sneaked through Middletown by night and fog like miserable tramps who shun every honest face. The young man alone had the courage to remain here and not return like an infant to his crib. One should send fellows like this one to America if one wants exact information about the country and the prospects that it offers.

I would not even have written this if I had not thought that perhaps someone opposed to immigration might take this opportunity to use this vivid example of the men from Bern to show how all favorable reports from America have been fabricated.

I am far from advising anyone to come to America, especially if it is to happen in this manner, which is unfortunately all too often the case: One comes today, the other tomorrow, one goes in this direction, the other in that direction. But when someone arrives in America and, because of an erroneous point of view or an attitude of superiority, disparages the real advantages which America does have over the old world and shows only the shady side in the darkest light, I cannot keep my mouth closed against such injustice. It is bred of the lowest purposes. The time will probably soon come when the man who now writes against immigration will set his pen in motion in its favor and with just as little honest motivation.

The location of Middletown and the beautiful seasons

MIDDLETOWN is a little city of about forty attractive houses and two very handsome churches. It lies in a little hollow by the side of the main road that goes from Baltimore to the western states. It is surrounded by a hundred oak groves. There are hidden, romantic little valleys in all directions around the town where the farmers have their peaceful, comfortable, and, on the whole, beautiful homes, among which are strewn orchards, farms, and meadows. A little river winds crookedly by, and there is one mill after another, each swiftly and quietly swinging its ingenious wheelworks. The land is rolling, and the whole is encircled by hills like a wall. The whole area looks somewhat like parts of Switzerland except that the stark, bold mountains are missing. Many little valleys here, however, do not have a regular form, and because of it they are that much more interesting and surprising. The highest ridges are forested with oak, chestnut, walnut, and hickory trees. Many kinds of blueberries, and a kind of alpenrose which in beauty and grandeur is perhaps superior to the Swiss kind, grow in among the bushes of the upper areas.

You get a very special satisfying feeling when you come upon the scattered plantations. You come upon a dark-green oak wood where the high-trunked trees spread their strong branches and offer you cool shade even in the hottest summer. You walk into these dim bowers of foliage and slowly refresh yourself in the cool breezes rustling the leaves. You walk thoughtfully on and see the cows pasturing in the grass and rich verdure. Occasionally you are amused to see pigs rush through the underbrush and last year's fallen leaves with stiff little hops. When you least expect it, the forest stops, and you see before you fields of grain or corn. Entwined in the strong, green stalks of corn the wild pea grows. Between the rows pumpkin plants creep. Beyond the fields of this waving sea of green you see tall poplars reaching to the sky and here and there a gigantic weeping willow sways gently.

As you walk on you see before you a magnificent farmhouse peeking through the trees; in Europe it would be considered the seat of nobility. Surrounding the house are broad fenced grounds, and within at least a half dozen smooth, glossy horses wander at will, a flock of poultry, hens, ducks, geese, and guinea hens stroll around, and a magnificent peacock struts proudly. Next to the house you see an orchard sparkling with its burden of golden fruit. In the valley there is a green meadow enclosed by thick bushes. The wild grape at the edge of the little stream climbs up into the highest trees and over its tops; it is hung heavily with millions of little grapes. Above the forest in an empty field a flock of sheep with wool as white as snow grazes its fill on the green plants growing between the old stumps.

I have experienced one American spring with its thousand joys and pleasures. When I walked with my dear friend Schweizer through the green valleys, the blossoming orchards, groves, and forests, I would have liked to call all our Swiss friends about us to show them what charms spring can also have in another and strange part of the world.

Spring, however, begins only at the end of April and the beginning of May. Until this time all life in nature seems dead. The winter has lasted four or five months. This is a period of alternate snow and rain, day after day, and biting cold north winds blow. Last winter there were few days in which the earth was covered with snow for the whole day. Occasionally it was lovely and warm for several days, so that it felt as though spring were about to begin. Yet we did not see a single blade of grass appear and no buds swelled on the trees. Nature knows its period of rest, and it will not awaken until the watchman Spring sounds the call.

It calls! The pastures, the meadows, and the planted fields respond. The sun sends gentle rays, the wind blows warm, and in a few days the fields are green. Flowers soon open their petals. It calls, and the trees stand forth in full blossom, and yet no greening leaf appears. It calls. The oak trees awaken and the delicate green leaves weave a shady canopy

over the cool halls of the woods. The call of spring draws you outdoors into awakening nature. You wander over the green fields, across the hills encircled with trees, down into the valley. There you rest on a boulder in the shade of cedar trees. Near you a brook flows gently and quietly down through the valley, its waters golden. It winds here and there and loses itself among the tall trees only to appear again, shining. All about you, on rocks and spots of green, you discover a multitude of different plants blooming — plants which you have never seen anywhere before. You learn to know them. There are some among them which smile up at you as friends from the old world. The infinite variety of magnificent color and form changes in this blooming meadow. You raise your eyes, and as far as you can see the plantations are framed with the rose-colored splendor of blossoming peach trees. You cannot imagine anything more beautiful or charming than a whole row of such trees in bloom. Certainly they must have been the most splendid ornament of the garden where Adam and Eve spent their innocent days. Before the peach tree has put aside its crimson mantle the cherry tree is hung with snow. Then the apple tree appears in pale pink blossoms. Thus before you stands the magnificent bouquet of May, filled with the most beautiful blooms and blossoms of nature. What heart could remain untouched in the midst of this temple of spring!

You may wander all spring and summer through the woods and forests, and you always discover new trees and bushes in bloom. You find an indescribable variety of plants in the American forests. The woods are populated with thousands of different birds. Their songs are really more shrieking and cackling than appealing in tone; they do not charm the ear like those of Swiss forest singers. But the eye is filled with joy and wonder at the multitude of colored plumages. All of nature sparkles with an infinite glory of color.

Autumn too is lovely. I would almost say it is the most beautiful time of the year. The oppressive heat of summer changes to a lovely mellowness. Until almost Christmas time and New Year's, when winter really begins, the sky is almost always clear as far as the eye can see. Oh, the most marvelous feelings of nostalgia and joy are awakened in one's soul when fall comes to the American woodlands! There is a very remarkable solemnity about this scene. There is an infinite variety of color to be found among the thousands of different bushes and trees; they take on their color at different times of year and have a unique splendor which can be admired only in the American world. And the morning and eve-

ning sun on the high autumn woodlands colors this painting with endl
glory and splendor. Schiller indeed spoke the truth when he said, "T
world is perfect everywhere that man has not entered with his torment
What disturbs you most in this autumnal season is the thousands or
pounds of fruit that lie under the trees; here the pigs grub about and the
cows munch and what remains rots.

The end of the song

I COULD have given many other striking examples of the fertility
of this land, but so much has been written about it that everyone must
be convinced of the astonishing harvest of the American soil, even though
he be the greatest enemy of this continent.

My dear friends, now you are going to ask me if I am happy in America
and if it in general pleases me. You could probably already judge quite
accurately from my account. Whatever your conclusion may be, I will
not answer your question with an unqualified yes. The point where everything pleases and where there is nothing left to wish for one must not
seek this side of the grave. This much I can tell you, I no longer wish
myself back in the old world and its circumstances. Even if you could
look deep into my eyes and ask me on my honor and conscience, I would
not answer you differently. Although I have yet no definite prospect of a
certain and assured livelihood, at least the hope of it is not trickling away
in sad futility as in the old world. Here it is still possible to get a piece of
good, fertile land without having to spend huge sums of money on it.
When one has this, then he can sing boldly with the poet Ambühl, "See,
what I have is mine alone. It is clear and free of debts," and "No prince
dare claim my land from me, the Lord be thanked for this," and, "I wear
my hat upon my head whichever way I please," and so on. Could I do
this in Europe even if a thousand acres were given me to command and
to work? And I would not reproach myself with having done it all for
nothing, if somehow conditions in Europe had improved while I've been
here. Would God it were so! I would then be more at peace in the lap
of American freedom. Unfortunately, however, oral and newspaper reports from there continue to bring news to the contrary. Perhaps soon
the man who formerly charged the emigrant with being an ungrateful
scorner of his native country will himself take up the wanderer's staff
and seek happiness and freedom in America — that is, if the pitiful idea
that for love of country one must bend one's bare neck to the yoke has

not already robbed him of too much money or aged him prematurely. It is true that a man owes his country everything, but to unjust coercion he owes nothing.

A complete evaluation of America, its situation and conditions, I do not yet trust myself to make. When I consider everything I cannot yet say if I should regard its liberty as a goddess furthering the happiness of mankind or as a hateful demon with the opposite consequences and effects. Sometimes I think one way, sometimes another. I do believe this, however; America is still capable of anything. I mean to say that it lies in the balance between benediction and curse. All that is required is an initial push and one of the weights in the scale will rise and the other will sink. Which way the balance will shift is not yet determined.

But whatever is to happen to America will, it appears, happen quickly. Will it meet the fate of the Greeks, the Romans, the Germans, or will it meet a fate uniquely its own? In either case, it will all happen in a much shorter period of time than theirs did. It seems, I might say, that its physical aspect foreshadows, as it were, the duration of its scientific and moral aspects. Plants grow with incredible strength and speed and in just as incredibly short a time they perish. A tall tree is full grown in fifteen to twenty years. If a tree is chopped down and the atmospheric conditions given full sway the tree is rotten in two or three years. It is the same with the flowering fruit trees; they are unusually exuberant and the fruit is excellent in flavor, but they do not last long. A peach stone set into the earth shoots up so quickly that it bears fruit as early as its third year. This is not because any particular care has been lavished on it. This happens generally.

Let things be as they may, I would like to see the wonderful working of destiny in America as long as the good Lord, who makes all things, grants me life. May God in Heaven grant that America remain a free, happy refuge for all those who are forced from the old world by oppression and misery and seek asylum here! And with this — period.

And so to you pages, written here in the new world, Godspeed! Go forth to our dear friends, and tell them truly, sincerely, and forthrightly the things which I have so confidently entrusted to you. Entertain each person pleasantly for an hour, as though we were there in person. May your trip to their homes be completed just as safely and happily as was our trip here when we left them. And ah, may you find them all in good health and contentment! Greet them all with a genuine Swiss handshake! Greet too our native valley and heights, meadow and field, forest, brook,

266

and lake where we once strolled happily in our youth. Greet every little spot that our memory cherishes like a sacred kingdom in the heart.

While you are making your journey, I will happily anticipate receiving from each of our friends a full dozen pages, closely written even to the corners, filled with all sorts of news. I too will have many more experiences and from time to time I will send a note. Perhaps I will even undertake a considerable trip to the western states.

Your unchanging friend and brother,

J. Jakob Rütlinger

Epilogue

THE Rütlinger family did not remain long on the farm he rented near Middletown, Maryland. In his *Tagebuch*, Rütlinger made clear his intention of moving westward. In 1826, shortly after the manuscript of the *Tagebuch* was sent to Canton St. Gallen for publication, he and his family began their travels in search of a place to settle. As in the past, he kept an account of his experiences and continued to write poetry. In 1841 Rütlinger sent a manuscript to Switzerland in which he described life in Ohio during the years from 1824 to 1838; also included were perhaps fifty poems written during these years, reflecting his experiences in America. The manuscript bore the title "Frischer Anklang lang schlummernder Töne der Erinnerung an seine Schweizerfreunde" ("A Fresh Chime of Long-Dormant Notes, for the Remembrance of His Swiss Friends").

The "Frischer Anklang" was never published.[20] The manuscript, dedicated to the Basel Missionary Society in appreciation of their work abroad, was last known to be in the hands of Rütlinger's descendants. In preparing his brief biographical sketch of Rütlinger's life published by the St. Gallen Historical Society in 1915, Oskar Frei had access to both the manuscript and a few surviving letters written by Rütlinger from Ohio. The contents of these Frei described briefly, giving some excerpts. Recent efforts to locate the "Frischer Anklang" and the letters have thus far been without success.

[20] A letter from Prof. Dominik Jost, St. Gallen, September 15, 1963, affirms a report from St. Gallen's city librarian, Dr. Hans Fehrlin, that the "Frischer Anklang" is not listed in any bibliography or catalog in Swiss libraries.

Their friends in Middletown gave Rütlinger, his wife, and their infant daughter many expressions of their friendship and best wishes at their departure for the west. "Even the poor Negro, a strong young slave who belonged to our landlord, extended his powerful hand and said, 'Farewell!' A great tear rolled down his shining black cheek."[21] They drove their covered wagon onto the road leading to Pittsburgh, some four hundred miles away. The travelers had provided themselves with coffee, bread, and ham. At noon they stopped at a spring or a little stream and the table was set with bread, ham, and water. In the evening they usually stopped at an inn. While Rütlinger took care of the horse and tended to the wagon, his wife went into the kitchen of the inn for milk, water, and fire in order to prepare a modest meal. They slept in the covered wagon at night. "So it went day after day. Nowhere were we asked for passports or other papers by policemen or officials or by any other bothersome hirelings making unabashed and officious demands to burden our lives; not a single beggar asked us for alms."

Although the Allegheny mountains were not as high as the mountains of Switzerland, they were impressed with the rich vegetation and the lovely, fertile little valleys. Whatever skill Rütlinger lacked as a driver he found that his faithful old horse was able to make up for by experience.

Before leaving on his journey, Rütlinger had read in a German-American newspaper of plans being formulated for the founding of an industrial communal society, and on reaching Greensburg, Pennsylvania, where the leader of this project lived, Rütlinger sought him out. After much effort the new prophet was finally discovered in a print shop — a little man with a prodigious nose and green glasses, who had been a rug-weaver in his native Aargau. The printer professed great pleasure at having an honest Swiss as one of his followers and instructed him further concerning the motives and goals of his movement. The following day, with three German farmers, plans were written down for a German-Christian Industrial Society. All that was lacking was the means by which the plans could be made reality. In his journal, Rütlinger recorded the principles of the movement in which each would get what "he was able to produce" but also "that to which he has a right in order to live a reasonably happy, comfortable life."

[21] Rütlinger, "Frischer Anklang," in Oskar Frei, *Johann Jakob Rütlinger von Wildhaus (1790–1856), Sein Leben, Seine Dichtungen und Schriften* (St. Gallen: Historischer Verein des Kantons St. Gallen, 1915), p. 20. The facts about Rütlinger's later career and the quotations from his letters in the pages that follow are taken from this work (our translation).

268

One of the interested farmers, J. G. Mayer from Swabia, invited the prophet to his home near Bull Creek in Springfield Township, Columbiana County, Ohio. Here he might remain until plans for the community came to fruition. Rütlinger decided to spend at least the winter in that area. When they reached the fertile farmland of Columbiana County, the Rütlinger family was invited to stay with Mayer's brother Johannes. This offer was gratefully accepted. Here they learned weaving and reed weaving.

Shortly after his arrival Rütlinger was sent out with the printer-preacher to look for land for the community, which was to be called "Concordia." "We saddled our horses in good spirits and for the first time in my life I started a journey as a cavalry man." Near New Philadelphia they found fertile land for sale which seemed ideal and they returned home contented. While efforts were being made to bring the plans to realization, the Rütlingers settled down to make their living. Mrs. Rütlinger earned money by weaving and making hats. The old horse was exchanged for a cow. "Gradually a sense of joy and contentment filled our souls as never before in America. Piano, violin, flute, and song resounded again." In this setting a second daughter, Mariannchen, was born to them on New Year's Eve, 1827.

Nothing came of "Concordia" and Rütlinger observed that although many are willing to help with the harvest, "in times of sowing they withhold their hands." The prophet went on to try his projects elsewhere but "poverty and need followed on the heels of the good man."

Rütlinger visited the Rappist colony at Economy and the Separatist colony of Zoar with which his old friend Vetter was connected. He was also seriously interested in the movement of "Count" Leon which split off the Rappist colony. When this came to naught he abandoned forever his interest in joining a communalistic enterprise.

Rütlinger then searched for a good farm. He spent some time near New Lancaster in the northwestern corner of Columbiana County. A compact colony of from sixty to eighty families, mostly from Basel, was reported to be living there.[22] Although he found the farmers from Basel somewhat "rough and raw" he was attracted by the fact that they maintained their language and customs. On the point of deciding in favor of "New Basel," he learned that in the neighborhood of his friend Mayer

[22] Knox Township was the center of the Swiss settlement. It was noted particularly for its production of cheese. See Henry Howe, *Historical Collections of Ohio* (Cincinnati: Krehbiel & Co., 1902), Vol. I, p. 463.

in Springfield Township a farm of twenty acres was for sale. He could not afford the whole piece but purchased the buildings and fifteen acres for $165. The remaining five acres were purchased by his friend.

Rütlinger found this area particularly pleasing, the most desirable he had seen in America. The gently rolling hill country, with streams flowing in all directions, was reminiscent of the Swiss midlands; "only the majestic panorama of the towering Alps and mountains in the background is missing."

The land was productive; the Pittsburgh market was only fifty miles away. "All the produce that is taken to Pittsburgh brings money." The area was well settled. "People from Württemberg, the Palatinate, Switzerland, Prussia, Hungary, Bohemia, and Bavaria are among our neighbors." There were Reformed, Lutherans, Baptists, Separatists, Methodists, Terstegians, Swedenborgians, Stillingnians, and others.

In a letter written to his sisters Anneli and Babeli in 1828, Rütlinger reported that his family was well and by this time in comfortable circumstances, although they had experienced many grave difficulties that had almost "made a hell out of life." "Now we live free and without debts – almost without worries on our own homestead." He reassured his sisters that "about saving bread we are not at all concerned. We live as well or better than the richest people over there. Things are cheap and earnings good." Rütlinger described his farm and the diversity of his agricultural enterprises. He raised pigs, sheep, and cows; he planted potatoes, wheat, rye, and corn. There were also various fruit trees. In addition the family income was supplemented by earnings from weaving.

In a letter written to his sisters in 1830, Rütlinger commented at some length about teaching and, more broadly, about schools in America. "It looks very much as though I will be asked to serve as the schoolteacher for our area," he reported. If he was not asked to serve in this position he was not much inclined, he added, to send his children to school. He was highly critical of American schools. He believed that he could teach his children more at home than they could learn in most American schools. The poems he wrote during this period of his life reveal his concern over the disrespectful spirit of youth in America. Apparently Rütlinger wrote articles on American schools which were published in contemporary Swiss journals.

In various ways Rütlinger expressed his continued attachments to the old homeland and friends and relatives. "For a long time I have been afraid that the precious old family house has been barbarically torn down

270

and that no trace could be found of where it had once stood." Nevertheless, he added, should he return later to Switzerland, he wanted to spend the last years of his life in a milder part of his homeland. By that time he would "no longer be readily able to accustom myself to winter storms and blizzards."

In January 1830 a third daughter had been born to the family. Rütlinger announced the birth to his sisters and expressed his wonderment at the brightness of his children. Later a fourth child, Barthel, was born. His family became the focus of his life and the source of deep satisfaction. Rütlinger wrote to a sister about coming to America with her husband and children.

His letters reveal that he continued to feel the concern he had expressed shortly after his arrival about the abuse of freedom. "Liberty is a noble daughter in this country for those who can love her purely, but whoever approaches her too closely with an impure and stained heart, she hurls into the abyss of ruination."

In his letters he sent greetings to various of his friends among whom was the organ maker Ulrich Ammann. Before leaving for America, Rütlinger along with Ammann had been part of a small group of musicians who gathered regularly on Sunday afternoons "to make music with might and main."[23] Ammann was a distinguished craftsman whose musical instruments were sold throughout Switzerland as well as in Germany, Italy, and even Lisbon.[24] Rütlinger on his Ohio farm had also become an instrument maker, among other things, and by 1830 reported to his sisters that he was working on his second piano.

The part of eastern Ohio in which the Rütlinger family lived was known for its fruits and berries. In a letter dated June 23, 1842, Rütlinger described his farm: "At this moment nature all around us is beautiful and inviting; the fields, meadows, and garden glow with promise. Here at the window where I am writing, ripening cherries smile at me and tempt my wife and children from their work to pick them — I shall never forget how much I enjoy them. Over my window hang blooming grape vines, affording me their fragrance and pleasant, cooling shade. Hardly six steps from me there is a beautiful apple tree whose branches are already bending under the burden of ruddy-cheeked fruit."

His letters gave an indication of the size of his farm and the amount

[23] *Illustrierter Kalender, 1851*, quoted in Albert Edelmann, "Vom frühern Musikleben im obern Toggenburg," *Toggenburgerblätter für Heimatkunde*, Vol. 23, Part II:2–3 (1962), p. 4.
[24] See Edelmann, *op. cit.*

of work involved in maintaining an agricultural enterprise of that kind. On small Swiss holdings there was no such diversity of tasks and no single task would absorb so much time and effort as was true of an Ohio farm. "There has been many a year in which I have used either a scythe or sickle or a pruning shears day after day for four weeks at a time," Rütlinger wrote in 1842. Splitting rails and building fences were important farm activities and he was proud of his prowess with the axe; he wrote to his brother-in-law, "Just come over here once and I'll challenge you at wood-chopping."

In his letter of June 23, 1842, Rütlinger mentioned an economic recession; trade and industry were at a standstill, but his own well-being was not affected. He observed that in the midst of economic and political complexities new prophets were rising to proclaim the dawn of a golden age and some "were trying to frighten mankind with the fear of all things on the surface of the earth."

Rütlinger was aware of religious controversies stirring in Switzerland. In Canton Zurich, the bitter differences between traditional Protestantism and the "disbelieving, un-Christian officials" and educators reached a crisis in 1839. The occasion was the election of Professor David Friedrich Strauss, a modernist, to a chair in philosophy at the University of Zurich. So strong was public reaction to Strauss as a symbol of Biblical criticism that he was pensioned off before he began his professorship at Zurich.[25] Rütlinger was concerned about the "famous or infamous Strauss in Zurich," although by the time he wrote this part of the general religious controversies had been resolved. "I don't believe that the evil stench of this Strauss is confined only to the borders of Zurich; no, he must certainly have spread his influence into St. Gallen and other areas of Switzerland. I have often thought about this dangerous Strauss because of you and wonder what you make of it. Write to me sometime concerning your views of this and what meaning and influence is brought to bear upon the people generally by this as well as what position the preachers and teachers find themselves in because of it."

In the spring of 1844, Rütlinger reported that he was still living "in the old spot" in Petersburg, Ohio. He noted in his letter of April 20, 1844, the increasing changes occurring in life about him and noted as well the striving of individuals to advance their fortunes by this expedient or that. "It is not to be found," he observed, "in the external things but rather, like the Kingdom of God, within us."

[25] Gitermann, *op. cit.*, pp. 456–460.

In the early 1850's Rütlinger and his wife, now that their children had established their own homes, moved four miles north from their farm near Petersburg to New Middletown.[26]

"For several years now we have been all alone on our little estate; in return for half the yield, we have it cultivated. We keep several cows and occasionally still busy ourselves with a little weaving. Thus we live in our older days, still fairly healthy, contented, living in simple peace and quiet. So far, thank God, we have not suffered from these hard times. Our children and grandchildren are also well and not in need; they visit us often and this pleasures us not a little."

In his last letter, written shortly before his death in 1856, Rütlinger concerned himself with some of the acute problems plaguing American society. He described the crop failure in 1854 which came as a consequence of drought and which occasioned widespread distress. He reported, as well, economic dislocations both in the large inland cities and in the coastal cities along the eastern seaboard; distress had reached shocking proportions and soup kitchens were being maintained to save innumerable unemployed from starvation. In New York, approximately ten thousand unemployed marched through the streets in battle formation "to show by their threatening bearing" what they planned to do if the city could not supply them with work or bread.

The rapid influx of German refugees arriving in the United States following the Revolution of 1848 concerned Rütlinger for several reasons. In the first place the refugees were ideologically disturbing, "attempting to spread broadly their crazy, harebrained schemes." The behavior of the new wave of immigrants, he observed, caused the German character to be viewed more critically than had formerly been true.[27]

[26] Both villages were in Springfield Township which in 1846 had been shifted from Columbiana County to the newly created Mahoning County. A few miles to the north lay Youngstown which by the late 1840's was experiencing an industrial expansion based upon the abundant coal mined in Trumbull and Mahoning counties. See Harlan Hatcher, *The Western Reserve* (New York: Bobbs-Merrill, 1949), p. 231.

[27] The failure of the Revolution of 1848 in Germany brought a remarkably varied stream of immigrants, including men of considerable eminence as well as ordinary clerks, mechanics, and farmers. There were all manner of political liberals, republicans, and radicals among them. The refugees were to have a significance in American intellectual history beyond their proportion in the population. Certain radical German elements supported fantastic plans for encouraging and directly supporting further revolutionary attempts in Germany. Efforts were made to gather funds and enlist men for this purpose. Sharp-shooting training was initiated among German radicals in Louisville in the early 1850's. Special attempts were made to recruit engineers and architects as well as veterans of other revolutionary movements. The most restless, tiring of delay, joined American filibustering attempts in

Finally, Rütlinger mentioned the aggravated nature of the controversy over slavery; unfortunately no excerpts relevant to this controversy are included.

Nicaragua. Other nationalities in this period had similar groups, but Germans were more conspicuous by virtue of their numbers. See Carl Wittke, *Refugees of Revolution: The German Forty-Eighters in America* (Philadelphia: University of Pennsylvania Press, 1952), pp. 94–96.

INDEX

Index

Agriculture: waste of fruit, 90, 226; careless husbandry, 90, 112–113, 226; meat improperly utilized, 96; prices, 96, 228, 231–233; American and European practices compared, 98, 101, 112–114, 271–272; American skill, 100, 226; mowing and harvesting, 100, 101; soil fertility, 108, 265, 268; meat curing, 113; cheese, 113; exports, 125, 138–140; scutching, 125; vineyards, 125, 252; milling, 126, 228; surpluses, 140; division of labor, 224; seasonal labor, 227; wages, 227; price of cleared land, 228; homesteading, 250–251; cotton, 252; pig raising, 252–253; neglect of cattle breeding, 253; orchards, 271; crop failure, 273

Ambühl, J. L., 82

America, appraisals of, 15–19, 21–25, 93–95, 108–110, 152, 156–158, 265–267, 273

American Colonization Society, 106

American social character: basic optimism, 21; love of freedom, 21; superficiality of friendships, 22; stability of, 22, 109; lack of discipline, 23; disrespect for law, 23, 214; wastefulness, 24, 90, 112–113, 226; skill at inventing tools, 24, 226; table manners, 87, 88; contradictions in, 93; practicality, 95; dexterity, 100; arts uncultivated, 100; dislike of walking, 127; cleanliness, 127, 157; mobility, 136, 158; weak parental authority, 138, 139; courtship, 138; sense of architectural beauty, 140; self-reliance, 142; love of luxury, 156–157, 229–230; concern for clothing fashions, 160, 229; democratic spirit, 222; lack of discipline in schools, 270. See also Family life, Fashions, Food and drink, Hospitality, Household management, Slavery, Standard of living, Women

Amsterdam, 47, 62, 64–69, 73, 173, 176, 181, 182, 183, 185–192, 198, 200, 218

Anabaptists, 104, 234

Army, 41, 45, 244

Arnhem, 64, 65, 67, 181, 182, 183

Aubigne, Merle d', 86n

Azores, 78, 205

Bacchus, 44n

Baden, 41, 116, 169

Baltimore, 70, 118, 128, 129, 138, 190, 201, 209–215, 218, 219, 235

Bank of the United States, 20, 119n, 119–120, 142

Baptists, 234, 270

Basel, 3, 38, 39, 167, 269

Baumgartner family, 164

Bavaria, King of, 47

Berks County, Penn., 115–116

Bibles, selling of, 61, 87, 97, 99, 108, 115

Bingen, 51, 53, 177

Blegen, Theodore C., 14, 19n

Böker, Mr., 57, 58, 61

Bonn, 178

Bordentown, 97

Botany Bay, 57

Brandy distilling, 59–60

Breisach, 169–170

Bridges: pontoon, 47, 51, 57, 62; flying, 183–184

Browe, Captain, 190–214 passim

Brugg, 166–167

Buffalo, N.Y., 134

Business speculation, 230

Bütschwyl, 166

Calais, 75

Camp meeting, 238–240

Canada, 49

Cape Norfolk, 211
Catherine II, 9–10
Catholics, 53, 58–59, 154, 175, 235
Chesapeake Bay, 211
Chillicothe, 118
Christophe, Henri, 138
Churches: of Cologne, 58, 180; farmers organize, 128; itinerant ministers, 128, 235; singing in, 154; weddings and baptisms, 154; of Mainz, 174; not established, 234; poor education of ministers, 235; adult baptism, 235; services in German, 236. *See also* Camp meeting, Religion, and specific denominations
Cincinnati, 104, 142
Colleges and universities, 237
Cologne, 50, 55–62, 69, 98, 180
Congregationalists, 235
Courts, 94, 242–244
Crèvecoeur, Michel-Guillaume Jean de, 25
Cumberland, 115, 121

Debtors, 243
Delaware River, 97–98, 102, 141
De Rahm, Henry C., 86, 87
Disease, 102, 108–109, 258–259
Distilling, 59–60, 125–126
Doctors, 258–259
Dover, England, 75
Düsseldorf, 180
Dutch, 57–73 *passim*, 87, 184–193 *passim*

East Indies, 138, 212, 213
Economic conditions, 19–21, 41–42, 46, 113–114, 227–229, 230–232
Eddy, Thomas, 89
Education, *see* Schools
Elections, 110–111, 241–242
Emigration and immigration: hazards of, 12–13, 124, 130, 185; advice on, 13–19, 32, 132–134, 139–140, 147, 250–253; patterns of, 15–19, 26–27; adjustment and assimilation, 123–124; attitudes toward, 123, 156; need for government regulation, 131; aid in, 146; emotions in, 151, 152. *See also* Occupational adjustment
Emmerich, 63, 180, 181
England, 75, 76, 87, 193
English language, 99, 158, 236, 256
Episcopalians, 235
Erie, Lake, 96, 129
Erie Canal, 128, 231
Erwin, Master, 170

Europe, 80, 91–96 *passim*, 110, 114, 117, 119, 130, 132, 140, 153, 194

Factories, *see* Manufacturing
Family life, 127, 136–139, 143–145, 221–226. *See also* American social character, Household management, Women
Farms and farming, *see* Agriculture
Fashions, 71, 93, 156, 160, 225, 229
Findlay, William, 110
Fire-fighting, 92
Florida, Gulf of, 79, 80
Flying bridge, 183–184
Food and drink: in Europe, 49, 59–60, 68, 180; at sea, 71, 72, 75, 76, 150, 151, 152, 191, 206, 210; in America, 88, 90–91, 96, 104, 113, 115, 118, 125, 126, 127, 144–146, 157, 158, 161, 217–218, 222, 224, 231–232
Forests, 261–265
Forrer, Johannes, 205
France, 6–7, 59, 75, 171, 193
Frankental, 49
Franklin, Benjamin, 55, 74
Frederickstown, 137
Frei, Oskar, 8n, 164, 267, 268n
Freiburg, 41–45

Gall, Dr. L., 214
Gallatin, Albert, 86
Garique, 99, 100
Gellert, C. F., 154
Geneva, Lake, 68
German language, 158, 179, 192, 236
Germans in America: American attitudes toward, 16, 105, 123; in Germantown, 100; newspapers, 111, 268; benevolence to poor, 124; views of American marriages, 138; warnings to prospective emigrants, 139; Society of Lancaster, 139; orient new immigrants, 215; establish schools, 223; churches of, 234; colonizing society, 268; critical of *1848* refugees, 273
Germans in Rhineland, 47
Germans in Russia, 9–11, 33
Germantown, 99–100
Germany, 55, 177
Germersheim, 46–47
Gesner, Conrad (von), 211
Gonzenbach, Maier, 86
Grünenwinkel, 45–46
Grymberg, Madame von, 48
Gun factory, 246–247

279

Neuhäusel, 171
Neuwied, 55
New Brunswick, 97, 98
New Jersey, 85, 97, 210
New Lancaster, 134, 269
New Orleans, 94, 116, 127, 129, 133, 231, 235
New York City, 84, 86, 97, 116, 129, 136, 137, 153
New York State, 95, 128, 134
New Vivis, 134
Newfoundland Banks, 80, 203, 208
Newspapers, 110–112
Niederholt, Captain, 69, 70, 86

Occupational adjustment: opportunities, 87–89; time needed for, 91; premium on practicality, 110; artisans try various trades, 117, 118, 221; advice on, 133; uncertainties of, 227, 253–258
Odessa, 33
Offenburg, 44
Ohio, 106, 119, 142, 198, 224, 250, 252, 271
Ontario, Lake, 96, 129
Orkneys, 77

Palmyra, 26
Pennsylvania, 96, 108, 110, 112, 119, 125–130, 214, 217–219, 250
Pennsylvania Dutch, 11
Philadelphia, 70, 97–99, 102, 106, 117, 126–129, 136, 140, 141, 146, 153, 219, 220
Pittsburgh, 118, 127, 132, 137, 270
Plattsburg, 94
Political life: emotionality of campaigns, 110; cycles of interest, 111; federal government, 241–242; state governments, 242
Postal service, 245
Presbyterians, 104, 234
Prices, 96, 231, 245
Prostitutes, 58, 191
Prussia, 59, 63, 88, 108

Quakers, 98, 99, 100, 104, 117, 121, 235, 241, 244

Rappite colony, 132–133, 269
Rastatt, 44, 45, 54
Reading, 111, 215
Readinger Postbothe, 111
Reformed Church, 154, 234, 270
Religion, 58, 59, 110, 177, 237, 272. *See also* Churches

Rhineland, 39–68 *passim*, 168–185 *passim*
Rhode Island, 143
Ringheim, 43
Roads, 245
Rotterdam, 59
Rousseau (ship), 73
Rückert, Frederick, 49
Ruhr River, 61
Ruhrort, 61
Russia, 9, 10, 33

Saart, 66, 69
St. Gallen (city), 56, 86, 162, 164
St. Gallen (canton), 3, 4, 7, 8, 30, 32, 164, 267
St. Jakob, 74
Sand, Karl Ludwig, 48
Sanitation, 127, 156, 225
Santo Domingo, 138
Saudersburg, 106
Schäfer, Pastor, 89
Schinznach, 167
Schmidt, Captain, 71–74
Schmidt, Prussian consul, 86
Schools, 109, 128, 161, 223; poor construction in, 236; farmers organize, 236; unruly children in, 270
Schuylkill River, 116, 117, 128
Sea voyage: on the *Xenophon*, 70–84 *passim*, 149–152; on the *Massasoit*, 71n, 190–214 *passim*; dangers of, 73, 151, 152; seasickness, 76–79, 204; storms, 78, 79, 206; pranks at sea, 204
Senate, U.S., 241
Separatists, 175, 176n, 182, 187, 198–199, 201–202, 244, 270
Sierra Leone, 106
Singing school, 160, 222
Slavery, 22, 232–245; transportation to Africa, 106; on farms, 225; and Negro literacy, 232; religious objections to, 234
South Amboy, 97, 98
Spain, 117, 171
Speyer, 46, 47
Standard of living: of unemployed, 95; compared with Europe, 109, 115; of unfortunate speculators, 120; of simple laborers, 157; of Mennonites, 158. *See also* Household management
Steamboats, 85, 89, 90, 98
Steinbeck, John, 16
Stoss, 74
Strasbourg, 168, 169